LYNCHING

IN THE WEST:

1850-1935

D1121291

LYNCHING

IN THE WEST:

1850–1935

Ken Gonzales-Day

Duke University Press

Durham and London

2006

© 2006 Duke University Press
All rights reserved
Printed in the United States of
America on acid-free paper ∞
Designed by Amy Ruth Buchanan
Typeset in Bembo by Tseng
Information Systems, Inc.
Library of Congress Cataloging-
in-Publication Data appear on the
last printed page of this book.

Frontispiece: Ken Gonzales-Day,
"Franklin Avenue (1920)," 2005.

Duke University Press gratefully
acknowledges the support of Scripps
College, which provided funds toward
the production of this book.

FOR GARY

CONTENTS

ILLUSTRATIONS

ACKNOWLEDGMENTS

ACKNOWLEDGMENTS

ACKNOWLEDGMENTS

This book grew out of a residency at the Rockefeller Foundation's Bellagio Study and Conference Center. The residency was a remarkable experience, but my favorite part was staying up late and talking with the many accomplished people I met there. Later, I had an opportunity to spend the summer in residence at the Smithsonian Institution where I was hosted by the American Art Museum and the National Portrait Gallery through the Latino Studies program. The Smithsonian provided me with access to a vast array of materials and gave me the opportunity to explore the many resources held in our nation's capital. Once the manuscript was underway, Courtney Berger and Ken Wissoker at Duke Press were extremely patient as I worked to complete *Lynching in the West* and guided me through each stage in the process.

With regard to the images, Robert Grahmbeek (Lemon Sky: Projects + Editions) in Los Angeles did a masterful job scanning many of the fragile old newspapers and photographs illustrated in the pages of this book, as well in producing an edition of images from the "Hang Tree" series. Dace Taube, the archivist in Special Collections at the Library at the University of Southern California, was also a valuable resource for both images and information. John Calhoon at the Seaver Center for Western History at the Los Angeles Natural History Museum in Los Angeles waited patiently as I finalized my image selection. Erin Chase at the Huntington Garden and Public Library made finding materials a breeze. Beth Guynn at the Getty Research Institute helped me to navigate the labyrinth of books at the institute. I would also like to thank the California Historical Society, Baker Research Library in

San Francisco, the Beinecke Rare Book and Manuscript Library at Yale, the Oakland Museum of Art, the California State Archive, and the Sacramento Archives Museum and Collection Center, each of which allowed me access to every manner of microfiche, scrapbook, and journal as well as a wealth of photographic images, not all of which could be included but which were essential to the research.

Subvention monies for color reproductions came from a Faculty Research Grant and the Mellon Faculty Renewal Dean's fund at Scripps College. I must also thank the Arnold L. and Lois S. Graves Award for Achievement in the Humanities, which allowed me to order research prints and scan original materials, and also assisted in the fabrication of the photographic series "Searching for California's Hang Trees." My thanks to both Tyler Stallings and Amelia Jones for their early interest in my research, and for feedback on chapter 4, portions of which were included in the exhibition catalogue for "Whiteness: A Wayward Construction." Special thanks to Cynthia Wilson, coordinator at the Archives of the Tuskegee Institute, for making the original files available to me.

Thanks to my colleagues Susan Rankaitis, Cheryl Walker, and Michael Deane Lamkin for their constant support, and my parents Peter and Nancy Gonzales whose own journey has shaped so much of my thinking about race. I would also like to acknowledge my late grandfather, Telesfor Gonzales, whose storytelling revealed a world that was both wondrous and terrible. Thanks to Michael Hutter and Juli Carson for our discussions; Bruce Yonemoto for his dark humor—and curating an exhibition of the hang tree photographs. Special thanks to Margaret Morgan and Wesley Phoa for always being there through this long process. Most importantly, I wish to acknowledge and express deep appreciation to my partner Gary Wolf for his unwavering belief in me, his honest feedback at so many crucial moments, and for the many hours he spent searching for images or reading through microfilm. Without him, I could never have completed such a remarkable journey.

Los Angeles, January 5, 2006.

LYNCHING

IN THE WEST:

1850-1935

Map of California Counties. Courtesy of California State Association of Counties, Sacramento, California.

The hang tree's leaves twinkled
as merrily as those of other
trees; its massed foliage held
the same sunny gleams and
cool shadows; it crooned the
same lullabies when the breeze
stirred its branches. But men
who admired its beauty, crossed
the street to avoid walking
beneath its haunted shade.

—Walter Noble Burns,
The Robin Hood of El Dorado

INTRODUCTION

Searching for California's Hang Trees

SLOW CIRCLES

I exited Union Station in downtown Los Angeles and began walking south. I was traveling to the intersection of Alameda and Aliso streets—barely a block away. To get there I would have to take one of several streets that extended over the freeway. This particular stretch of freeway had been carved out of one of the oldest parts of the city when urban planners decided that running a multilane highway through a few blocks of crumbling adobe buildings could serve two purposes: lead visitors through town and shield them from an unsightly past. But like an old wound, it still scars the landscape, forming an artificial barrier between Los Angeles's raucous past and its sprawling present.

Eighteen-wheelers hummed and hissed their way through the slow traffic below me—modern day woolly mammoths trapped in rush hour tar pits. Once across the freeway, I realized that I was standing at the very intersection I had been searching for. I walked in slow circles and squinted helplessly at the bleached gray asphalt, vaguely aware of how random my actions might appear to those passing by—but I could see no one.

I knew *he* wouldn't be there. I had gone to see, to witness his absence, as I had done for a hundred others, in a hundred places. What did I expect to see? The broken circle of blood-soaked dirt that would have formed beneath his feet as the wind pushed his body in slow circles? No, there was nothing to see, no clues to what had happened here. Perhaps it was the saccharine smell of hot tar, smoldering brake pads, and diesel fumes that was making me nauseous, but I had to leave.

AN ORDINARY CASE

It was just weeks before the great deluge that would define the winter of 1861–62, a year when the Los Angeles River would overflow its banks and store owners like Mr. Meyer or the Hellman brothers would face ruin as adobe walls melted under torrential rains.[1] On October 17, Mrs. Leck, or Frau Leck as she was sometimes called, was working in the small shop that she and her husband owned in downtown Los Angeles when she was brutally stabbed and robbed.[2]

According to one account there were no witnesses; another suggested that her young children may have been present in the store during the heinous crime. People began to assemble in front of the small storefront after she was discovered. Word spread through the crowd that a suspect had been identified. He was rounded up and brought before the angry crowd. A rope was placed around his neck. One eyewitness detailed how the angry mob dragged the accused down Alameda Street, observing that by the time they had turned onto Aliso Street the loathsome creature had been stabbed so many times that he was nearly dead already.

In spite of his rapidly declining health, he was strung up by the vigilantes just blocks from the sheriff's office. The newspaper summarized the popular sentiment surrounding the case when it wrote, "A butchery such as he committed was enough to stir our citizens to call aloud for instant vengeance. This was no ordinary case. A helpless and feeble woman, a mother, with two little children playing around her, is set upon by this devil in human form, and mangled and mutilated until life is extinct, for the purpose of gain. No death is too horrible for such a monster, and the yawning gates of hell opened to receive him none too soon."[3]

This particular monster was named Francisco Cota and he was fifteen years old. In uncovering the details of the case, I would learn that he was Mexican, that he had been denied due process, and that he was stabbed, dragged, and hanged with a rope by a group of European and Anglo-Americans that had chosen to take the law into their own hands. Afterward, his body was left to hang on public display for an undisclosed period of time. If the boy was lucky, and there is no reason to believe that he was, his family members would have found his body in time to provide a proper burial.

In considering the details of the case, I wondered if *justice* could really be served if the law was not. In Cota's case, all legal alternatives had been blatantly ignored. And how might race or ethnicity have contributed to the outcome of a case? The 1861 claim that this had been "no ordinary case" was ironic because, as the history of lynching makes clear, Cota's treatment by the enraged mob was nearly identical to the treatment received by thousands of other persons lynched across the nation.

A LANDSCAPE WITHOUT MEMORY

Of the many books published on the history of lynching in the United States, only a handful give much thought to the Western region of the nation; when Western states are included, the information is usually out of date or inaccurate. This book attempts to correct the historical record in one of these states and to reveal to the nation that—like the lynching of African Americans— Native Americans, Chinese, and Latinos of Mexican and Latin American descent were lynched in California. This book demonstrates that many of these public killings were guided by anti-immigration sentiments, the fear of miscegenation, a deep frustration with the judicial system, or in combination with white supremacy. Thus, the goal of this study is twofold: first, to provide a broader understanding of the transracial nature of lynching in the United States; and second, to consider those factors which may have contributed to the nearly complete erasure of this history from national consciousness.

In their introduction to *Remaking a World: Violence, Social Suffering, and Recovery*, Das and Kleinman theorize the creation of a "public space" in the wake of such collective tragedies, recognizing that "the experience of victims and survivors can not only be represented but also be molded," and they insist that the "repair of relationships" must begin "in the deep recesses of family, neighborhood, and community" before they can be incorporated into the "narratives of larger entities such as the nation and the state."[4] Therefore, acknowledging lynching in California is only the first step in addressing the legacy of violence and terror experienced by racial and racialized communities in the West.

However, before such reparations can be realized, it will be necessary to establish the precise impact of race on this history. Seemingly counterintuitive, the discussion of race in chapter 1 begins by exploring the evolution and emergence of the "Anglo-American" and the United States as a race nation because this formation was directly linked to the degradation of blacks, Asians, American Indians, and persons of Mexican or Latin American descent — racially, ethnically, and legally.

THE LAW OF THE LAND

The first state constitution, written in 1849, guaranteed that "the right of trial by jury shall be secured to all, and remain inviolate forever. . . ."[5] It asserted that in a court of law, no person shall be "subject for the same offence to be twice put in jeopardy of life and limb; nor shall be compelled in any criminal case to be a witness against himself, nor be deprived of life, liberty, or property, without due process of law. . . ."[6] In spite of such precautionary measures, the history of lynching reveals that in many cases those charged with a crime would be denied these basic rights and were often compelled to confess their crimes from the end of a rope. In one well-known case a man was lynched twice for the same crime, one for which he may have been completely innocent.

On February 8, 1857, a volunteer posse was returning to Los Angeles from Santa Barbara, where they had just lynched a man by the name of José Jesús Espinosa, when they decided to pay a visit to a certain Encarnación Berreyesa, following rumors that he was an escaped villain.[7] Arriving in the middle of the night, they saw that a rope had scarred his neck and quickly hanged him to a nearby tree. The men would later claim that Berreyesa had been tried and found guilty of escaping the hangman's noose.[8]

Accounts confirm that three years earlier a different posse of men had visited Berreyesa's house, then in northern California, and that he had been questioned from the end of a rope, but there is nothing to suggest that the posse had tried to kill him, only that they had questioned him. Several days later, on July 21, 1854, a similarly masked posse went to visit his brother at another of the family's nearby ranches in Santa Clara County.[9] Presumably accused of the same crime, the posse either succeeded in gaining his brother's confession or killed him in the effort because the next morning he was found, by his wife and children, hanged to a tree.[10] If all of this wasn't confusing enough, Encarnación's brother Nemesio was misidentified as "Derrasio Berreyesa" in one of the earliest newspapers accounts of the incident.[11] Given the proximity and similarity between the two cases one can reasonably conclude that Nemesio was the Berreyesa the 1854 posse had been searching for.

One newspaper article expressed great scorn for Nemesio's killers: "When vigilant committees must go, like thieves, at night in disguise, it is time for them to be hung. . . . When honest men take the law into their own hands they don't steal about in the dark."[12] Significant in several respects, this criticism of the lynching demonstrates that this "vigilant committee" was not only indistinguishable from a *hanging party* but that the term *vigilance committee* was used far more broadly than has generally been recognized. This is not to suggest that lynchers and vigilance committees were indistinguishable, but simply that they could be.

The Los Angeles account is disturbing for another reason as well, because it suggests that the Los Angeles posse decided to hang a man simply because his neck was scarred.[13] Even if he were guilty of a crime, it seems unlikely that a single man could have presented a serious threat to such a heavily armed band, and he should have been brought to Los Angeles to stand trial.

In recognizing that the deaths of these brothers were linked to one another, the Berreyesa case is able draw attention to the biased nature of both "trials," revealing that neither was the result of a true vigilance committee but was merely the anticipated results of a hanging party that had gone in search of "Mexicans."[14] The Berreyesa family, once a wealthy and highly respected California family, is a tragic and frequently cited example of bias against Latinos. At least nine members of the extended family died at the hands of Anglos.[15]

OTHER SOURCES

Examining a handful of surviving documents, newspaper accounts, and other forms of ephemera, including lynching souvenir cards, view cards, postcards, sketches, published illustrations, and scrapbooks, this history provides a unique opportunity to observe the power of racist pleasure, first in shaping Western racial stereotypes, then, as they were echoed in the journalistic texts, legislative measures, and finally in the photographic images they inspired. Though comparatively rare, particularly when compared with images of African Americans in other states, these images are material clues to a history that has long been cloaked and obscured by regionalist narratives.

This book must also consider the relation between the aesthetics of the event, from the physical act to the creation of the lynching photograph and its progeny, the souvenir card, view card, and postcard, each of which remains trapped somewhere between memento and evidence.[16] Bound within the politics of race, such images stood in direct contradiction to what can only be characterized as an emerging and expanding judicial system throughout the latter half of the nineteenth century.[17] Given the necessity for a complex and multivalent analysis, the chapters will traverse a number of disciplinary fields, setting regional, racial, and legal histories alongside of photographic and art historical ones.

After the war with Mexico, and compounded by the nation's fascination and disdain of indigenous populations, California became the first Western region to draw international attention as newspaper correspondents reported on everything from the daily emergence of mining camps, spawned by the discovery of gold at Sutter's Mill in 1848, to conflicts with "Indians," to tracking the going price of eggs, and finally, to even noting the location of the nearest hang tree.[18] These hang trees would continue to cast their haunted shade well into the twentieth century.

While the West was still a U.S. territory, bandits, murderers, and horse thieves from China, England, France, Ireland, Italy, Mexico, and other countries were summarily executed and lynched alongside African Americans, American Indians, and Mexican Americans. But contrary to the popular image of the American West as a lawless frontier—encountered everywhere from the dime novels from the 1860s to Hollywood Westerns still in production over a century later—in California, those areas with the most law enforcement had the greatest number of summary executions, vigilance committees, and lynch mobs.[19]

Although persons from many different races, ethnicities, and nationalities died at rope's end between 1850 and 1935 (the period from statehood to the last documented lynching), new data suggest that persons of color were statistically more likely to die by lynching than those of northern European descent.[20] There was a report of a lynching as late as 1947, but it could not be confirmed in time for publication.[21]

Lynching in the West compiles the most complete list of California's legal and extralegal executions published to date, revealing the lynching of persons of color alongside Anglo-Americans, Australians, and Europeans from three continents. The data suggest that lynching and other forms of community-driven violence were deeply linked to the formation of our young nation; from vigilance committees to the antilynching movement, the history of lynching has touched many communities and continues to serve as a powerful catalyst for thinking about race, ethnicity, and national identity.

The summary execution of Richard Cronin (Crone), also known as "Irish Dick," was one of the earliest Gold Rush accounts to be published. Cronin was said to have dealt monte in the El Dorado Saloon, and most accounts agree that he killed a miner in a quarrel over a wager. A later account described what followed: "The miners took him in charge, tied a rope round his neck, then giving him the other end, compelled him to climb a tree, go out on one of the limbs, fasten the end of the rope, and at the drop of a handkerchief, jump off. He complied with apparent cheerfulness, and died without a struggle."[22] But this image stands in stark contrast with the majority of accounts that suggest that death at the hang tree was among the worst deaths imaginable. Often misdated, the Cronin case occurred before California was recognized as a state and is not included in the final statistics, but as one of the earliest cases involving a hang tree, it provides a valuable point of comparison to the many cases that follow.[23]

After the Gold Rush, the vigilance committee or lynch mob was most likely to surface in response to an alleged capital offense. Rather than leaving the judgment or sentencing to a legally recognized court of law, the committee or mob would intervene on behalf of the *people* when guilt was presumed, and if there was insufficient evidence to ensure a conviction, or if there was the perception of unwarranted legalese, such as a request for a change of venue. Unlike the Southeast and East Coast, where lynch victims rarely saw the inside of a courtroom, in California, legal trials were not an uncommon precursor to a lynching or summary execution. Even when trials resulted in a death sentence, there were cases where the *people* were driven to action rather than allow the accused to appeal to a higher court or have the opportunity to petition the governor for a reprieve or pardon.

In some cases, the actual workings of the law provoked the community to action, as in an 1854 case in which two men were legally tried, found guilty, and sentenced to be hung in Los Angeles. One was a "mestizo" by the name of Féliz Alvitre, and the other was an Anglo by the name of Dave Brown.[24] On January 12, 1855, a stay of execution arrived for Brown but not for Alvitre.[25] On the day scheduled for Alvitre's execution, and in keeping with the law, he was taken to the jail yard and executed. There was, however, the perception of differential treatment among the city's gathering Latino residents, and matters were only made worse when the execution was badly bungled and Alvitre's body fell to the ground in the middle of the execution. Apparently the rope had broken, and the executioner had to run out, lift the body, and knot the ropes back together before he "once more drew aloft the writhing form, to the delight of the mob."[26]

The mayor, a man by the name of Stephen Foster, had stopped a previous attempt to lynch Brown by promising to resign as mayor and resume the lynching should a higher court reverse the Brown decision. With the stay of execution in hand, he was called on to keep his promise.[27] He resigned his office "from a beer keg" and led a crowd that was described to be composed of "Latin Americans and Yankees" to storm the jail.[28] A Mexican man by the name of Juan Gonzales was assigned to pull the cord but Brown objected to being hanged by a "greaser," so the mayor gave the job to an Anglo-American.[29] Alvitre's stay of execution arrived a week after he had been hanged—it had apparently been delayed in the mail.[30] Foster was later reelected as mayor.

But not everyone lived in a region that had a mayor, let alone a sheriff. Consider, for example the lynching of a Swede known as David, "DG," or William Brown, in fall 1851.[31] He was tried for stealing nearly $600 in gold dust in Rich Bar, a small mining camp located on the Feather River.[32] Because the nearest judge was two days' travel away, a judge and jury were appointed from among the miners, and after the trial, the jury handed the judge a paper saying that Brown was to be hanged in one hour's time.

"Dame Shirley" (Louise Amelia Knapp Smith Clappe) was one of the few women to have kept a record of her time in the gold fields and left a description of the events that followed. "The whole affair, indeed, was a piece of cruel butchery," she wrote, "though that was not intentional. . . . In truth, life was only crushed out of him, by hauling the writhing body up and down several times in succession, by the rope which was wound round a large bough of his green-leafed gallows."[33] She concluded that the trial was performed by some of most reckless members of the community, in spite of the fact that another eyewitness insisted that the sheriff and constable had been present throughout the whole proceeding.[34]

This second witness was a German sailor, turned miner, by the name of Adolphus Windeler, who, given his professional training, had been responsible for the handling of the ropes in at least two lynchings. His journal confirms details from Shirley's account and matter-of-factly notes that Brown had to be "forked up and down several times to break his neck."[35]

According to his journal, he was also responsible for one of the earliest recorded lynchings of an African American in California. Recorded as Joshua

Robertson, or "Josh," he had been, like Brown, accused of robbery and was brought to Rich Bar to be tried by the miners[36] (color plate 1).

"Josh" had been Shirley's cook for three months, and in a letter to her sister, she doubted the veracity of the charges.[37] Writing on the episode, she gives a sense of the futility that must have been shared by all lynch victims when she wrote, "He said, very truly, that whether innocent or guilty, they would hang him; and so he 'died and made no sign,' with a calm indifference, as the novelists say, 'worthy of a better cause.'"[38]

AN AMERICAN TRADITION

Those familiar with the history of lynching will not be surprised to learn that the number of African Americans lynched in California is extremely small when compared to the southeastern United States. In fact, three of the most widely cited sources on lynching identify only two cases of African Americans being lynched in California as compared to the over five hundred cases recorded in Mississippi during the same period.[39] These same sources placed California's total number of lynchings somewhere between twenty-five and fifty cases.[40] The remaining cases have been repeatedly, if curiously, identified as white, regardless of the fact that American Indians, Asians, and Latinos (including at least one Mexican national) were counted in their number.

I identified at least eight cases that involved the lynching of African Americans in California, and when I combined these with the lynchings of American Indians, Asians, and Latinos from North and South America, the number of racially or ethnically motivated lynchings increased from 2 to 210.[41] This number does not include the 22 cases in which the race, ethnicity, or national origins of the victims could not be determined.[42]

In addition, *Lynching in the West* includes many new cases involving the lynching and summary execution of persons of European origin or descent, bringing the total from a recorded 48 cases to 120.[43] If all these cases were included in the national statistics on lynching, California's ranking would move from the twenty-first to the sixth worst state in the nation.[44] The greatest problem encountered in compiling these statistics was the time frame represented in the most widely cited studies; many of these case lists begin in the 1880s, and as the Cota case suggests, California's ranking would be very different if all of the state's cases could be acknowledged. This is not to suggest that the number of cases recorded in other states wouldn't be expanded by extending their lists back in time as well but that California's most turbulent years occurred prior to the dates conventionally covered in the most widely cited sources. *Lynching in the West* seeks to not only correct the historical record but to wrestle with the question of *erasure* itself, a historical (but not irreversible) phenomenon whose impact can be seen in the national statistics on lynching.

LIFE IN THE GOLD FIELDS

The first Anglo-American, African American, Latin American, Australian, Chinese, and European fortune hunters borrowed mining techniques from Chilean and Mexican miners, learned how to brew acorns into "coffee" from Indians, bought tortillas and chili from Mexican women, and had their laundry washed in Chinese camps.[45] There were also Latinos or *native Californians*, as they were known, who already lived on ranches or who lived in the small towns that had sprung up around the handful of still-functioning parish churches. These Spanish speaking *Californios* sold beef, produce, and wine to the miners and occasionally even tried their hand at mining. Beneath this lofty image of intercultural exchange, racial, ethnic, and national biases were being reconsidered, revised, and newly formulated; whether taking on new forms or solidifying long-held beliefs, these constructs would leave an indelible mark on the region for generations to come.

In California, as immigrants continued to flood into the state in the 1850s and 1860s, American Indians were constantly and increasingly being targeted for removal from their lands. These conflicts led to numerous Indians wars and outright massacres, and for every Indian killed by acts of aggression, many more died from disease. Those that survived took jobs on ranches, wandered in the city squares, or were relocated to reservation lands. Likewise, Chinese immigrants were driven from their claims, denied the opportunity to own land, and characterized as "heathen Chinee" for their spiritual beliefs. Even those who lived on Mexican and Spanish land grants found their long-held privileges weakened as land grants were challenged, overturned, or lost from taxes owed. In the gold fields, Mexicans, Peruvians, and Chileans were driven from their claims, and Mexican and native-born Latinos were repeatedly characterized as mongrels and bandits.

Given such overt challenges, one of the greatest obstacles to understanding the history of lynching in the West must be traced back to the concept of vigilantism itself. The irony is that while terms like "frontier justice" or "popular tribunal" still invoke images of cattle rustlers and stagecoach robbers meeting justice on a lawless frontier, they also mask a history of racial violence in a region that was not only culturally diverse but still is.

Coined by later historians, the term "frontier justice" has been applied to everything from racially motivated lynchings to urban vigilantes: dandies that dressed in finely tailored suits and vests and held mock trials that paralleled court proceedings in every manner—except for being legally constituted. Even the most ambitious researchers are challenged to distinguish substantial differences between the practices referred to as vigilance committees, lynch mobs, kangaroo courts, hanging parties, and sheriff's posses.

Often perceived as the sole expression of law in Gold Rush mining camps and in the region's burgeoning new cities, vigilantism could be willed into existence with chilling efficacy, punishing horse thieves and gamblers in a moment's notice or unseating corrupt city officials in places like San Francisco.[46] A reasonably accurate description for some of the most celebrated cases, this malevolent presence could not exist without lasting repercussions to the judicial system, and in subsequent decades, lynch mobs and self-appointed committees of vigilance would become so commonplace that sheriffs would be forced to hide, disguise, or move their prisoners to keep them from the impassioned mob.

To make matters worse, in the nineteenth century, the term *lynch law* included numerous forms of vigilante justice, ranging from hanging to flogging, banishment, branding, ear cropping, and other forms of summary justice that have complicated the study of lynching in the American West. The cases from which the chapters draw include only those that conform to the Tuskegee Institute's definition of lynching, a definition which reads, "There must be legal evidence that a person was killed. That person must have met death illegally. A group of three or more persons must have participated in the killing. The group must have acted under the pretext of service to justice, race or tradition."[47] The greatest advantage to using the same definition that guided previous scholars in establishing the national statistics on lynching is that California's case list can now be compared and contrasted within a national context.

With regard to the availability of legally sanctioned punishments, the first state prison opened in January 1851 on a ship named the *Waban*, and construction began on a new city jail in San Francisco in February of that same year; in spite of these early advances, funding and labor issues would delay the completion of the state prison at San Quentin until 1854.[48] In the interim, the newspapers were filled with accounts of prisoners escaping from these floating prisons, which, when combined with the embryonic state of the legal system, helps to explain the apparent explosion of extrajudicial activities in the 1850s and 1860s. But why there were vigilance committees and lynch mobs in the West is not questioned as much as why these practices were uncritically accepted well into the twentieth century — nearly a century after the legal system was first established?

Even as new courthouses and county jails were being completed in the 1860s and 1870s, lynch mobs and vigilance committees continued to meet, but unlike their predecessors, many of these new collectives shifted their actions from the light of day to the anonymity of night. Indeed, these extralegal proceedings were increasingly performed by masked mobs whose lawless acts could be worse than the criminals they prosecuted. To give one example, in 1879, Elijah Frost, "Bige" Gibson, and Tom McCracken were legally arrested for the larceny of a saddle and some pieces of harness.[49] Though guarded by two deputy sheriffs at Brown's Hotel while awaiting trial, at one o'clock in the morning on September 4, 1879, a gang of vigilantes overpowered the guards and escorted the prisoners to the nearest bridge, where they were hanged with a well rope that had been borrowed from a neighbor.[50] From a legal perspective, stealing "some pieces of harness" can hardly be said to merit the death penalty — even by the staunchest of death penalty advocates.

FRONTIER JUSTICE AND RACE

The most significant data to emerge from this study have to do with the impact of race on the history of lynching in California. Some may question the comparison of the self-appointed vigilance committees and necktie parties of frontier justice to the race hatred and brutality of lynch mobs in the South. However, national statistics on lynching have always included the lynching deaths of both blacks and whites; some of the most widely cited sources record over fourteen hundred Anglo-American deaths by lynching out of a total that hovers around five thousand cases nationwide, depending on the source.[51] The presence of whites, or Anglos, in the national statistics has not diminished the impact of lynching on African American history. Asians, American Indians, and Latinos of Mexican and Latin American descent were lynched in the West, yet no one has acknowledged that racial bias may be as integral to the study of Western lynching as it has been to the study of lynching nationwide. This historical erasure has been heightened by the fact that lynching has become conflated with white racism against blacks. This observation is not intended to diminish the significance of lynching to the history of African Americans; it instead attempts to acknowledge that the history of lynching has touched other racial and racialized communities in other historical moments. Even though the number of cases recorded in the

West is considerably smaller than the number recorded in the South, these lynchings were no less fatal.

That lynching has long been thought of in terms of black and white racial categories has contributed to the general absence of information on cases involving other nonwhite communities, and it has ultimately served to lock blacks and whites in a false binary of race.[52]

Although race was once seen as a biological fact, many race theorists now recognize that ethnicity, class, and nation are the three categorical paradigms that have guided race and race relations in the nineteenth and twentieth centuries.[53] Whether one uses race, ethnicity, or nationality as a guiding principle, the record suggests that lynching was far more deeply ingrained in the national consciousness than has been previously acknowledged.

Likewise, questions of class alone cannot explain lynching in the West. In the nineteenth century, race hatred was driven as much by the pseudo-sciences as by class privilege and social Darwinist models; and concepts such as Manifest Destiny were invoked to justify war with Mexico, the killing of thousands of American Indians, and the taking of thousands of acres of land from Mexican and Spanish land grant holders. The case studies in this book also make it apparent that such concepts contributed to the lynching of hundreds of persons in the American West.

MARKING THE TERRITORY

In the American West, communities that were identified as nonwhite were regularly targeted by exclusionary acts that placed restrictions on who could mine, own land, buy a home, vote, serve on a jury, become a citizen, and even get married.[54] Even the names of the mining camps revealed something about the new social order. Chinese Camp, French Camp, and "Chili Gulch" (named after the people from Chile, not the pepper) emphasized national identity, but nationality was not the only source of inspiration for camp names. There were others with names like Poverty Hill, Mormon Island, Yankee Hill, Nigger Hill, Murderer's Bar, and Hangtown, which literally mapped out the new economic and political landscape.[55]

As mining towns gave rise to new cities, it was not uncommon to read about the emergence of Mexican "Sonoratowns," named for the many Mexicans who came from Sonora, or the many new "Chinatowns." Meanwhile, the wealthiest "Yankee" and European settlers took up residence on higher ground, creating, for example, Nobb Hill in San Francisco or Bunker Hill in Los Angeles. Many of these original communities have migrated or witnessed the displacement of older immigrants (as they were replaced by more recent arrivals), but the basic principals have remained constant; each community created, or was forced to create, separate markets, separate schools, and separate economies, and with varying success, each attempted to provide opportunities for self-improvement to its members.

Distinguishing between race, ethnicity, and nationality was not always as straightforward as it is today, and in the nineteenth century it was not uncommon for the term "Mexican" to be employed as either a racial, class, or national marker, or all three. This is nowhere more true than in California's history of lynching, where Mexicans, Chileans, Peruvians, native Californians, and other immigrants from Latin America might find themselves called Chilean in one account and Mexican in another.

The lynching of African Americans has been recorded in many Western states and, as stated, is regularly included in the national statistics on lynching. Likewise, the lynching or summary execution of Anglos has long been recognized as a part of vigilantism, and countless examples can be found in regionalist texts on the rough-and-tumble days of the Old West. So one of the fundamental goals of this book is to allow the nation, and the many communities it represents, to finally acknowledge that when taken collectively, the lynching of American Indians, blacks, Chinese, and Latinos constituted the majority of cases of lynchings and extrajudicial executions in California. Perhaps this history may even inspire other researchers, students, and history buffs to look anew at their own states and hometowns.

SEARCHING FOR CALIFORNIA'S HANG TREES

The initial research for this book grew out of an interdisciplinary approach that sought to pair the case records with the analysis of photographic and historic images.[56] In addition to tracking down historic photographs, drawings, and prints, I began looking for any kind of official documentation that I could find: an announcement in a newspaper, published leaflets, or first-person narratives which could be confirmed in multiple sources.

In California, there is only one official historical marker. It is located in Placerville, or "Hangtown" as it has long been known.[57] The sign marks a spot that is just yards from where one of California's most infamous hang trees stood.[58] The marker is in front of Hangman's Tree Bar, and inside, next to the jukebox, a small papier-mâché tree branch spouts from the wall and is said to mark the site of the original tree. As recently as 2005, a manikin was

1. Ken Gonzales-Day, "Historical Marker #141," 2002, chromogenic print, 8 by 10 inches. Courtesy of the artist.

tethered to the building with a hangman's noose and dangled above the bar's entrance. According to the bartender, this Western clad creation must be re-lynched each year due to the bleaching effects of the sun—a crime for which he is surely not guilty (figure 1).

The historical record clearly indicates that while telephone poles, bridges, corral gates, and, in at least one case, a wagon could be used to hang a person, the method of choice for lynch mobs and vigilantes usually involved throwing a piece of rope over one of the low hanging branches of California's many native oak species.[59]

As a practicing artist, a photographer, and an avid researcher, I set out to travel to and photograph as many of the sites as I could. I photographed oak trees in rustic and urban settings, in strip malls, and amid tract housing. Sadly, California's native oak species are plagued by sudden oak death, a mysterious disease that can be carried on the shoes and clothing of hikers and local residents. It attacks the frail immune systems of California's native species, and as a result, these last living witnesses to California's history of lynching may one day be gone.[60] The California oak grows extremely slowly, and some preservation groups have claimed that a large tree can be several hundred years old, which means that many of these trees would have shaded the lynch mobs and hanging parties as they passed under their branches (figure 2).

Over the past five years I have retraced the steps of the lynch mob and vigilance committee, and these photographs have become an irrefutable record of my journey. Standing at these sites, even the most beautiful landscape is undone. Sometime a natural landmark or the mention of a street name guided me, but often I had no way of knowing whether I was photographing the exact site or not. In my own journey, the photographs have come to symbolize points of resistance in a vast landscape, both physical and historical, over which I have no control. A solitary figure on a solitary journey, I have documented the empty space that lies between the historically unseen body of the lynch victim and my own unseen body. Standing on the side of the road, tucked beneath the old-fashioned black hood that covers my camera's ground glass, cars slow and people stop to ask what I am doing. What can I tell them?

Once at a site, I gaze into the haunted shade and try to remember the names of those who died—if known. I also try to remember the names of their victims. In visiting the many different locations and regions of the state I have been able to see this history with new eyes. Sleeping at a roadside hotel or camped in some pristine wilderness area, I can sometimes understand how isolated and threatened these small communities must have felt. In the Gold Rush town of Columbia, now preserved as a state park, travelers can wander down Main Street or sit in the cool dampness of the old jail cell. There is a courtroom wedged in a long narrow room a few short blocks from both the jail and the saloon. Scarcely wider than a modern hallway, it is filled with small chairs. One begins to understand the degree of isolation that the people in these communities must have felt as they crowded into the courtroom, huddled side by side, to pass judgment on murderers and thieves—in between rounds of whiskey at the saloon.

Part pilgrimage and part memorial, my work has taken me to hundreds of California's lynch sites, and no matter how pristine or developed these sites may be, my experience of the landscape has been forever transformed.

THE CHAPTERS

Using the history of lynching as a point of departure, chapter 1 examines the historical misrecognition of lynching from two perspectives, first, by looking to popular conceptions of frontier justice and the Wild West, and second, by exploring the antilynching movement's role in shaping the history of lynch-

2. Ken Gonzales-Day, "Aqua Fria Road," 2005, chromogenic print, 46 by 36 inches. Courtesy of the artist.

ing nationwide.[61] To give a sense of the amount of information that was previously available on the history of lynching in the West, one must look to the National Association for the Advancement of Colored People (NAACP) and the Tuskegee Institute Archive in Tuskegee, Alabama, each of which generated some of most widely cited statistics on the history of lynching in the United States.

Under the Tuskegee definition of lynching, the actions of some of the most respected vigilance committees, typically excluded from the history of lynching, would become recognizable as lynching, if for no other reason than the vigilance committee was regularly invoked as a regional "tradition" as early as 1851. Later committees bypassed most, if not all, of the procedures followed by the state's most celebrated vigilance committees.[62]

Chapter 2 looks to the history of capital punishment from its midcentury decline in Europe to its simultaneous emergence in California. During the first five decades of California statehood, legal executions were mostly administered by individual counties, and as a result there is no single registry or source from which to gather information as to whether a given execution was legally constituted or not. Luckily, the newspapers were often adamant about distinguishing legal executions from lynchings because legal executions were seen to emphasize California's progress toward becoming a modern state. However, unlike a growing number of other states which passed laws that demanded that all legal executions be conducted beyond the public view, California's legal executions continued to draw crowds that numbered in the thousands well into the final years of the nineteenth century.

Once seen as a neutral depository for regional, individual, and institutional records, in an age of increasingly limited resources and ever-expanding audiences, the archive has itself become a subject of study.[63] Its collecting policies, its requirements for access, and its methods of indexing and organizing materials can have an impact on which histories get told. The contemporary historian David Montejano states: "The death or resurrection of race divisions is fundamentally political" because "the notion of race does not just consist of ideas and sentiments; it comes into being when these ideas and sentiments are publicly articulated and institutionalized." The question of how race and vigilantism have been "publicly articulated and institutionalized" is specifically taken up in chapter 3, which considers the archive.[64]

Moving from the categorization of race to racial categorizations themselves, chapter 4 looks at the intersection of race and lynching from a very different perspective than that found in the previous chapters. Comparing the evolution of "the American type" with its nemesis, the *greaser*, chapter 4 explores the tensions between these two groups, noting that as Anglo-Americans began to search for their own national identity they increasingly sought to distinguish themselves from their European ancestors as well as from the "barbarian" hoards that infested the West—Indian "savages," Mexican "greasers," and Chinese "celestials," among others.[65] Drawing from an analysis of physiognomy and a wide range of pseudosciences, chapter 4 demonstrates how "the American type" evolved in response to social Darwinist fears that Americans might someday devolve into "primitive" dark-skinned beings.

Finally, chapter 5 looks to some of the most turbulent episodes from California's past and details specific examples from the compiled case records in its consideration of *the wonder gaze*, a concept, it is argued, that contributed to shaping the image of the "Mexican" bandit and murderer as exemplified by the public display of the "head preserved in spirits" or the public hanging of the only woman to be lynched California's history.

More than a history of Gold Rush miners or cowboys, *Lynching in the West* revives a past that had nearly been lost as lynching and other forms of vigilantism faded from historical view. But should this past be forgotten? In examining the relationship between the evolution and development of the Anglo-American as a national type and nineteenth-century attitudes about race, this book looks beyond the spectacle of lynching to the social histories which made these acts possible in the first place. This book also serves to remind the nation's many communities that it is never to too late to reclaim your past or to acknowledge the past of your neighbors.

DISGUISED BANDIT

Analyze punitive methods
not simply as consequences
of legislation or as indicators
of social structures, but as
techniques possessing their own
specificity in the more general
field of other ways of exercising
power. Regard punishment as a
political tactic.

—Michel Foucault, *Discipline
and Punish*

CHAPTER ONE

Counting the Dead:
Frontier Justice and the
Antilynching Movement

CORPORAL PUNISHMENT

In *Discipline and Punish*, Michel Foucault (1926–84) tracked corporal punishment as it moved from a medieval spectacle of hot irons, flesh-pulling pincers,
and other marvels of the grotesque to an increasingly discrete and sanitized
practice performed away from the public gaze. He detailed the evolution and
subsequent decline of public execution, along with other methods of corporal punishment, once so common throughout Europe.[1] In his text, Foucault employs a vast array of gruesome details, and with each appearance of
phrases like "drawn and quartered," "flogged," and "flayed," he makes palpable
the modern disdain for public torture. However, while the analysis of capital
punishment in Europe may be familiar, less obvious are the myriad ways that
corporal punishment came to shape the image of the American West in the
national consciousness.

This study begins a half a world away from where Foucault's ends and extends the discussion of public execution (legally or otherwise constituted) to the Western region of the United States. In the epigraph, Foucault insists that one must analyze methods of punishment, including capital punishment, not merely as consequences of legislation or as indicators of social structures but as proof that power is systemically dispersed. This principle holds true in California, where the public display of lynch victims and those legally executed continued until the final years of the nineteenth century, yet the impact of racial bias within these histories was masked; a realization that confirms not only that power is systemically dispersed but that it can be measured on the branches of each hang tree.

As the spectacle of capital punishment began its retreat in the middle of the nineteenth century from the public square to the cloistered halls of an increasingly legislated, modernized, sanitized, and highly regulated penal system in much of western Europe, this dark legacy had already managed to stow away in vessels leaving ports throughout Europe and make its way, first across the Atlantic and then around Cape Horn, before finally landing upon the shores California's Barbary Coast, as San Francisco's waterfront was known from the first days of the Gold Rush to its material destruction in the great earthquake of 1906. Once on land, this modern plague crept like the rats carried in the ship hulls to the mining camps and growing townships throughout the region.

In California, the comparison of capital punishment and extralegal executions also provides a remarkable point of departure for the discussion of race because each of these histories speaks to the differential treatment received by persons of color throughout the second half of the nineteenth century, and even extended into the twentieth. The cases (recorded in the appendixes) reveal that inequalities in power were often drawn along racial lines and that questions of race, ethnicity, and nation were, more than has been previously acknowledged, obscured by the near-mythic image of frontier justice and Western vigilantism.

THE GREASER ACT

The Anti-Vagrancy Act of 1855, also known as the Greaser Act, was renamed only after it had been on the books for a year.[2] Section two of the statute explained that this new law was directed at "all persons who are commonly known as 'Greasers' or the issue of Spanish or Indian blood . . . and who go armed and are not peaceable and quiet persons."[3] Less about the behavior than the "racial" construction of a specific group of people, it should be kept in mind that while the Spanish were recognized as part of the Caucasian races, they, and southern Europeans more generally, were often characterized as inferior to northern Europeans while the indigenous peoples of the Americas (North and South) were characterized as "savages." In the cited passage, "Spanish" was intended to include Mexicans. Reflecting the cultural mores of the time, laws like the Greaser Act went so far as to conflate race and racial mixing with criminal behavior itself.

Even before the Anti-Vagrancy Act, the most damaging of California's early legislation may have been the creation of the Foreign Miner's Tax of 1851 which actually required that all foreign-born miners pay a monthly license fee of \$20 and which was intended (according to its authors) to booster the state's empty coffers and reclaim some of the great wealth that was flowing out of the state in the form of gold dust.[4] However, the fee was to be paid whether the miners made money at mining or not, and it is this aspect of the law which also served to punish those who were driven from theirs claims or otherwise denied equal protection in a fledgling legal system in which laws like the Anti-Vagrancy Act were sometimes authored in order to reduce legal access and not to expand it.

In theory, the tax was supposed to apply to all foreign-born miners regardless of their country of origin, but in practice, the tax really served to drive thousands of Mexican and Latin America miners from their claims. Mexicans born in what had become California were promised U.S. citizenship under the terms of the Treaty of Guadalupe Hidalgo, but according to the Miner's Tax, they were required to pay the tax in direct contradiction with the rights they had been promised.[5] For native Californians, this racial and national double consciousness would find parallels in their differential access to due process as well.

To give a snapshot of the state's other inhabitants, one recent study has claimed that contrary to prior estimates, the American Indian population may have been as high as 150,000 in 1848, a number estimated to represent half the precontact number and which would be reduced to a mere 20,000 by the century's end.[6] The discovery of gold and the subsequent annexation of California into the Union would ignite a mushroom cloud of immigration that would take the non-Indian population from approximately 10,000 in 1846 to over 100,000 just three years later, reaching 1.5 million by century's end.[7]

Mexican and Mexican Americans were not the only "foreign-born" persons to protest the Miner's Tax, and among the many stated injustices of the provision, one mountaineer complained that no distinction was made between those foreigners who had brought their families and intended to become citizens and those "degraded Asiatics and South Sea Islanders, who are not fit and who do not desire to become citizens."[8]

However, the greatest cries against the tax came from those who made their livelihoods by selling goods to the miners, and it was only through their complaints that the tax was eventually repealed. In the end, the Foreign Miner's Tax was credited with having driven from the country "many thousands of the most industrious miners, especially Mexicans and Chileans, whose labors the state could ill spare."[9] An unexpected compliment for the time, the statement acknowledged the fact that Mexican and Chilean miners brought much of the initial mining technology with them from Latin America.

The Greaser Act and the Foreign Miner's Tax are concrete examples of how racial theories could extend their influence beyond the gibbet and hang tree and demonstrate that such practices were only the most extreme manifestations of bias in a systemic continuum whose influence could be felt from the halls of legislature to the aisles of the general store.

RACING THE WEST

Trying to quantify racial or racialized experiences in the West in the later half of the nineteenth century is no easy task, but the history of lynching provides a historical glimpse into life in California in a way that the U. S. Census records and first-person narratives cannot. That persons of color were statistically more likely to be lynched than legally executed, in spite of their small numbers, reveals something about the impact of race on this dismal history, and while race has had an undeniable influence on the history of lynching in the region, I have also been able to document 120 persons of Anglo-American or European descent from this continent, Europe, and Australia who also died at the hands of lynch mobs and vigilance committees. This number constitutes slightly more than one-third of the total caseload of extralegal and summary executions.

The most striking statistic to evolve from the research has been the lynching or summary execution of 132 Latinos or Hispanics (Chileans, Peruvians, Mexicans, and other persons of Latin American descent or origin) who died at the hands of impromptu vigilance committees and lynch mobs and who have somehow managed to be completely erased from the popular image of frontier justice.[10] This in spite of the fact that, depending on the source, even as early as 1850, long before countless waves of Anglo immigrants entered

California, Latinos may have constituted less than 10 percent of the state's population.[11]

The lynching of African Americans has long shaped the discussion of lynching in this country, and as noted in the introduction, I was able to document eight cases in California, six more than were previously recorded by either the NAACP or the Tuskegee Institute Archive.[12] But I was equally surprised to discover that in addition to blacks and Latinos, twenty-nine Chinese immigrants were lynched in California.[13] Perhaps most disturbing of all, the new list documents forty-one cases of lynching or summary execution involving American Indians.[14] This isn't counting the untold thousands massacred or "cleared" from the land throughout the state.

The ethnic, racial, or national origin of California's lynch victims is also revealed in the case list, and this information has been summarized in appendix 1, which shows that Latinos were nearly five times more likely to be lynched than Chinese immigrants, three times more likely to be lynched than American Indians, and nearly sixteen times more likely to be lynched than African Americans. At seventy-eight cases, the total number of lynchings and summary executions for these three groups is well below the number of cases involving Latinos of Mexican and Chilean descent or origin. In fact, Latinos identified as "Mexican" outnumber all other groups, including Anglos.

According to the 1850 California census (completed in 1851), the total number of African Americans in California was 962, as compared to the 92,597 "whites."[15] The Anthenæum, an association of African American men based in San Francisco, reported 1,500 African Americans in San Francisco in April 1854 and provided and extensively detailed list of their trades, possessions, and property.[16] Unfortunately, the 1850 census makes no specific mention of Asians, American Indians, or persons of Mexican or Latin American descent. With regard to the Chinese, *Harper's Magazine* reported that between February 1848 and May 1852, 11,953 Chinese arrived in San Francisco, of which 7 were women and 167 had returned or died.[17]

The 1860 census didn't fare much better than its predecessor, but out of 397, 994 persons recorded, it included 52,731 persons who were recorded as neither black nor white.[18] This number is in keeping with the general statistics found on American Indian and Chinese populations, and it is not without significance that Mexicans and Mexican Americans would be subsequently recorded as "Mexican," white, or Caucasian, depending upon the year and region in which the census was conducted.

Referring to persons of Mexican, Spanish, or Latin American descent or origin, one author has noted that in the early 1850s it was not uncommon to hear "Yankees" refer to all "Spaniards" as "half-civilized black men."[19] Such insults sought to parallel the racial mixing of the Moors and the Spanish in Europe with the racial mixing of Spanish colonials and the native peoples of the Americas. Beyond the question of miscegenation, terms like "Mexican" or "Spaniard" could also be deployed to signal class status, the nation of origin, and even the specific ethnic origin of the person referenced. Ethnography was a rapidly growing field of study throughout the second half of the nineteenth century, and the question of race was increasingly being debated throughout the United States and Europe. Beginning as early as the 1840s, scholars and humanists tried to wrestle with a number of related issues, not the least of which was the "slavery question," and it has long been acknowledged that California's decision to become a free state greatly aided its rapid admission into the Union.

In the 1840s, before the war with Mexico, the Western frontier was largely seen as a barren and godless wasteland inhabited by "savage" Indians and "mongrel" Mexicans whose removal from this continent was seen as inevitable.[20] Anglo-Americans increasingly came to see themselves as a race-nation that was destined to represent the greatest achievements of the "Caucasian races" through the popular, if fictive, construction of the "Anglo-Saxon."[21] Borrowed from European race theory, it has been argued that the Anglo-Saxon race was literally willed into being by northern and western Europeans who sought to link themselves back to a more distant Teutonic and Aryan past while distinguishing themselves, not only from the peoples they had subjugated and enslaved, but also from Asians, indigenous Americans, southern Europeans, Gypsies, Moors, Jews, and Mexicans.[22]

The contemporary historian Reginald Horsman has noted that the legacy of "Puritan colonists, Revolutionary patriots, conquerors of a wilderness, and creators of an immense material prosperity" had taken hold of national consciousness by the 1850s.[23] Mexicans, who inhabited many of the farthest reaches of the new territories, were thought of as being a half-breed race, scarcely above the indigenous "Indians" who were regularly portrayed as primitive or savage peoples. Much more could be said about the origins of these terms, but suffice it to say that after 1848 and the end of the war with Mexico, a war which can now be recognized as the willful invasion of a vast area that the United States had increasingly come to believe was its God-given right to possess, these terms were integral to the concept of Manifest Destiny and the massive westward expansion that followed.

Most surprising of all, some advocates for American expansionism actually imagined that the Mexicans and Indians would magically melt away as the Anglo-American race took its "rightful" place at the helm of the nation, and it was not uncommon to find such statements as "the Indian and white races in California and Mexico . . . must fade away; while the mixing of different branches of the Caucasian family in the States . . . must stride the continent."[24]

By the end of the nineteenth century, physiognomy, phrenology, and various contradictory theories of evolution would further modify popular conceptions of the "Anglo-Saxon" race, ultimately generating a uniquely "American" evolutionary *type* known simply as "the Anglo-American."[25] The term was intended to refer to those "inhabitants of America in whom English blood predominates . . . and may therefore be considered as being practically descriptive of a national type—the American of the Great Republic."[26] In recognizing the evolution of a new "national type," one realizes that the Western frontier was not seen as being uninhabited as much as being inhabited by the wrong people.

In England, the Victorian biologist and early social philosopher Herbert Spencer (1820–1903) and the British Naturalist Charles Darwin (1809–1882) would add more fuel to the fire, as they and others continued to wrestle with the theory of evolution throughout the 1850s and 1860s. Their ideas, and their further interpretation by the social Darwinists, as they have come to be known and who will be discussed further in a later chapter, would have a lasting impact on secular and religious interpretations of everything from the creation story found in Genesis to debates about the age of the earth.[27]

While Darwin's theory of natural selection may be familiar to most readers, it is Spencer's version that concerns us here. Spencer, who was more interested in philosophy than science, would claim, or at least imply, that he had published his own theory of evolution before Darwin, and he continued to expand his ideas over the next three decades. It is generally agreed that Spencer was greatly influenced by Darwin's work and not the other way around, but what is significant about Spencer was the emphasis he placed on the idea of "inherited characteristics," and his concept would be essential to all manner of social Darwinists. For Spencer, evolution was only half of the equation, and he went to particular pains to articulate what he considered to be its complement; that is to say, the concept of *dissolution*. As it turns out, this concept would have as much if not more impact on Western racial formation than Darwin himself. Spencer argued, "An entire history of anything must include its appearance out of the imperceptible and its disappearance into the imperceptible."[28] This concept of "disappearance" lay at the heart of his *dissolution* theory, and it is relevant to the study of lynching in the West because it would be openly applied to the indigenous and Mexican populations throughout the Americas in a wide variety of sources that imagined that these populations would somehow wither and vanish with the arrival of the "Americans." In an 1857 article published two years before Darwin's *Origin of Species*, Spencer laid out his fundament claim that each of the "races" represents a distinct phase of human evolution. He writes:

> The advance from the simple to the complex, through a process of successive differentiations, is seen alike in the earliest changes of the Universe . . . it is seen in the geologic and climatic evolution of the Earth, and of every single organism on its surface; it is seen in the evolution of Humanity, whether contemplated in the civilized individual, or in the aggregation of races; it is seen in the evolution of Society. . . . From the remotest past which Science can fathom, down to the novelties of yesterday, that in which Progress essentially consists, is the transformation of the homogeneous into the heterogeneous."[29]

In his fourth edition of *First Principles*, he expands upon this initial view, writing that "the species, as a whole, has been made more heterogeneous by the multiplication of the races from each other," and he goes on to compare various races, noting the "underdeveloped" legs of the Papuan and the "more complex" nervous system of the "civilized man," assertions which he uses to support the now-long-discredited claim that humans evolved from "several separate stocks" or species of man.[30] These "separate stocks" were considered to be inferior to the "civilized" races, and should there be any doubt about the speed with which the races could appear and disappear, Spencer writes that with the "Anglo-American" one finds an example of a "wholly new variety arising within these few generations."[31] Indeed, Spencer's ideas would eventually migrate to the West Coast where they would be used to expand upon old biases and be directed against one of the most reviled of American types, the greaser.

The greaser is an interesting racial slur because it so clearly acknowledges the impact of miscegenation in "Spanish America," as it was sometimes called. The term greaser was intended as an insult to those of Spanish, Mexican, and Latin American descent. It was used as early as 1846 and as late the 1970s, at which point it fell from popular usage.[32] It was the equivalent of calling someone a "half-breed," a "mongrel," and, as already suggested, it was intended to highlight the presence of indigenous or "primitive" bloodlines.

The precise origins of the term greaser are unknown, and some have argued that the term derived from the shiny skin and hair of the darkest

Mexican Indians. Still others have tried to attribute it to the oily content of Mexican food, but this second explanation is unlikely given the overarching simplicity of frontier cuisine, which primarily consisted of tortillas, beans, and dried or roasted meat.[33] If its origins are unknown, its meaning isn't, and the nineteenth-century adventurer, writer, conservationist, and historian Charles F. Lummis (1859–1928) noted an equivalence between calling a Mexican a "greaser" and calling an African American a "nigger."[34] Employed as a derogatory term by Anglo-Americans against California-born Latinos and Hispanics even before California became a U.S. territory, the term evolved into a full-blown racial slur long before its reappearance on the East Coast in the twentieth century, where it referred to the slicked-back hair of semi-rebellious Anglo youth who reeked havoc by, among other things, donning black leather jackets, wearing their hair long, and riding their hogs, or motor-cycles, up and down manicured suburban streets. Not surprisingly, given the question of erasure, this popular usage of greaser may have even helped to obfuscate what was, even then, nearly a century of racial violence in the West.

In an article that appeared in the *Atlantic Monthly* in 1899, the author, a William R. Lighton, left us the following description:

> The mestizo, the Greaser, [is the] half-blood offspring of the marriage of antiquity with modernity. Time cannot take from him the unmistakable impress of old Spain. But his Spanish appearance is not his dominant characteristic. His skin has been sunbrowned for centuries; his nose and cheeks are broad; his lips are thick; his brows are heavy, sheltering eyes soft, passionate, inscrutable. . . . Anomalous as he is, he is one of the few distinct types in our national life whose origin is fully known to us.[35]

In case there were any doubts about how this invocation of the "type" relied upon evolution theory, Lighton specifically invokes Spencer's theory of *dissolution*, flatly stating, "And the Greaser is passing [from this earth]. It is now quite in order to write his obituary."[36] He writes:

> Some one—I think it was Mr. Herbert Spencer—has declared that the unmistakable mark of a high race of men is individualization, differentiation, heterogeneity, and variation from type. If that be a test, then we need not hesitate to say of the Greaser that he stands very low in the scale; for, . . . he is all alike. Choose one, and you a have a pattern from which all his brethren could be drawn, with only slight modifications in the items of beard and adipose.[37]

That is to say that, aside from facial hair and fat deposits, all Mexicans are alike.

Many Americans have long imagined that California was populated with Spanish Europeans, and indeed some families can trace their lineage back to the cobbled streets of Madrid. But as the case lists (appendixes 1 and 2) make clear, Spanish, Mexican, Chilean, or native Californians of Mexican and Latin American descent or origin could, and were, regularly referred to as "Mexicans" or greasers in the newspapers and historical texts from which the case lists were drawn.[38] Where possible, I have noted whether a lynch victim was identified as coming from Spain, Mexico, California, or Texas, but the question of exact origin would not have been as important to the lynch mob as it is for readers today.

The contemporary expectation that this text will confirm beyond all doubt the racial origin of the "Mexican" lynch victim may be part of the same phenomenon that led to the erasure of this history in the first place. In the nineteenth century, appearance was everything, and tracking the impact of this phenomenology of difference in the Anglo-American imaginary not only contributed to the history of lynching but to the legacy of racial formation on the local and national stage. In going through the case histories, one inescapable fact emerged: in the absence of modern evidentiary proof, being perceived to be "Mexican" was often the only material clue considered in determining a person's guilt or innocence. Beyond the question of race, one must also recognize that the research was gleaned from texts which themselves reflected the racial, ethnic, and nationalist models of the eras in which they were authored.

Scholars have come to recognize that the notion of "race," once seen as deeply problematic, has less to do with biology than it does with social and historical conventions. Given this recent shift, one may now go beyond the mere acknowledgment that the perception of race, real or imagined, could have a deadly impact. If race is a construct, a fiction, a practice, then this project has set out to excavate the many racist and racializing representations (whether found in text or image) hidden in the Western landscape. In specifically considering the Latino body in California, which has endured and been shaped by discourses of race, ethnicity, and nation over the past one hundred fifty years, this text begins to suggest more than historical correction alone.

In their groundbreaking book entitled *Racial Formation in the United States from the 1960s to the 1990s*, Michael Omi and Howard Winant define race as "a concept which signifies and symbolizes social conflicts and interests by referring to different types of human bodies."[39] But part of the question here is, how has the question of racial mixture, once driven by the phantasm of the other, transformed in this new era? If race is a concept whose time has gone, what is one to do with those identities, socially, politically, or otherwise constituted, which derive from racial admixture?

Returning to the nineteenth century, it must be acknowledged that many Anglo-Americans and Europeans demonstrated great disdain for the real (and perceived) presence of indigenous bloodlines throughout every level of what had been Spanish colonial society. T. J. Farnham stated: "The law of Nature which curses the mulatto here with a constitution less robust than that of either race from which he sprang, lays a similar penalty upon the mingling of the Indian and white races in California and Mexico."[40]

In the American West, Spanish immigration was never more than a trickle, and over time many of those families with the purest of bloodlines intermarried with America's indigenous peoples, along with other Spanish-speaking populations from Peru, Chile, Mexico, and a handful even married Anglos. After annexation, the use of the term "Spaniard" decreased as "Californio" and "native Californian" came into greater popular usage, but, like "Spaniard," these terms could refer to Californians of Spanish, Mexican, or Latin American origin or descent.

Finally, and most importantly, what are the multivalent meanings of the word "Mexican," and how might this term have an impact on the research? As already noted, it could be invoked to signal ethnicity, class, or nationality, and yet this slippage was reduced by going through the many case histories. The appended case list is able to identify the racial, ethnic, or regional origin of many of those summarily executed in California from 1850 to 1935.

With regard to Chileans, it is worth looking to a description given by a forty-niner by the name of Vincente Pérez Rosales who, in 1878, ridiculed the logic of how Anglos perceived Chileans. Summarizing their views, he wrote, "Chileans were descended from Spaniards — Spaniards were of Moorish ancestry, therefore a Chilean was at the best something like a Hottentot."[41] This passage is fascinating because, given the ridiculousness of the logic, one can now see that in the West, Chileans, Spaniards, Moors, blacks, and Latinos of Mexican and Latin American descent or origin were less linked by some fantastic racial fantasy than they were by the real history of lynching in the West.

Of all of the communities touched by this history, persons of Chinese descent may have been the easiest to identify because their names and national original were relatively transparent in the first decades of statehood. American Indians were also present in the case list, and even when their surnames were of Spanish origin, most journalists went out of their way to note their Indian ancestry.

Many will be surprised to learn that one of the greatest challenges to creating an accurate case list was encountered in identifying persons of northern and western European descent because, in many cases, their names, state, or country of origin were the only clues to their racial or ethnic origin.[42]

The appendixes also reveal that twenty-two cases remain completely unidentified, either by name or origin, and were apparently hanged without even being given the chance to say their names, as in the case when an unnamed escaped convict from the state prison stole a mule and was apprehended. He was allowed to leave unmolested, and it was only when he stole a second mule near Shasta that he was brought back to the scene of the original theft (in Red Bluffs) and summarily hanged. He requested to be shot, saying that if allowed, he would reveal his real name, but the crowd denied the request and so he reluctantly entered the ranks of those lynched.[43]

The term Spaniard was regularly applied to Mexicans, Latin Americans, and American born Latinos of indigenous and European descent, as in the hanging of a "Spaniard" named "Charley the Bull Fighter," whose proper name and country of origin remain unknown to this day. Thus, in the absence of additional information, I have recorded Charley the Bull Fighter as Spanish in the final list.[44] As in the Charley case, someone identified as Spanish or Mexican in the source material has remained so in the final list. If someone was identified as a Spaniard, a Mexican, or a Californio in different sources, I have included those terms as well.

LYNCHING AS CAPITAL PUNISHMENT

Beyond the slippage between "Mexican" and "Spaniard," the historical record also reveals that the term "lynching" has undergone many changes over the past century and a half. One cannot imagine how two such diverse interpretations can be applied to the same punitive method. No one tries to defend the lynching of African Americans in the South as a popular form of capital punishment (as many Anglo-Americans once did), but the lynching of blacks, Asians, Indians, and Latinos continues to be defended in many historical texts and popular representations as an unavoidable part of the taming the West. Why? To find the answer to this question it will be necessary to revisit two of the most dominant forces in shaping the popular understanding of lynching and other forms of popular justice in the United States. The first is the nearly mythic presence of frontier justice in the American West, and the second is linked to the five-decade struggle of the antilynching movement, which sought to bring an end to the lynching of African Americans across the nation.

Before considering the lasting impact of these historicizing forces, it may be beneficial to consider some of the similarities and differences between lynching and capital punishment in the American West. Unlike Europe and an increasing number of Eastern states, in California, capital punishment continued to be performed in public throughout most of the second half of the nineteenth century. Initially these executions took place in public settings because there were few places secure enough to escape the public's view, and may have also meant to demonstrate, to the viewing public, that the law could be as vigilant as any popular tribunal.

In California, lynching was always a public act, though after 1860, it increasingly took place under the cover of night. Both lynching and capital punishment made use of hanging as the favored method of execution. Legal execution was an example of what Foucault described as a legislated measure, while lynching, committees of vigilance, and other forms of summary execution, whether driven by community outrage or racial bias, were never legally constituted or recognized.

To add a little historical perspective, the punishment of hanging for those convicted for stealing a horse or a sheep was abolished in England in 1832, and burglary was completely removed from the list of capital offenses in 1836, only to become one of the first capital offenses in California in 1851.[45] One can understand how larceny came to be ranked as a capital offense in those first days of statehood, particularly during the height of the Gold Rush when a tent might be the only thing standing between one's belongings and a covetous neighbor.

One cannot really begin to understand the degree to which England and California differed in this period without addressing the image of vigilante justice made popular in the travel logs and eyewitness accounts which began to flow from gold fields in nearly the same remarkable quantities as the gold itself.

If, as Foucault suggests, we are to see each technique as an exercise of power, then one must also ask why California residents were so insistent upon keeping both forms. The familiar answer is that extralegal or summary forms of execution helped to bring law and order to the West. It has also been argued that these practices added to the economic and social stability for Anglo-American miners, farmers, and businessmen alike, as private property was increasingly protected. Their property would be legally and socially privileged over those Californians of Mexican and Latin American descent as well as from those who were excluded from citizenship under federal law.

Indigenous communities were regularly removed or relocated from their traditional lands, and the murder of Anglo-Americans by "Mexicans" could result in whole communities having their houses burned to the ground and being driven from their lands, as in the 1855 Rancheria tragedy in which reports claimed that between eight and sixteen Mexicans were hung without a trial of any kind. The Rancheria tragedy began because five Americans, one of whom was a woman, and one American Indian were murdered by a small band of bandits that included eight Latinos and one man "with red hair and whiskers" called Gregorio.[46] The band was generally represented as consisting of Mexican bandits in the newspaper and press of the time. Shortly after the "tragedy," three suspects were apprehended and summarily tried; their names were recorded only as Puertovino, Tancolino, and José. They were hanged to an oak tree. Afterward, the crowd proceeded to burn down every "Spanish" house, and a resolution was passed that "no Mexican shall hereafter reside at the above place"; any Mexicans found would be requested to leave—and receive one hundred fifty lashes to help them on their way.[47] The entire Mexican population quickly complied and left their homes forever. This much-touted example of frontier justice was specifically referred to as "mob law" in its own day and was attributed to "the terrible reign of Judge Lynch."[48] Speaking to the lynching of the Mexicans, one newspaper editorial complained, "No inquiry is made as to the guilt of one of the proscribed race, but they are hanged as unceremoniously as the huntsman shoots down the deer or the coyote. . . . Nearly every man in that region is under arms and ready to level on the first unfortunate greaser that comes across his track."[49] Meanwhile, the volunteer guard at Sutter tore down every house inhabited by Mexicans and ordered the entire Mexican population to leave town.[50]

Another newspaper reported that as many as sixteen Mexicans and Chileans were hanged and that after it was over not a single Mexican remained in the towns of Sutter or Rancheria. One newspaper would later assert that of all those hanged, only one had been connected with the murders.[51] As for poor Puertovino, it turns out that his accuser would take over his mining claim shortly after he was hanged, suggesting that he may not have been as guilty as the crowd supposed.[52]

Sheriff Phoenix of Amador County had gone in pursuit of some of the Mexicans connected with the Rancheria tragedy when on August 13 he was killed in a shootout. Two of the suspects escaped, and a third took refuge in a house. After some effort to get him to come out, the house was set aflame. As the house filled with smoke he was said to have sprung from the house with a six-shooter in each hand. He was reported to have fired ten shots. Having received several shots himself, he remained standing until he "became so weak that he could not cock his pistols, and after staggering about, he was cut down by an axe, in the hands of an American."[53]

One newspaper noted that Anglos were so enraged after the death of the sheriff that some were threatening to drive all Mexicans from the country.[54] In retaliation for the killing of one of their own, the local Indians had independently attacked and killed Mexican men, women, and children and left their bodies where they lay, only to be devoured by hogs.[55]

In an unrelated case from the same period, two Chileans were summarily executed because they were alleged to have been involved in the killing of a man by the name of John Sheldon. Sheldon was believed to have killed one of their friends at the "riot" in the Tigre, back in 1851.[56] According to the account, the two men had "dogged him with sleepless and unforgiving vengeance" for four years, until he was finally muffled in a cloak and fatally stabbed.[57] After the murder, the two suspects were taken at Tuttletown where their guilt was proved "principally by means of the dropped hat," and they were sentenced to death before a crowd reported to have been three thousand strong.[58] One can't help but wonder if the death of their friend was the only justification for their actions, or perhaps they imagined that no Anglo would ever be tried for killing a Mexican.

In addition to blatant acts of violence and retaliation in the 1850s, Mexican land grants were also overturned and denied, and others would eventually be sold off piecemeal for taxes owed. In a speech to the California Senate in 1855, the Hon. Pablo de la Guerra of Santa Barbara summarized the challenges faced by Mexican land grant holders (like himself) when he criticized the 1851 law that provided for the settlement of the land claims in California. He stated, "I regard the law as injurious, for it compelled every land owner to carry his case to the Supreme Court of the United States, and when a claim was worth no more than $6,000 or $8000 (the case with two-thirds of the claims), of what use was the law to him."[59] The cost of defending a land grant often exceeded the value of the land itself.

In attempting to compare the history of legal execution with the history of lynching, this text is able to highlight a number of similarities and differences between the two practices and provide a framework from which to examine the lingering confusion surrounding the sliding scale of difference between legal execution, committees of vigilance, lynch mobs, volunteer police, mounted volunteer rangers, and the various manifestations of the sheriff's posse.

"Frontier justice" is regularly invoked as the precursor to the establishment of a legal code of law, but while the concept of an empty frontier has been the subject of much scholarly criticism—because of its obvious disregard for those American Indians, Mexicans, Latin Americans, Spaniards, and the handful of "Mexicanized" Anglo and European settlers who already lived in the West prior to its annexation by the United States—surprisingly little attention has ever been given to the second half of the phrase.[60]

POPULAR JUSTICE

Extralegal or popular forms of justice have been described in everything from the five-penny novels of the nineteenth century to the great American Westerns of the silver screen in the twentieth. In reading dozens of first-person narratives from the later half of the nineteenth century I was surprised to find that in addition to the rugged frontiersmen, miners, sweet-talking gamblers, trigger-happy outlaws, overworked sheriffs, and earnest homesteaders, there was the repeated mention of legal executions, lawyers, and grand jury hearings in capital cases.

As one "special correspondent" wrote in 1852 regarding the lynching of Carlos Eslava by the vigilance committee in Mokelumne Hill, "We have lawyers, judges, sheriffs, but alas! No justice, unless we fight for it ourselves, treating our own law-officers as aliens, and becoming a mob."[61] The account also suggests that Carlos "cheerfully" helped out with his own execution, a characterization that is strangely reminiscent of the 1849 Cronin case, noted in the introduction.

Before discussing the question of justice, one might want to briefly consider how it is portrayed in the United States: A blindfolded woman in neoclassical attire, justice is, at least in principle, blind to religious, economic, or other forms of bias. Her highly coded image is meant to reflect the nation's belief that whether guilty or innocent, all will be treated equally under the law. Ironically, it is perhaps fitting that justice is portrayed as a woman since in the nineteenth century lynch mobs and committees of vigilance were almost exclusively male pastimes.

American Indians, Asians, blacks, mulattos, and mestizos could not testify against Anglos for much of the nineteenth century. The precise dates vary from group to group and state to state. Delegates to the 1849 constitutional convention drafted a charter that would establish California as a free state, but after admission to the Union, the state legislature enacted legislation that would severely disenfranchise blacks. They were denied the right to receive a public education, to homestead public lands, or to vote. The Civil Practice Act, Section 394, which passed into law in 1852, made the testimony of blacks inadmissible in cases involving a white person.[62] Without the right to give testimony, blacks could not protect themselves or their property in a court of law.

In 1855, California's state legislature allowed American Indians to testify against whites; the law was repealed in 1863 when Indians, Chinese, and "Mongolians" were prohibited from giving testimony against whites. Surprisingly this was also the same year the state legislature ruled that blacks could testify against whites.[63]

Historically, frontier justice has been used to identify a wide range of extralegal and extrajudicial practices that include everything from branding to summary execution. Summary executions were those executions that were performed without legal or judicial sanction, and the variety of terms that have come down to us reveal a degree of acceptance that often belies the brutality of the practice. Known as cowboy justice, kangaroo courts, and necktie parties, these extralegal practices often took less than a quarter hour to perform, and being tried in "the court of Judge Lynch" often took place only moments before the execution. In all of the cases uncovered in creating the case list, there was not a single mention of an accused criminal ever being returned to his cell after the "trial." From a strictly legal perspective, each of these practices was unsanctioned, and as such, each must be recognized as part of the history of lynching nationwide. The record also demonstrates that few of these lynchings could be seen as precursors to the legal system and should therefore finally be recognized as its rival. Unlike the lynching of African Americans in the South, these often-brutal killings have been romanticized in popular and historical texts, comics, television Westerns, and motion pictures. Idealized as frontier justice and mythologized as cowboy justice, such summary executions have been largely mischaracterized as an inevitable consequence of Western expansion.

Audiences accustomed to thinking about lynching in relationship to African Americans often ask, how it is that the lynching of Latinos, Native Americans, and Asians could have been overlooked all this time? Part of the answer lies in the general confusion over the procedural differences implied by the many variations in the terminology itself, and while trying to distinguish between a hanging party and a vigilance committee might be a fascinating exercise in semantics, it has little bearing on the illegality of these practices. The only definitions of interest are those that help to distinguish a legally constituted execution from one constituted by the self-interest of the mob, but a critical analysis of the Wild West cannot fully explain this historical erasure. The second greatest influence on this history must be traced to the antilynching movement itself, a movement that was, understandably, more concerned with stopping the abominable practice of lynching African Americans than with addressing its historical usage in the American West.

Less concerned with the familiar debate about whether such activities were a necessary step in the establishment of law and order during the Gold Rush, this book sets its sights on the period after California statehood, once due process had been established. The book tracks lynchings into the twentieth century and suggests that such summary executions were a conscious act of collective will rather than the brutish innocence usually associated with frontier justice. As part of the mythology of the West, the many terms continue to disrupt the ability to distinguish between legal and extralegal proceedings and doggedly shadow the question of justice itself.

Harris Newmark (1834–1916), in his frequently cited text *Sixty Years in Southern California*, invoked one of the most popular justifications for vigilance committees and lynch mobs, but unlike later accounts, he attempted to acknowledge the role played by class. Most significantly, he employed the terms vigilance committee and lynching interchangeably when he wrote:

> While upon the subject of lynching, I wish to observe that I have witnessed many such distressing affairs in Los Angeles; and that, though the penalty of hanging was sometimes too severe for the crime (and I have always deplored, as much as any of us ever did, the administration of mobjustice) yet the safety of the better classes in those troublous times often demanded quick and determined action, and stern necessity knew no law. And what is more, others besides myself who have also repeatedly faced dangers no longer common, agree with me in declaring, after half a century of observation and reflection, that milder courses that those of the vigilance committees of our young community could hardly have been followed with wisdom and safety.[64]

Stanley Berkeley (1855–1909), in his painting "Judge Lynch: California Vigilantes, 1848," managed to suggest some of the fear experienced by the lynch victim when confronted with the rage of the mob and the inescapable fate of the hang tree before him. The painting depicts a slain man in the foreground as the murderer recoils from the approaching mob. His shirt has been torn,

3. Stanley Berkeley, " 'Judge Lynch,' California Vigilantes, 1848," n.d., oil on canvas, dimensions unknown. Courtesy of the Library of Congress.

referencing either his struggle with the fallen man or with the mob itself. In either case, this image seems to question the benevolent wisdom of which Newmark wrote (figure 3).

Theodore Henry Hittell (1830–1917), in his four-volume *History of California*, also provided a useful analysis of the practice of "Lynch law" when he summarized that it resulted from one of two forces, the first a "violent prejudice against foreigners" and the second the presence "of a new judiciary as, provided for by the state constitution, and having assumed office by as early as 1850." Remarkably, he blamed the very existence of the American legal system, because of all the "technicalities . . . that had grown up in the body and substance, as well as in the procedure, of the criminal law."[65]

Sonora's 1851 committee of vigilance may have summarized this view best when it claimed, "We are not opposing ourselves to the courts of justice already organized. We are simply aiding them or doing work which they should do, but which under the imperfect laws of the state, they are unable to accomplish."[66] In the first years of statehood such claims were frequent, but as the decades rolled by there was little justification for the community taking the law into its own hands.

Hittell's indictment of the legal process, while undeniably a factor in some cases, does not bear out under historical scrutiny, particularly if one considers that even the partial list of legal executions included in appendix 2 records that nearly fifty legal executions had taken place in the first decade of statehood.[67]

Hittell also argued that it was next to impossible to convict persons of a crime, however guilty, if they had money or influential friends to secure a lawyer,[68] suggesting that Anglo-Americans, more than any other community, would have been the natural targets for the lynch mob. But, as the record makes clear, persons of color were almost twice as likely to die at the hands of the lynch mob, a fact that had nothing to do with influential friends, money, or good lawyers.

The "violent prejudice against foreigners" of which Hittell writes was not only directed at those arriving in California from the Americas or Europe but was regularly directed at Latinos who had been born and raised in California as well. American Indians had neither influential friends or economic wealth nor could they be seen as foreigners, and yet their presence in the history of lynching can surprise no one.

Having suggested at least a cursory view of how the image of frontier justice may have helped to cloud historical memory, I would like to consider the possible impact of the antilynching movement in shaping this history.

THE TUSKEGEE DEFINITION

The historian Jacqueline Jones Royster defined frontier justice as occurring primarily in one of two situations, and her analysis echoes aspects found in Hittell over one hundred years ago. She wrote:

> The first situation is when law and order does not exist, as in the early western frontier. In such cases people are compelled to take justice into their own hands in paving the way for the establishment of legal systems. When legal systems are in place, "frontier justice" is expected to end. The second situation is when law and order does not satisfy the needs of justice and can therefore be "rightly" ignored or circumvented.[69]

These two conceptions continue to permeate the study of the West, but neither of these rationales can explain why, if the practice of lynching was an extension of frontier justice, it continued well into the twentieth century?

In trying to understand this peculiar metamorphosis, it is necessary to define lynching as a term. Commonly recognized as a means of prosecuting and sentencing criminals without the delay of a legal trial, the most widely cited definition is not the one found in a standard dictionary but is one credited to the Tuskegee Institute, an all-black college in Tuskegee, Alabama. Their definition reads, "There must be legal evidence that a person was killed. That person must have met death illegally. A group of three or more persons must have participated in the killing. The group must have acted under the pretext of service to justice, race or tradition."[70] Succinctly stated in four chilling sentences, this definition provides the essential bridge between lynching and frontier justice.

The Tuskegee definition is significant in that, in addition to the means of death, it recognized a sociological dimension to lynching by insisting that "justice, race, or tradition" could be determining factors. The remaining question here is, what was intended by the invocation of "tradition" in the Tuskegee definition? Historically, the practice of extrajudicial execution dates from before the American Revolution, though the specific use of the term "lynching," or what was originally known as "Lynch's law," has been traced to the Tory revolt of 1780.[71]

LYNCH'S LAW

The first application of Lynch's law was believed to have taken place under the walnut tree at Green Level, the Charles Lynch home in Chestnut Hill, Virginia.[72] Today there is a historical marker commemorating the site. Colonel Charles Lynch Jr. (1736–1796), his brother-in-law, Capt. Robert Adams Jr., Colonel William Preston, and Colonel James Callaway are the four men credited with putting an end to the Tory Conspiracy of 1780.[73] Tories were those who remained loyal to the King of England after the outbreak of the Revolutionary War, and freebooters were those who profited by selling (often stolen) goods to the highest bidder, who, as it turned out, were usually Tories. Tradition had it that their flogging stopped when the Tory or freebooter screamed "Liberty!"[74]

Philip Dray, in his book entitled *At the Hands of Persons Unknown*, traced the use of the term back to 1780 when the British troops under General Lord Charles Cornwallis invaded Virginia. Lynch was reported to have ordered the incarceration of local British sympathizers, and he was sued afterward. The Virginia legislature supported Colonel Lynch and decided that Lynch's law was reasonable given the circumstances.[75] In 1782, the term appears again, but this time it specifically referenced acts of corporal punishment in connection with a Tory organizer by the name of John Griffith, who had "stirred up trouble" among the lead miners.[76] The account stated that his subordinate in charge at the mines used Lynch's law in order to punish the men. This was not a hanging but a flogging of thirty-nine lashes, or stripes, as they were called.[77]

At the most basic level, Lynch's law was an example of military law that was extended to nonmilitary personnel, but unlike later uses of the term "lynch law," Lynch's law was administered by military personnel in accordance with the principals of "line of command" military protocol and not simply in response to the collective will of the citizenry.

At the end of Reconstruction in the late 1870s, Southern whites were determined to end Northern interference and curtail black participation in what they believed to be the exclusive rights of whites. This was compounded by growing indifference of Northerners toward the civil rights of African Americans. In this same moment, the federal government ended its oversight of the recently reconstructed South. Southern legislators took advantage of this moral vacuum and authored a slew of laws that have since come to be known as the Jim Crow laws.[78] From 1882 to 1920, cases of lynching were recorded with ever-increasing frequency across the nation, and lynch mobs began to exercise degrees of cruelty that were almost completely absent from the West.

THE ANTILYNCHING MOVEMENT

The origin of the antilynching movement has been credited to a speech made by Frederick Douglas on September 24, 1883, in which he denounced lynch law before three hundred delegates gathered in Louisville for the first "national Colored Convention."[79] In fact, even before the convention took place, regional state conventions in Texas, South Carolina, and Arkansas had already recognized that the lynching of African Americans had a direct impact on black civil rights.[80] In addition, in 1883, the Supreme Court voided the Civil Rights Act of 1875, a decision that would be widely credited with increasing violence against blacks.[81]

Fixing an end date to the antilynching movement is a little harder to do, but it is sometimes given as 1932, the year Franklin D. Roosevelt was elected president, though the NAACP continued to promote antilynching bills as late as 1938.[82] The lynching of African Americans would not actually stop, but it continued to decline over the next three decades.[83] A number of other elements contributed to the end of the antilynching movement: the decline in the number of lynchings, the increased role of European Americans in the movement, and the growing recognition of profound parallels between Hitler's anti-Semitism in Germany and the treatment of blacks in the South.[84]

The period addressed in *Lynching in the West* overlaps with existing lynching records but it also reaches back an additional three decades before the antilynching movement began. Chronologically and regionally distant, these cases had no recognizable impact on the antilynching movement. It is hoped that by making the history of lynching in the West visible, this project will contribute to the important work being done, and yet to be done, on the history of lynching nationwide.

In 1882, the *Chicago Tribune* began to include lynching in its summary of the year's crimes, and that statistical data would find their way into a number of studies on lynching.[85] A quiet man by the name of Monroe N. Work began to keep track of the *Tribune* statistics, accumulating the data until 1908 when he took up a position at the Tuskegee Institute.[86] After 1908, he began adding news clippings to his file, and in 1927 his figures were incorporated in the 1927 World Almanac.[87] According to the NAACP and the Archives of the Tuskegee Institute, lynching has occurred in at least forty-four states and territories.[88]

One cannot discuss the antilynching movement without crediting Ida B. Wells-Barnett (1862–1931) for her many writings on the subject, including her own use of the *Chicago Tribune* statistics. One of two women to have been present at the founding meeting of the NAACP in 1909, her paper, titled "Lynching, Our National Crime," would influence generations of activists and scholars. For seventeen years, Wells-Barnett struggled, through lectures, articles, and leaflets, to raise public awareness and put an end to lynching.[89] It would be another twenty-one years before the Southern Commission on the Study of Lynching would finally take lynching seriously. The commission published its findings in 1931, officially recognizing 3,753 cases of lynching for the period 1889–1932 (figure 4).[90]

THE CASE LISTS

Walter White (1893–1955) is credited with having initiated the NAACP's publication *Thirty Years of Lynching in the United States: 1889–1918* while assistant secretary of the NAACP.[91] First published in 1919, it recorded 3,224 cases of lynching in the United States.[92] Ten years later, White would publish his own analysis of the historical record entitled *Rope and Faggot*, and it would increase

4. National Association for the Advancement of Colored People, "Stop Lynching: N.A.A.C.P. Legal Defense Fund," circa 1930, metal pin back, 0.75 inches in diameter. Collection of the author.

the total number of cases to 4,951 for the period between 1882 and 1927; of this number he identified 3,513 as black.[93] Included within the total are seventy-six African American women and sixteen Anglo-American women.[94] As of 2002, the Archives at the Tuskegee Institute recorded 3,445 instances of African Americans being lynched out of a total of 4,743 cases nationwide.[95]

Born in Atlanta, White was a graduate of Atlanta University and would eventually serve as the executive secretary of the NAACP from 1931 to 1955. He was also well known for lobbying politicians in Washington in order to gain support for antilynching legislation. White set the total number of cases for California at fifty, identifying two as African American, and the remaining forty-eight as white.[96] Unfortunately his list does not supply the names for the individual cases, but he does at least identify them by year. According to White's records, Mississippi led the nation with 561 cases, and Georgia ranked second with 549 cases.[97] By extending the start date of my case list back to 1850 instead of 1882, the number of cases recorded for California increases sevenfold, bringing the new total to 352 cases.[98]

The antilynching movement sought to bring national attention to the lynching of African Americans, a point that is made doubly clear when one considers that as recently as 2003, the discussion of lynching suddenly re-appeared in the national press after the mysterious "suicide" of Ray Golden, a thirty-year-old black man living in Belle Glade, Florida. The controversy surrounding the case makes clear that lynching may not yet be as much a part of the past as one might hope.[99]

With fifty or less cases recorded for the state of California, the records kept by White, the NAACP, and the Tuskegee Institute Archive all under-represent California's historical caseload and, as a result, largely overlook the impact of lynching on California's diverse communities.[100] In reexamining the early antilynching literature one is surprised to find Mexicans, Mexican Americans, American Indians, and Chinese included in *Thirty Years of Lynching*. They are present in appendix 2, but are recorded as "white" in appendix 1.[101] Seemingly contradictory, the appendixes were each configured with a particular emphasis in mind. Rereading the "Number of Persons Lynched, by Geographical Divisions and States and by Color, 1889–1918" table in appendix 1, it becomes clear that, given the time frame of the study, "Color" was synonymous with "Negro," and indeed, each of the terms is linked within the table. In this black/white binary, Mexicans, Indians, and Asians became indistinguishable from whites, or put more succinctly, they were not black. This emphasis, while understandable, given the goals of the antilynching movement, has, at least partially, contributed to the erasure of these histories from public awareness. This is largely because the various case records generated during the antilynching movement have remained primary sources for information on lynching nationwide. It is my hope that the cases recorded here may one day appear in the NAACP and Tuskegee records.

Even within the twenty-six cases listed in *Thirty Years of Lynching* for the state of California, three were parenthetically identified as Chinese, one as "Mexican," and one as "Indian."[102] But unidentified in their list was one Mexican national, one Native American, and one "half-breed" of mixed Indian and European ancestry.[103] Aside from correcting the existing records, this project also adds many new cases. The new case list incorporates a number of previously unrecorded cases, and where possible, it identifies Latinos, Native Americans, Asians, and Anglos. It is hoped that this new information will contribute to the understanding of lynching and correct the common misconception that African Americans, Europeans, or European Americans were the only persons to be summarily executed or lynched in California.

In all likelihood, a complete list may never exist. But by the 1850s, a lynching was recognized as a powerful event that could threaten the reputation of the community and the state because many of these cases were covered in the local and national press. By the 1860s, law enforcement struggled to assert its authority over the bloodthirsty mob, and one historian has argued that local sheriffs would go to Herculean efforts to protect prisoners:

Losing a prisoner to a lynch mob was the greatest affront to the professional lawman's authority and the most embarrassing incident that could befall him. . . . The existence of such vigilantism was considered to be a personal insult for two reasons. First, it showed that the community did not have sufficient faith in the sheriff's ability to put together a criminal case that would stand up in court and result in legal punishment. Second, and more important, it demonstrated that the vigilantes believed the sheriff was impotent to protect his prisoners.[104]

METHODS AND MEANS

Hanging a man from a tree, pole, or gibbet was no easy task. The case records reveal that two techniques were commonly employed. In the first, the accused would be placed upon a horse, cart, or barrel; the rope would be adjusted and secured; and then the support would be removed and the accused would fall a short distance—hopefully far enough to break the neck on the first try. In the second, the body was pulled up and down multiple times until the neck finally broke.

In an unidentified image of one early lynching, a newspaper "correspondent" created a drawing that depicted the crowd of onlookers, with rifles in hand, as they encircled the condemned man. The man was shown standing on the back of a mule moments before his end. The image is startling because it makes clear just how short the fall would be, allowing for a drop of only a few feet, or the average height of a mule. It has been calculated that a man of approximately one hundred forty pounds (or ten stones) requires a six-foot drop in order to effectively break his neck. A man of approximately one hundred seventy pounds (or twelve stones) requires a four-foot drop to accomplish the same end.[105] It is impossible to accurately determine the man's height or weight from looking at the drawing, but one can only hope that he was heavier than the drawing suggests. If the neck was not broken in the fall, the victim might be left to hang until he slowly suffocated as the rope cut off all airflow, but suffocation was a slow and arduous death (figure 5).

In a legal execution, the hangman's job is to end the condemned man's life as quickly and painlessly as possible; it is for this reason that gallows are constructed with a trap door. This unique design feature allows the hangman to precisely calculate the length of the fall. Furthermore, the noose must be carefully adjusted and the knot must be properly placed. If the noose is too tight or is poorly placed, the condemned may be decapitated. Such details,

A MURDERER LYNCHED BY CALIFORNIAN EMIGRANTS—FROM A SKETCH BY OUR OWN CORRESPONDENT.

5. Unidentified artist, "A Murderer Lynched by Californian Emigrants—From a Sketch from Our Own Correspondent," n.d. Courtesy of the California Historical Society, FN-28951.

while unpleasant, help to explain why extrajudicial executions were undeniably much more gruesome and violent than legally performed ones.

To add one ready comparison between lynching nationwide and lynching in the West, one should also note that in the South there were many accounts in which the lynch victim was shot first and then hanged or hanged and then shot. Undeniably disturbing from any perspective, at least being shot could curtail the victim's suffering. There are no statistics on the frequency of this practice in the South, but in the West, there appear to have been less than a handful of cases where the lynch victims were shot, usually when the rope broke. Thus, the majority of those killed had to rely solely upon the unskilled actions of the mob.

The second method usually began when someone from the mob or vigilance committee would throw a rope over a branch, or erect a makeshift gallows, as seen in a photograph depicting the double hanging of the Ruggles brothers in 1892. The rope would be thrown over the branch, one end fastened to the accused, and at the opposite end, a group of men would give the rope a hearty tug, often sending the accused into the air. If the accent was fast enough, the earth's gravity would do the rest on the way down and the muffled snap of the neck would (presumably) appease the mob or vigilance committee that justice had been done. Unfortunately, this method was inefficient and prone to error, regularly resulting in the prolonged suffering of the accused. The rope could stick to the branch, or the ascent or descent could be unexpectedly slowed by any number of factors. If the fall was too great, the victim might touch the ground and the whole procedure would have to be repeated from the beginning. In the Ruggles case, it would appear that each was tied to a harness and then hanged simultaneously (figure 6).

THE MOST BELOVED VIGILANTES

California's most celebrated committees of vigilance formed in a period when there was little legal recourse for criminals, and with the general knowledge that summary executions had been performed both under the alcalde system of Mexican California and in the Gold Rush camps which were scattered throughout the inhospitable and isolated nooks and crannies of the Sierra Nevada mountains. In addition, San Francisco had been plagued by the misdeeds of the Sydney Ducks. The Ducks, as they were known, were a loose knit collection of ex-convicts who had been released from England's penal settlement in Sydney, Australia. One such Sydney Duck, a man by the name of John Jenkins, brazenly stole a safe from a shipping office but was promptly captured, tried, sentenced, and hanged at two A.M. on June 11, 1851.[106] The second man to be hanged by San Francisco's committee of vigilance was James Stuart, a former resident of Sydney as well; he was hanged one month later, on July 11, 1851.[107] In his characterization of Stuart, Bancroft cites Johann Caspar Lavater's physiognomic treatise: "Fear the boisterous savage of passion less than the sedately grinning villain," and in doing so draws a link between the actions of the vigilance committee and the nineteenth-century fascination with reading the criminal body, a concept that will be more extensively taken up in a later chapter.[108]

Less than two months later, Samuel Whittaker and Robert McKenzie (also one-time residents of Sydney) were detained without the authority of the law before being turned over to police custody; whether accurate or not, the citizenry was convinced that if tried in a court of law that the men would be acquitted.[109] So while they were awaiting their court date, members of the vigilance committee broke into the prison during Sunday services, a time when few guards would be on duty, and the prisoners were removed from

Franklin

REDDING.
CAL.

6. Franklin Studio, "John and Charles Ruggles, Stage Robbers and Murderers of Buck Montgomery. Taken From the Jail of Shasta County, Redding and Lynched by a Mob, Sunday 2:30 A.M. July 24, 1892." Courtesy of the California Historical Society, FN-33890.

their cells and then promptly hanged.[110] Having completed their work, California's first committee of vigilance disbanded abruptly on June 30, 1852.[111]

In 1856, rampant allegations of city corruption and the murder of James King of William, the editor of the *Evening Bulletin*, by James P. Casey drew out the former members of the 1851 committee, who quickly organized a new "committee of vigilance." This time, they organized along a military model and even raided the city's militia armories and uniformed some of its members.[112] More than fifty notorious or suspected criminals were banished from the city, suffered lesser punishments, or were turned over to the legal authorities, but by far the most sensational cases are those which resulted in summary executions before enormous crowds.[113]

On May 22, committee members hanged Casey (born in New York City) and Charles Cora (born in Genoa), a gambler who shot and killed U.S. Marshall William Richardson, from the committee's offices, also known as "Fort Gunnybags."[114] The building was located on Sacramento Street between Front and Davis Streets in San Francisco. On July 29, they hanged two more murderers, Philander Brace and an Englishman by the name of Joseph

EXECUTION OF JAMES P. CASEY AND CHARLES CORA,
BY THE VIGILANCE COMMITTEE, OF SAN FRANCISCO,
On Thursday, May 22d, 1856, from the Windows of their Rooms, in Sacramento Street, between Front and Davis Streets.

7. "Execution of James P. Casey and Charles Cora," n.d. Courtesy of the California Historical Society, FN-04446.

8. Dressler, "The capture of the 'Law and Order' armory at the N.E. corner of Kearny and Clay Streets, San Francisco, California by an armed detachment of the Committee of Vigilance, June 21, 1856." Courtesy of California History Room, California State Library, Sacramento, California.

Hetherington.[115] As many historians have noted, the iron fist of the vigilance committee was good for the city coffers as well, and forcibly extricating corrupt city officials, the vigilantes had reduced the city's expenditures from $2,646,190 in 1855 to $856,120 in 1856, and finally to a startling $353,292 in 1857.[116] Given their remarkable success, it is not surprising to find that vigilance committees began to spring up throughout the state, but it must be emphasized that few, if any, followed the procedural rigor practiced by California's most beloved vigilantes (figures 7 and 8).

PUBLIC DISPLAY

The much romanticized and frequently misrepresented image of summary execution as the only means of taming a lawless and Wild West was understandably less distressing to the imagination than the realities of choking the life out of a living human being. Likewise, this practice has been disproportionately credited with providing a civilizing force to the rough-and-tumble of life on the frontier. The truth is that police, prisons, an evolving penal code, legal execution, and a burgeoning infrastructure of property taxes, water rights, agricultural production, small businesses, and even barbed wire may have contributed more to taming the West than the summary execution of criminals ever did (figure 9).

The public display of legal executions was outlawed in many states but continued in California until 1872 when capital punishment was fully incorporated into California's Penal Code.[117] To place this shift within a slightly broader context, it may be useful to note that with the passage of the Act of 1868, England ended public executions altogether, insisting that they be held away from public view and within prison walls.[118] In May 1868, England saw its last public execution when a twenty-seven-year-old Irishman by the name of Michael Barrett was executed before a crowd described as "an incarnation of evil persons with perverted sympathies."[119]

In California, it would not be until 1891 that the penal code would be further amended to insist that all executions take place within the confines of the state prison, although the last county-run execution would be recorded as late as 1895.[120] Though legally required to be held outside of public view after 1872, the practice of public display continued; primarily, it was argued, due to the material constraints of individual county prisons. It was only when the execution of criminals was moved to the state penitentiaries that the element of public display finally ceased.[121]

The significance here is that for much of the nineteenth century, both legal and extralegal executions were public spectacles. As early as 1854 there were those who questioned the merits of state-sanctioned executions being held in public. One newspaper article decried this fact: "There is no law in this state similar to the one which has been adopted in nearly every other state in the Union requiring that executions should be in private."[122] The article noted: "It was formerly supposed that executions of criminals had a salutary effect upon the beholders, and had a tendency to deter others from crime, but experience has proved the fallacy of this idea."[123] The article also went on to state that there were no private spaces available in most of the counties, but that such spaces should be established as soon as possible.

Four years later, on December 25, 1858, Henry F. W. Mewes, alias Charles Dowse, was executed in the county jail yard, and one newspaper strongly praised the fact that the execution was carried out in a manner that was "entirely private," except for several officers of the law and two representatives of the church.[124] It is in light of these early successes that one must wonder

9. Misidentified as "Lynching of Leo Grover, CA 1890," in the records of the California Historical Society, San Francisco. The image is more widely known as the 1884 lynching of John Heath by the Bisbee Mob in Tombstone, Arizona. Photograph courtesy of the California Historical Society, FN-33891.

why so many of the most celebrated executions, in some instances occurring decades later, would continue to boast to having thousands in attendance.

To better understand what was intended by this notion of a private space, it may be useful to consider a photographic postcard that was produced to commemorate the execution of two "Mexican Murderers" in 1904, in nearby Arizona. In it one sees that a simple wooden fence was erected around the scaffold in order to guarantee some degree of privacy for the two condemned men.[125] The irony, of course, is that while the execution was held in private, a postcard of the condemned bodies became its own kind of spectacle, and the caption "Adios Amigos!" added a sarcastic flair to an otherwise distasteful entrepreneurial venture. Identified as "Mexicans" in the caption at the bottom of the postcard, one wonders if they were Mexicans or Mexican Americans, particularly since executing people from other countries is not only inhospitable but as the Yreka quadruple lynching demonstrated (discussed in the next section), it could be costly (color plate 2).

THE PHOTOGRAPHER'S ARSENAL

Edgar Wade Howell, a well-known photographer from the Yreka region, captured the quadruple lynching shortly after it occurred, sometime after two o'clock in the morning of August 26, 1895.[126] Identified in the photograph from left to right, the names of the four men were William Null, Garland Stemler, Luis Moreno, and Lawrence Johnson.[127] Moreno was a Mexican national, and his lynching would be followed by a demand from the Republic of Mexico for an investigation and the payment of an indemnity for Moreno's family. Needless to say, the "investigation" never identified a single member of the mob, but the indemnity was written into the House Appropriation Bill of 1898, which ultimately paid $2,000 to Moreno's relatives in Mexico as compensation[128] (color plate 3).

The men were being held in the county jail awaiting trial when the crowd decided to hang all four to a railroad tie they suspended between two trees. One newspaper editorial went so far as to suggest that the lynch mob was guiltless in crime by insisting that "the body responsible for this is the Supreme Court of the state, which has established numerous technicalities for the protection of the guilty."[129]

The charge against the court derived from the fact that Johnson was waiting for his third trial to begin. Johnson had murdered his wife for "unfaithfulness," and it was feared that the question of adultery might cloud the judgment of the third set of jurors. According to some sources he also attempted to murder his daughter, a detail that couldn't have helped his odds with the mob. But the courts had not yet heard the cases of Moreno or Stemler, who were each charged with robbery and murder and were still awaiting their preliminary hearing when they were lynched.[130] Null had murdered a miner in Calabasasa and had already been arraigned.[131] His trial was scheduled to begin in less than two weeks from the day he was lynched.[132]

Lynchings and summary executions were obviously intended for public viewing, but what did a photograph of a lynching communicate beyond the sunken contortions of a lifeless face or the angle of a broken neck? Photographed, printed, mounted, and sold, such images were frequently embellished with details about the case, usually with a handwritten note across the back, or as in this case, around the edges of the image. The comments usually sought to celebrate the actions of the vigilantes. Most viewers will be drawn to these editorial comments, but the most surprising aspect of this image isn't the text or even the bodies themselves.

Recognized but unseen in an age teeming with technological advances, it is the presence of the photographer's flash which will go unnoticed by most viewers, and yet, it is the most striking feature of the image because flashbulbs (though a relic of the recent past) would not become commercially available for another thirty-seven years.[133] Thus, to a professional photographer like Howell, one of the surest ways of illuminating such a macabre scene would have been to use some form of commercially available flash powder.

Magnesium flash powder was available as early as the 1880s, but it could be dangerous to use. Other kinds of metal and aluminum shavings were briefly *en vogue* in Paris in the 1890s, but for the most part, magnesium remained the standard.[134] Recipes varied, but at its simplest, flash powder could be created from potassium chlorate, powdered metal, and table sugar. This mixture could then be placed on a metal armature and ignited with a swath of cotton. Prior to the invention of the commercially available flashbulb, nighttime images of lynchings were rare because of the necessity of professional equipment or training.

By 1890, the Scovill Company of New York began selling magnesium cartridges that were completely self-contained and even had a fuse attached, and by 1900, they would market the Solograph Flash Pistol.[135] Designed to incorporate a conventional trigger and pistol handle, the advertisements for this curious weapon gleefully claimed that it "shoots sunshine all over"; unfortunately, it could also badly burn the bearer's hand and face if aimed in the wrong direction.[136] Though short lived, as an object its design still speaks to the curious parallel between photography and firearms; after all, each tar-

10. *"The Solograph Flash Pistol,"* Scovill and Adams Co. of New York, *American Annual of Photography and Photographic Times,* 1900. Collection of the author.

gets many of the same subjects. The makers of the flash pistol recognized that the flash would become an essential weapon in the photographer's arsenal[137] (figure 10).

Thirty-two years after the Flash Pistol appeared on the market, General Electric would make a slightly different claim when it introduced one of the first commercially available battery powered flash units in 1932. Known as the "Mazda Photoflash," the slogan read, "Make . . . pictures that are alive with Mazda Photoflash lamps."[138] There is little doubt that flashbulbs would dramatically broaden not only the number of images that could be captured on film but the number of people that had access to the technology, and flash photography may have had the greatest impact on law enforcement and photojournalism because police and freelance photographers were able to quickly document not only the criminals but the crime scene as well. A lynching is, after all, a crime scene.

The glow of photographer's flash, whether achieved with powder or bulbs, was deceptive in at least one respect because in real time, it faded as quickly as it appeared, but in the Yreka quadruple lynching as in all lynching photographs, the infernal scene will remain illuminated for all eternity. Remarkably, the flash provided a view of the lynching that would not have even been available to the mob itself, because prior to the use of the photographic flash, the scene would have had to have been illuminated by torches, flashlights, flares, and later, by car lights.

Given the early date of this lynching, it is possible to see that the impact of the flash on lynching photography was just beginning, and for the next five decades the use of the photographic flash would be almost as integral to lynching photography as the mob itself. Beyond the spectacle of a light in the darkness and the promise of creating pictures "that are alive," the flash would make a spectacle of death as well.

PHOTOGRAPHIC ECSTASY

Fascinated by the ways that the photograph can conjure the "frail rewards" of life, Roland Barthes (1915–80) concluded *Camera Lucida* by suggesting that all photographs fall into one of two categories: they are either mad or tame. He defined "tame" as an image whose realism "remains relative, tempered by aesthetic or empirical habits."[139] Examples might include the photographic portrait found in a high school yearbook or the evidentiary value of a crime-scene photograph. For Barthes, an image that was "mad" was one whose realism was absolute, "obliging the loving and terrified consciousness to return to the very letter of Time: a strictly revulsive moment which reverses the course of the thing."[140] For Barthes, this madness results in nothing less than "photographic *ecstasy*." He then concludes by asserting that the viewer can assign either definition to a given image. He explains, "The choice is mine: to subject its spectacle to the civilized code of perfect illusions, or to confront in it the wakening of intractable reality."[141] Given such a proposition, the lynching photograph must be the ultimate form of photographic ecstasy, not only because in the click of the shutter, or in the flash of light, it is sealed in the "letter of Time," but because this particular *revulsive moment* is so utterly final. Can there really ever be tameness to such images? Naturally, any object, act, or phenomenon can be aestheticized or fetishized, but in a democratic state, the terror embodied in these images resists any "civilized code," and it is the repulsiveness of these images that has contributed to the shame, silence, and ultimate erasure of the very histories they so adamantly depict. Like the portrait image of a living body, the lynching photograph offers something Barthes had called the "Spectrum" of the photograph, a term that he argued retained, through its root, a relation to the "spectacle," but added to it, "that rather terrible thing which is there in every photograph: the return of the dead."[142] In the portrait photograph, a loved one can be returned their youth or brought back to life in the imagination of the viewer. But what can the lynching photograph offer the living, if not the irretractable violence of the lynch mob?

With the introduction of the flash to lynching photography, the photographer was able to capture the last traces of life as they leaked from the convulsing, pissing, dangling shells which swayed before the camera's lens. In such images, there can be no youthful smile, no innocence, no eternal return—only eternal denial.[143] In such cases, the photographic flash is less a tool than a weapon which symbolically strips its victim of all humanity.

The invocation of a "leaking" body is a not-so-subtle reference to Julia Kristeva's concept of the "abject" from which she explored the delicate boundary between "I" and "other," self and nonself. She argued that "the corpse, seen without God and outside of science, is the utmost of abjection."[144] In invoking Kristeva, I simply wish to take up the question of choice posed by Barthes because lynching images confound interpretation in a way that other photographs cannot. And as such, they do more than simply document what Foucault called the exercise of power—they embody it.

Capital punishment is the
result of a mystic idea, totally
misunderstood today. The death
penalty has not as its object to
preserve society, *materially* at
least. Its object is the *preservation*
(spiritually) of society and the
guilty one. In order that the
sacrifice be perfect, there must
be assent and joy on the part of
the victim.

—Charles Baudelaire,
Baudelaire: His Prose and Poetry

CHAPTER TWO

The Greatest Good:
Capital Punishment or
Popular Justice?

THE GREATEST GOOD

In the shadow of Enlightenment humanism, eighteenth-century Europe
would make great strides toward standardizing legal codes and punishments
so that each person, no matter what the circumstances, would receive equal
treatment under the code of law.[1] This simple premise was a radical departure
from the reliance on religious doctrine, royal proclamation, or traditions that
in some regions of Europe dated to the Middle Ages.

Perhaps the most significant contributing factor for this change was the
publication of *Of Crimes and Punishments*, which completely reconceptualized
punishment and laid the foundation for modern criminology. Surprising for
its time, it also argued against the death penalty. Its author was Cesare Bonesana, Marquis of Beccaria (1738–94), and as his title suggests, had been born
into an aristocratic Italian family. Beccaria is also considered to be one of the

fathers of Utilitarianism, and his theories on economics have been credited with anticipating the wage and labor theories of Adam Smith, but it was the suggestion that Beccaria's work had led Catherine the Great to consider abolishing the death penalty in Russia that made his text irresistible.[2] Addressing the question of capital punishment, Beccaria wrote:

> By what alleged right can men slaughter their fellows? Certainly not by the authority from which sovereignty and law derive. That authority is nothing but the sum of tiny portions of the individual liberty of each person; it represents the general will, which is the aggregate of private wills. Who on earth has ever willed that other men should have the liberty to kill him? How could this minimal sacrifice of the liberty of each individual ever include the sacrifice of the great greatest good of all, life itself?[3]

Beccaria not only rejected capital punishment but went one step further and argued that supporting the death penalty was in conflict with the religious doctrine (and one can presume he was speaking of the Roman Catholic Church) that instructs its followers that no person has the right to commit suicide. Beccaria argued that in collectively accepting the death penalty, every individual has inadvertently accepted the possibility of their own execution, and that since forsaking the divine gift of life to individual will is a sin, then ceding even the smallest portion of one's life to the collective good must also be seen as unacceptable. He concluded that the only possible justification for taking a life would be if the absolute security of the nation was at stake, if liberty was threatened for all (as would occur in a state of absolute anarchy).[4] Arguing against the death penalty he wrote, "One may posit as a general rule that violent passions grip men strongly but not for long," insisting that justice had less to do with passion than it did with reason.[5]

Beccaria's text would greatly influence John Adams, William Penn, and Thomas Jefferson in North America and even find its way into the U.S. Constitution.[6] Written at a time when few nations had a penal code, Beccaria was faced with many of the same questions that nearly eighty years later, would be encountered by the migrating waves of miners, adventurers, and settlers in California. Sparsely populated, the only law that existed prior to the American annexation had been handed down from the Mexican legal system or the U.S. military. Thus, one of the first challenges facing the new state was establishing equality under the law while preserving individual liberty.

The history of lynching in California reveals that not all racial or racialized communities had equal representation within the legislative system. Noncitizens were regularly excluded from many of the benefits of these new laws or, worse, targeted by them. The race of the alleged criminal, and in many cases the race of the victim, would be contributing factors in determining who would receive the benefits of due process or be "liberated" from their jail cells in the middle of the night and escorted to the nearest hang tree.

In extending Beccaria's views on capital punishment to the history of lynching in the West, one begins to see that the "violent passions" of the mob were regularly invoked to justify their actions, but as Beccaria predicted, these passions were often little more than a ruse to justify the cold-blooded— and often premeditated—lynching of an accused criminal. Taken as a whole, the case list demonstrates that by and large, lynching had as much to do with vengeance as with the pursuit of justice.

The frequent invocation of San Francisco's vigilance committees in many of the case records is clearly intended to link extrajudicial execution to "tradition," an essential element found in the Tuskegee definition of lynching. On a formal level, well over 50 percent of lynching cases that give a time, record that the lynching took place between midnight and 2 A.M. when the accused was usually encouraged to confess his or her crimes before being strung up. Sometimes they were allowed to make a statement, to smoke a cigarette, or confess to a priest, and after it was over, the bodies would usually be left to hang through the night. This public display of the body can be found in every case, with the shortest times usually lasting around thirty minutes, and the longest, until the bodies decayed.

In one instance, in the small village of Newtown, an African American man known only as "Brown" was apprehended for stealing money. The evidence was completely circumstantial but he was found guilty and sentenced to be hung by the mob on March 4, 1852.[7] Unfortunately for Brown, the rope was a little too long, and once he was hanged to the tree, the branch slowly gave way—until his legs dangled to the ground. Struggling in agony, the poor man was cut down in order to be properly hanged. Once he was fully revived, he was tied to a higher branch and the whole process was repeated. When he was finally cut down, a physician was asked to examine the body, at which point he announced that if Brown's body was left above ground for five minutes that he would regain consciousness. As a result, "he was therefore hastily dumped into a grave that had been dug and was half full of water, and quickly covered from sight."[8] Whether completely true or not, it's hard to imagine that anyone could argue that this killing really served the greatest good.

Less than a year after the state's official acceptance into the Union one of California's first pieces of the legal code was on the books. Known as the Criminal Practices Act of 1851, it authorized capital punishment and made grand larceny a capital offense.[9] On July 9, 1851, James Wilson, a resident of Consumnes township, was knocked down and robbed by four men in the streets of Sacramento.[10] The four men were arrested, and on July 12 each submitted a plea of "not guilty." A motion was made by the defense to move the trial to July 15 to give council time to prepare, but the assembled crowd objected, and a vigilance committee was formed.[11] Four men from the crowd went to call on the court and gave it one hour to resume the trial while a second committee was appointed to guard the prisoners.[12] The court had no choice but to proceed with the trial of the first suspect, and William Robinson (real name William B. Heppard, born in New York) was found guilty and sentenced to death. The second and third men, James Gibson (real name Hamilton) and John Thompson (real name McDermott), were tried on the 15th and also found guilty.[13] The judge then sentenced all three men to be hung on August 22, 1851, and gallows were constructed at Fourth and O Streets in Sacramento City.[14] The fourth man was sentenced to ten years in prison.

On the appointed day, the roads to Sacramento were lined with people on horseback and pedestrians on their way to witness this execution. Rumors began circulating among the crowd that the governor had already given Robinson a reprieve until September 19.[15] A meeting of citizens was quickly organized at the Orleans Hotel, but remarkably, the vigilance committee voted to leave the prisoners in the hands of the authorities. As news of the decision spread through the crowd, the mob became unwieldy, and someone cried out, "Hang the Rascal, He is the worst of the lot! Lynch him!"[16]

The other two men were legally hanged under the supervision of the sheriff when the drums began to play for a second time and suddenly Robinson appeared before the crowd. According to reports, the sheriff recognized that he could no longer control the crowd and quietly slipped out of sight. The crowd had been willing to support the decisions of the vigilance committee until the moment they agreed to leave Robinson in the hands of the legal authorities. After he was lynched, the crowd hanged an effigy of the governor and then lit it on fire and cheered exuberantly as the flames engulfed it.[17]

The public burning of either effigies or lynch victims was extremely rare in the West but, as the previous case makes clear, it was not unheard of. In California, the first actual account of a man being hanged and then burned occurred on the first day of July 1855 when a twenty-one-year-old Irishman by the name of John Fenning was taken from his boarding house by over a dozen men. The sheriff went in pursuit of the vigilantes but was only able to find the young man's hat. The next day the burned and hollowed out shell of his body was seen dangling from a tree.[18]

In the South, accounts of burning lynch victims were reported as early as 1851 when a black man was burned to death in Paudling, Mississippi.[19] The account claimed that "having committed an outrage upon the person of a white lady, and afterwards murdered her son, the citizens turned out *en masse*, arrested the Negro, and burned him alive."[20] Allegations of "outrages" against white women persisted throughout the twentieth century, but the antilynching movement broadly contested the accuracy of such claims.[21] In 1853, an unnamed slave belonging to H. France, of Pettis County, Missouri, was publicly burnt on July 13 for murdering the wife of a man by the name of Rains. Apparently, the slave owner had conceived the murder and then instructed the slave to carry it out, for which the owner was merely ordered out of the state.[22]

Some of the most violent cases are actually found in the twentieth century, as in the 1909 double lynching in Cairo, Illinois, when some 10,000 men and women lynched an African American man named "James" in the town square.[23] His body was reported to have received 500 shots after the rope broke, the crowd then "paraded" his head on a pole, and distributed "pieces of his heart" and sections of the "blood-soaked" rope as souvenirs, before burning his remains in the street.[24]

LEGALLY CONSTITUTED

In January 1852, a "Sonoran" by the name of José Corrales was legally executed in Sonora, California.[25] News of the sentencing appeared in the *New York Times*, making this one of the earliest nationally recognized cases of a legal execution in the state's history. The article simply stated that a horse thief by the name of Corrales was to be executed.[26] Still, the presence of the case appearing in the *New York Times* does suggest that the notoriety surrounding the 1851 extralegal executions conducted by San Francisco's vigilance committee had made an execution performed under legal sentence noteworthy to readers in the East.

On July 16, 1852, a few months after Corrales was executed, another legal execution took place when John Barrett (also known as Garrat) was hanged in Marysville, in Yuba County.[27] In fact, Barrett had been arrested in Nevada City while the jail was still under construction, so he was taken to nearby Marysville, where he received the full benefits of due process. He was found guilty and legally executed under the supervision of the sheriff, in keeping with state law. In this same period, two Mexicans were reported to have also been sentenced to be hanged in Stockton, and still a third in Monterey. Since the state keeps no records on legal executions from this period, I have been unable to determine if they were actually executed. As a result, they have been excluded from the appended case list, but the fact that they were sentenced confirms that legal prosecution was possible.[28]

To the northwest, the first execution in Contra Costa County took place on August 20, 1852, when an American Indian known only as José Antonio was sentenced to death for the murder of a man named Aparicio Morales.[29] He was hanged to a sycamore tree and only supplied with a barrel and an old cart for his makeshift gallows. Hardly standard procedure for legal executions, the case is notable on two fronts: the first that the sheriff oversaw the entire proceeding and the second that the sheriff had actually transported Antonio to the county seat to be legally tried.

The murder for which Antonio was executed was committed on May 29th, 1852, and with less than three months between his arrest and execution, the case challenged the already popular sentiment that legal execution was a slow and inefficient process.[30] In spite of the fact that the arrest, trial, sentencing, and execution could range from a few days to a few years, such cases suggest that a functioning code of law should have meant the end of extrajudicial executions. It did not.

Significantly more expedient than the current system of capital punishment, it is the speed between sentencing and execution that continues to be idealized in popular representations of frontier justice, but unfortunately, the expediency of lynching and other forms of summary execution was no guarantee of justice.

Writing in the later half of the nineteenth century, the French poet and art critic Charles Baudelaire (1821–67) wrestled with the question of capital punishment. Unlike Beccaria, his critique actually targeted what he interpreted to be the religious symbolism of the execution itself. In the epigraph, Baudelaire refers to capital punishment as a "mystic idea," in which the life taken functions symbolically, since the life of the victim can never be returned. In this, Baudelaire argues that the symbolic exchange serves to cleanse both society and the individual of their sins but that in order for this spiritual "*preservation*" to work, the accused, like the sinner in certain religious practices, must willingly accept his or her penance in order to be cleansed: "In order that the sacrifice be perfect, there must be assent and joy on the part of the victim."[31]

Nineteenth-century advocates of capital punishment on both continents regularly invoked the preservation of society as the primary justification for the practice. This was particularly true in the West, where society, was itself, largely symbolic. Banks, prisons, or walls for that matter (since the first miners lived in canvas tents) all tested the limits of the social contract. There was, however, a second and even more pressing reason for creating capital punishment at such an early date in California history. Before statehood, the miners regularly organized their own vigilance committees and had taken the law into their own hands on numerous occasions, and it was hoped by many that legalizing capital punishment would diminish the necessity for such extra-judicial executions.

Baudelaire's rejection of capital punishment split the argument in two. First, it acknowledged that, as a practice, it was intended to preserve the *material* conditions of society or, put more bluntly, it was intended to protect private property; and second, Baudelaire's invocation of capital punishment as a "mystic idea" bitingly equated prosecution and sentencing with confession and penance and sought to foreground the underlying metaphor of spiritual transcendence. In invoking the "joy" of the condemned, Baudelaire satirized the illusion of spiritual redemption underlying the criminal's acceptance of a human judgment.

Addressing the execution itself, he argued, "As a torture, it is born of the infamous side of the heart of man, a thirst for voluptuousness. Cruelty and voluptuousness, identical sensations, like extreme heat and extreme cold."[32] Ironically, Baudelaire was writing at the precise moment when public execution and the spectacle of the scaffold were nearing their end in France and the practice of public execution, both legal and extralegal, was just beginning to take hold of the American West. Even with all his poetic liberties, Baudelaire touched on one of the most striking differences between judicial and extra-judicial execution, that dragging a man from his cell in the dark of night to be hanged from the creaking branches of an oak tree or gibbet intentionally sought to deny the victim even the illusion that justice was being served.

In lynching, as with other forms of summary execution, there can be no moral cleansing, real or imagined, for the victim because the judgment is not sanctioned by religious beliefs, state law, or even the county sheriff; it is simply guided by the will of a small collection of individuals, who, as be-came clear in the Robinson case in Sacramento, weren't even bound to their own appointed representatives—a situation which reduced civil society to mob rule.

In the complete absence of what Baudelaire derided as the religious meta-phors of "assent and joy" in legal and state executions, the lynch mob sought to replace the frail veneer of justice-being-served with what Baudelaire rec-ognized as "the thirst for voluptuousness," a phrase which reveals, with bone cracking clarity, that the lynch mob has absolutely nothing to do with justice as a social contract and everything to do with cruelty and voluptuousness: extreme heat and extreme cold.

OF HIS OWN RACE

Los Angeles would see its first legal execution on February 10, 1854.[33] Ygna-cio Herrera was tried and convicted of murder in a court of law. According to most accounts he had gotten into a fight with another man "of his own race," and the brawl ended in death.[34] One account states that the execution was carried out with "much solemnity and propriety" and was witnessed by thousands. The details of the case fall somewhere between Baudelaire's cyni-cal characterization of capital punishment as a metaphor for moral transfor-mation and Foucault's emphasis on execution as a display of power.[35]

Herrera had been a well-respected Mexican soldier, and standing on the gallows, he denounced the legal system in his address to the crowd. The news-papers noted that the Latino community believed his execution to be un-just, but this is hardly surprising when one considers that not a single Anglo had yet to be legally executed in Los Angeles. On the day of the execution, thousands of spectators streamed into town, Anglos and Latinos shoulder to shoulder before the gallows, but as close as they may have been, each community perceived the event very differently. For European Americans, Herrera's case was perceived as an open-and-shut case, tried in a court of law—a cold-blooded murderer was to be served justice. For the many Mexicans and native Californians, the judicial system appeared to be the latest justification for the unequal treatment of the Latino community.

The crowd dispersed after the execution, and the body was taken by members of the Mexican community to be prepared for burial. Another group of Mexicans held a vigil at the execution site, and as they whispered the rosary, they must have struggled to understand the significance of this modern day crucifixion. Burning candles through the night, they would bury Herrera at daybreak with martial music and full religious rights.[36]

Too late to help Herrera, by 1854 the state legislature had begun to worry about the possibility that local bias might indeed influence court decisions. New legislation was introduced that would move the jurisdiction in capital cases from being shared concurrently by both the local court of sessions and the district court to a new system that placed all capital cases under the jurisdiction of the district court.[37]

In the 1850s, local bias could take several forms, and the antagonism between Anglos and Latinos was not restricted to Los Angeles. Farther up the coast, the "Honorable" Walter Murray, in a series of letters written and published in a San Francisco newspaper, considered what he believed to be the failings of the judicial system—but from a slightly different perspective. A judge himself, Murray complained of the difficulty of empanelling a jury in what may have been the last region in which Latinos still outnumbered Anglos. He had this to say about the Mexican and native Californian community in San Luis Obispo County, "We are helpless. At an election, or at the empanelling of a jury, it is very easy for an unwashed greaser to swear he came to this country before the treaty with Mexico. That oath makes him a citizen. . . . The Frenchman, the Englishman, the Irishman can't do this. His conscience won't permit it."[38]

THE "UNWASHED" CITIZENRY

From 1790 to 1870, naturalization in the United States was restricted to "any alien, being a free white person," so long as he or she had resided in the United States for at least two years.[39] One of the most interesting anomalies in U.S. naturalization law may be the fact that citizenship was theoretically granted, if not yet legally tested, to those individuals already living in the territories ceded by Mexico at the close of the Mexican War.[40] However, as Murray notes, Mexicans and other Latin Americans may have continued to arrive in California, and indeed other states, after 1850. The question posed or, rather, answered by Murray was whether these new arrivals had the right to citizenship. He answered with a resounding no!

There is however, a second question here. If only whites could be citizens, could those Mexicans who legally qualified as citizens have been classified as "white?" Again, for Murray and many others, the answer would be no! If they had been considered white, they wouldn't need a guarantee of citizenship because like the many new arrivals from Northern Europe, they would eventually become naturalized citizens. Since qualifying Mexicans could only claim the right to citizenship through the treaties signed with Mexico at the close of the war, one must conclude, as Murray insists, that "Mexicans" were seen as nonwhite. Some may even wonder why such a small group would have been granted citizenship in the first place, but by extending citizenship to the native Californian, the U.S. government had sought to ensure that the region's transition to statehood would be smooth, primarily because it would be able to take advantage of the economic, legal, social, and religious infrastructures that were already in place.

Beyond the contemporary recognition that there is no significant biological difference between the races, race does still continue to function as a legal category. One wonders what Murray would have thought if he had lived long enough to learn that in 1897, for the purposes of immigration, a federal judge in Texas would rule that all "Mexicans," assuming that they did not belong to any other legally recognized racial category, must be legally recognized as "white."[41] In a subtle piece of historical irony, this ruling was based on the very same treaties that Murray had used to argue the exact opposite, but Murray may have at least been pleased to know that the Texas judge noted that while such treaties may have ensured the right to legal citizenship for many Mexicans, it did not, in his opinion, change the fact that Mexicans "would probably be considered non-white from an Anthropological perspective."[42]

DEATH ROW

Populated with a disproportionate number of persons of color, even in the twenty-first century, California's death row is a constant reminder of just how difficult it is to eliminate race from the discussion of capital punishment. The debate began with Herrera in 1854 and resurfaced again when Ramón Amador was tried, sentenced, and executed in the San Leandro Jail in Alameda County under the supervision of the much-celebrated Sheriff Morse on September 22, 1871; Amador questioned whether justice was blind to social and cultural difference.[43] Rebuking the criminal justice system, he was reported to have said: "There is no course at all for a poor man. They are down on Spaniards. There are hundreds of cold murderers, but they don't hang them. Others go to state prison only, and are pardoned out. Now, sir, the first time they hang, they hang me."[44] Sadly, it was necessary for the sheriff and his deputies to use force to cover his head with the black cap. Once on the scaffold he "cursed, wept and prayed, in turn, and was totally unnerved."[45] The historian Leonard Pitt has argued that even twenty years after statehood "the Spanish-speaking still claimed—and with good cause—that the guardians of Yankee justice discriminated against them."[46] Pitt insists there may have been some truth to Amador's claim when he notes that a grand jury refused to indict a man by the name of Frederick W. Clarke in the same year because he was the son of a wealthy San Francisco lawyer.[47]

The execution of a human being is hard to imagine, perhaps because we have seen it re-created countless times in movies and films, but six unidentified and undated photographs from California's past provide a fragmented vision of a legal hanging. In the first of the images, one can see the condemned man standing on the gallows, a rope draped about his neck. The executioners appear distracted, one gazes downward, another to the side. The image is badly damaged but one can make out the condemned man's upward gaze as he stares to the heavens, moments before the fatal drop. His expression stands out in stark contrast to those of his executioners, and in examining the image I was unwittingly reminded of Amador's pleas.

By the fifth image, two of the men have begun to place the black hood over the condemned man's head while the others look on. The images are all a little blurry, which may suggest that the photographer was hurriedly attempting to change film holders. In the sixth image, the condemned man's body has been replaced, or displaced, with a single line of rope. Standing in their long coats, hats in hand, the remaining men peer down into the deadly void, one presumes to ensure that the executed man has died without complication (figures 11, 12, and 13).

In the history of the West, there are many accounts in which, due to unforeseen circumstances, the execution went poorly and the unfortunate recipient lingered painfully from the gibbet or hang tree. In reading hundreds of accounts, I was horrified to discover that if the knot is poorly placed or if the rope is too long, the unfortunate person may be unintentionally decapitated. It was as a result of such errors that hanging was eventually banned in every Western State except for Washington, where it is still on the books.

II–13. Unidentified photographer, "Unidentified Execution," numbers 3, 5, and 6 of 6, n.d. Courtesy of California History Room, California State Library, Sacramento, California.

Writing in 1880, the historian Harry Laurenz Wells (1854–1940) restated a sentiment found decades earlier when he argued that capital punishment did little to deter crime. He went so far as to propose that some other method of punishment should be devised because "the barbarous practice of hanging" will be regarded, "by our posterity with the same horror inspired in us by the tortures of the Inquisition."[48] Wells died before the last legal hanging took place in San Quentin Prison, California, on May 1, 1942.[49]

In California, hanging was eventually replaced with gas chambers and electric chairs. In 1968, California would begin a twenty-five year hiatus on executions that would not resume again until 1992.[50] Between 1883 and 2002, 510 executions were recorded in the state prisons; four were women.[51] Lethal injection was adopted as the default method of execution after the 1994 Supreme Court ruling that determined that the use of cyanide gas was cruel and unusual punishment and therefore unconstitutional.[52] In California, electrocution remains an optional choice for death row inmates. According to the California Department of Corrections there were 640 persons on California's death row on January 7, 2005; 228 men and 2 women were identified as African American, and 121 men and 6 women were identified as Hispanic.[53] The final impact of the appeal process is unknown, but the statistics provide a snapshot of the contemporary criminal justice system and offer a glimpse at our own historical legacy. As an interesting side note, the European Union will not consider admitting a nation that practices capital punishment.[54]

Nationwide, as of June 2002, 108 people, including 12 death row inmates, have been exonerated since DNA testing became available in 1973.[55] Because of recent advances made in DNA testing, many of the thirty-eight states that still have a death penalty are embroiled in debates surrounding the merits and challenges posed by capital punishment; many are authoring legislation to provide DNA testing to all eligible death row inmates.[56]

In some states that continue to practice capital punishment Amnesty International has calculated that the total financial cost of capital cases can be up to three times the cost of life imprisonment; a recent Florida study estimated that the cost to the state was approximately $3.2 million for each execution, as opposed to the $600,000 price tag for a life sentence.[57] A 1993 study of Los Angeles County claimed that the total cost for capital punishment cases was just over $2 million per case, as compared to the approximately $1.4 million price tag for a sentence of "life without parole."[58] The study also insisted that these costs were not a result of frivolous appeals but were simply the result of constitutionally mandated safeguards. In light of the increased public awareness of this topic, and in response to the general confusion surrounding the differences between legal executions, vigilance committees, and lynching in the West, it may be beneficial to briefly summarize the development of California's judicial system.

THE COURT OF LAW

After statehood, and contrary to the popular image of the American West as a lawless frontier, it was those areas with the most law enforcement that had the greatest number of summary executions, vigilance committees, and lynch mobs.[59] The primary reason for this was not that larger towns were more populated and could inspire more drunken brawls and vigilance committees, but was due, in part, to a legislative change that required all capital cases be tried in the county seats.[60] This meant that the criminal had to be brought to town and housed near the courthouse. In rural counties, the criminals had to be placed in local jails, tents, houses, and even hotels, where guards could be stationed in the lobby or in the prisoner's room. The larger towns were also more likely to have a newspaper or local correspondent to record the event. Contrary to the popular image of California as a wild and lawless frontier, by 1860, vigilance committees and lynch mobs usually occurred in towns that had a constable, sheriff, or a justice of the peace.

El Dorado County had twelve townships right in the center of the diggins' or gold fields, as they were known, and had two justices each, making for a total of twenty-four for the county by 1851.[61] The new jail opened in Marysville in January of the same year; it was made of timber that was twelve inches thick and the interior was lined with heavy sheet iron.[62] In nearby San Francisco, a police force had begun to take shape as early as 1849, and to the south, the Council of Los Angeles formed the "City Police" by 1853, though, at this stage, it has been characterized as a "vigilance committee organized under the auspices of the law."[63] New Orleans and Cincinnati didn't have a city police force until 1852, Boston's didn't start until 1854, and Chicago's police officers wouldn't hit the beat until 1855.[64]

That fully legal trials were possible in California as early as the summer of 1850 may surprise some readers, but one of the California state legislature's first tasks was to elect Charles M. Creaner as judge for California's fifth judicial district, an area that included the townships and settlements of Calaveras, San Joaquin, Mariposa, and Tuolumne counties. Creaner held the first session of the Tuolumne County Court in Sonora in July of that same year.[65]

The state constitution gave the district court jurisdiction to inquire into all criminal offenses by means of a grand jury, but it also gave them the authority to try the indictments of the grand jury. The first grand jury began on May 6, 1850—although it didn't actually achieve a quorum until October of that year.[66] In 1851, the power of the grand jury was extended to the county court.[67]

Consideration of candidates for federal judgeships began in 1848, two years before California became the thirty-first state in the Union; long before word of acceptance into the Union could reach San Francisco Bay, Congress had already begun working on California's federal court system.[68] The state legislature pronounced September 9, 1850, as California's official admission day, but news of California's admission into the Union didn't actually reach San Francisco until the steamer *Oregon* pulled into the San Francisco Bay on October 18, 1850.[69] San Francisco hosted California's first admission day celebration on October 29, and one-time Mexican Governor Andrés Pico proudly marched within the first division of the parade[70] (figure 14).

Ogden Hoffman Jr. (1822–91) received his bachelor's degree from Columbia College in 1840 and his law degree from Harvard in 1842. He was nominated to the federal bench on February 1, 1851; he was confirmed in the Senate a little over three weeks later and became the first federal judge in California within months of statehood.[71] His court opened on May 19, 1851, a mere two months after his appointment, and only five months since the creation of the courts themselves.[72] Admittedly, one federal judge hardly constituted a police state, but his presence does challenge the popular image of a lawless frontier. More than just an extension of the status quo, Hoffman had begun his career as a practicing lawyer and earned a pro-legal reputation when he opposed San Francisco's 1851 vigilance committee by defending a state judge who had defied the committee by joining with a number of lawyers to draft a counterresolution intended "to vindicate the supremacy of the Constitution and the Laws of [the] Country."[73] Such a stance would have only heightened the difficulty of Hoffman's job, particularly given the extreme popularity of the 1851 committee.

It must also be noted that Hoffman ruled in both circuit and district courts from 1851 to 1855.[74] The implications of this dual responsibility may not be completely self-evident, but the result was that, as the only federal judge, Hoffmann would have to hear appeals on his own lower court rulings. Nevertheless, in addition to the many local and county courts, the presence of

14. Francis Marryatt, "Admission Day Celebration," 1850.
Courtesy of the Library of Congress.

a functioning federal court highlights the fact that a legal system not only existed but had, as in Hoffmann's case, specifically sought to curtail extrajudicial and summary executions in the state.

VIGILANTISM: LYNCH MOBS AND COMMITTEES OF VIGILANCE

The vigilance committee has held a unique position in the imagination of Western writers and historians; positioned somewhere between legal and extralegal proceedings, the general acceptance of these practices was recorded as early as June 1851, when a letter from a miner in Stockton appeared in a newspaper published in Washington D.C. In it, he provided an account that was fast becoming the canonic image of Western vigilantism, that is to say, the image of justice manifested in the absence of legal means. He wrote:

> The miners go in for Lynch Law in almost all quarters. A man on the Calvaras, some fourteen miles from Winter's Bar, stole six pounds weight of gold dust a fortnight ago last Saturday; the Tuesday following he was hung. Two others were expected to be hung the following day at Carson's. Horse, mule and gold stealing are all punished by death. A man stands a better chance to save his life if he has committed a murder than he does if he has committed a theft. The same course is commencing in the cities, and, if not carried too far, is likely to produce a good effect—making life and property more secure.[75]

Unfortunately, the actions of the vigilance committee and the lynch mob were not always so glorious, and in August 1852, another newspaper carried an article under the heading "Infamous Outrage" and detailed how one such "committee" had flogged a seventy-year-old woman charged with having stolen $1,200.[76] According to the report, the local "vigilance committee" had resolved to hang her but before they carried out the sentence, they sought to extort a confession with lashes. According to the article, they stripped her body and proceeded to give her one hundred lashes, a punishment that was followed by "other villainous outrages," the details of which, perhaps thankfully, were not disclosed. It was later discovered that the poor woman was innocent of the charges made against her. In return for their actions, the "legal authorities" fined the offenders $120, an amount which hardly seems adequate, even by 1850 standards.[77]

Various historians have asserted that between 1836 and 1875, the city of Los Angeles saw between thirty-two and thirty-five summary executions performed by vigilance committees and conventional lynch mobs.[78] This number does not normally include the fifteen to twenty-two Chinese that died in Los Angeles in the Chinese massacre of 1871.[79] Unfortunately, none of these sources cited provide a precise list of which cases they were referencing, and as a result substantiating their exact findings is difficult, but my own list includes thirty-three cases, and could be extended to thirty-six, if one included Santa Ana (now in Orange County) and two cases that occurred near Ventura (now Ventura County). Most of the previously published statistics also include the execution by firing squad of Mariá de Rosario Villa and her paramour Gervasio Alipás in 1836, but they have been excluded from the appendix because the date lies outside the period covered.

By contrast, the actions of the San Francisco vigilance committees have been surprisingly well documented, and as I have argued, it was the extreme notoriety of their cases that may have contributed the most to the continued presence of vigilance committees and lynch mobs throughout much of California. In the best instances, the San Francisco committees of vigilance provided a model for judicial reform and expediency; in the worst, they were invoked as a justification for some of the cruelest spectacles of mob violence recorded on the West Coast.[80]

In spite of the quality and quantity of valuable research that has already been completed on these two regions, no complete accounting of California's many cases had been attempted since Bancroft's *Popular Tribunals* of 1887. One of the primary challenges of beginning such a list is the fact that not every account has been identified, and today, many of the early newspapers that recorded such events have been lost. Another problem, at least for southern California, is that the Los Angeles County Coroner's records have been "misplaced" for nearly all cases occurring prior to 1890.[81] The value of such documents is only multiplied by the fact that these records might have included accounts from a county that once included, not only most of Los Angeles County, but parts of present day San Bernardino, Orange, and Ventura counties.

15. Unidentified photographer, "Scene of the Chinese Riot," n.d. Reproduced by permission of the Huntington Library, San Marino, California.

CHINESE MASSACRE

By the 1870s, Chinese immigrants were being targeted by lynch mobs and vigilance committees in the state. There have been many theories about the rise of anti-Chinese sentiments, but most agree that racial and cultural differences, combined with the willingness of the Chinese to work for cheap wages, was increasingly perceived as a threat by Anglo workers. On October 24, 1871, a brawl broke out between two rival Chinese gangs in the oldest and perhaps seediest part of Los Angeles.[82] Things quickly got out of hand and Policeman Bilderrain, who had arrived at the scene, collapsed to the ground, mortally wounded from a pistol shot. Robert Thompson heard his calls for help and quickly came to Bilderrain's assistance when he too was struck by an equally fatal round (figures 15 and 16).

Night fell, and news of the shooting brought an ever-growing crowd of men to assemble around the old Adobe building, within which some of the Chinese men had barricaded themselves. One man tried to escape but was dragged and hanged to a nearby corral gate. By 9 P.M. several hundred men had assembled around the structure. They battered a hole in the eastern end

And he went for that heathen Chinee

16. Joseph Hull, "And he went for that heathen Chinee," from *The Heathen Chinee* by Bret Harte, 1870. Courtesy of the Library of Congress.

of the building and discovered eight Chinese men huddled in a corner.[83] Extracting them one by one, no less than three were killed from gunshots and as many as four others died later of wounds received that night. When the tally was done, it would be discovered that no less than fourteen Chinese men and one Chinese boy (Chee Long Tong) had been hanged in what has come to be known as the notorious Chinese massacre of 1871.[84] Among their number was a physician who was said to be only half clothed, and it has been suggested that he might have been sleeping when the trouble began. The young boy who was hanged lived with him, and so it seems unlikely that either of them had been directly connected to the shooting. Writing on the massacre, Cecilia Rasmussen captured the horror of the scene when she wrote:

> One by one, more victims were hauled from their hiding places, kicked, beaten, stabbed, shot and tortured by their captors. Some were dragged through the streets with ropes around their necks and hanged from a wooden awning over a sidewalk, a covered wagon or the crossbeam of a corral gate.[85]

The case records also reveal that the number of American Indians that were lynched spiked when tensions rose between settlers and indigenous communities over land. Sadly, those remaining Native communities that continued to survive into the 1860s and 1870s became increasingly incapable of sustaining themselves through age-old ways of life as new areas were settled by California's ever-expanding population. Numerous accounts confirm that American Indians were regularly driven from their lands and shot on sight. They also figured prominently in California's history of lynching.

Looking to the case record one finds that American Indians were most commonly lynched when specific crimes were attributed to specific individuals or small bands. The most common accusations appear to have been for murder or for stealing livestock. This is not to suggest that they were guilty of the charges but to simply note that they were believed to have committed the crimes. The fact that due process was rarely extended to "Indians" was complicated by their legal status. Because they were rarely brought to trial, one will never know the truth of the charges.

In 1852, three Native Americans were lynched in Bridgeport for murder.[86] According to the reports, a European or European American man was shot through the chest by four American Indians. They were reported to have then beaten the man with wooden clubs and stones, "breaking his cheekbone" before they left the scene; the man died within an hour.[87] The reason for their attack was never stated but the criminality of the case was unquestioned; four "Indians" had attacked and killed a white man. A posse of Anglos was organized, and the men set off toward the "Indian rancheria." Rather than searching for the individual men, the posse chose a more direct approach; they captured the chief of the band. The posse threatened to kill him if he did not identify the murderers, and only set him free once he agreed to turn the suspects over to the posse. On the following day, the chief brought four men to their civilian accusers. He explained that he knew they were the murderers because he had compared their arrows to the ones taken from the dead man's body. An impromptu court was assembled, and after it was over three of the accused were summarily hanged while the fourth was released on insufficient evidence.

Recurrent throughout the case list are instances in which a suspect was being held for legal trial when the machinations of due process were interrupted by a lynch mob or vigilance committee. In still other instances, the accused may have been captured by a posse, mob, or vigilance committee and should have been turned over to the legal authorities, but was not. In each of these scenarios, the criminal no longer presented an immanent threat to the safety of the community but was willfully denied due process.

On two consecutive days in June 1852, two "Spaniards" were tried and "hung by the people" from an old oak tree in Jackson.[88] Located in the heart of gold country, this particular mob was said to have been composed mostly of Frenchmen. The two "Spaniards" (José Cheverino, Cruz Flores), also identified as "Mexican," were accused of stabbing and killing two French men while they slept.[89] According to several accounts the judge was so inebriated that once word of the case got out, a grand jury investigation was called for.[90]

As the case record reveals, Anglo-American and European criminals also felt the wrath of the lynch mob and not surprisingly, with a few notable exceptions, it is these tales of stagecoach robbers, bank robbers, and gamblers that have shaped the Western image of cowboy justice. One of the earliest recorded appearances of a masked mob can be found in 1860, near Downieville, when a man named John O'Donnell was taken by a mob estimated to include some one hundred forty "ruffians."[91] They rushed into the house where he was being held in custody, and he was still eating his supper with the constable when he was dragged off to a nearby livery stable and hanged; his body was left suspended until the morning. The irony of the case is that it demonstrates that the necessity for jails had as much to do with keeping the criminals safe from the mob as from escaping.

Another strange case occurred in 1876, on May 9, when an unknown number of hogs had managed to escape their pen and wandered into a neighboring yard.[92] Tireless omnivores, they were more attentive to their appetites than to the property lines. Unfortunately, these nonruminant beasts had wandered onto the property of a man by the name of Charles W. Henley. The hogs belonged to James Rowland, and apparently the two men were engaged in a long-standing feud. According to Henley's testimony, Rowland had approached him in a threatening manner and so he shot him. He claimed it was self-defense. Whether true or not, he turned himself in and was placed in the county jail to await the action of the grand jury of Sonoma County. Over a month had passed and no decision had been made when a mob of "two hundred" men assembled outside the jail, on June 10, at one o'clock in the morning.[93] They wore masks but somehow managed to persuade the jailer, a man by the name of Wilson, to open the door, and then they overpowered him. They forcibly escorted the prisoner out of town and hanged him. The image of some one hundred fifty to two hundred masked men dragging a fifty-eight-year-old man (and one account said he was sixty) a mile down a dirt road on a summer night was summarized in one San Francisco paper as follows:

> The word was given, a moment more and a score of arms bent down willingly and quickly. Up went the struggling figure groaning, gurgling, staring, gasping; and there they left him hanging, a silent, ghastly spectacle of man's stern retribution, unguided by the hand of law, and therefore more awful in its crudity.[94]

The county board of supervisors approved a $500 reward for information leading to the arrest and conviction of the person or persons engaged in the act, but as might be expected, the reward was never claimed.[95] At their August meeting, the grand jury announced that the investigation into the lynching had been closed and, like the hogs, not one member of the mob was ever found.

A number of cases also resulted from public frustration with the legal system itself. In one rather notable case, Hamilton J. Tucker, his wife, and William Johnson were out riding near Long Tom in Kern County on the afternoon of April 13, 1878, when shots were heard.[96] A moment later Mrs. Tucker saw the two men collapse at her side. Though horrified and in shock she saw two gunmen run up a nearby hillside.

She had no choice but to leave the two men where they lay and ride to town, where she identified the two shooters as Thomas and William Yoakum. According to her testimony the brothers had been in a mining dispute with the two slain men. A posse was organized and the two brothers, not realizing they had been spotted, were apprehended and brought to the county jail.

The trial was to begin on November 1, 1878, but the defense asked for a continuance. When it was refused, they withdrew from the case, forcing the judge to postpone the trial anyway.[97] The next session of the court would not be for three months, and when January finally rolled around the two men were tried separately. William Yoakum's trial lasted nine days and ended in a hung jury. His brother Thomas was tried and convicted of murder in the first degree, but the ruling was appealed and actually overturned by the Supreme

Court on May 25, 1879.[98] A new trial was ordered and a change of venue was finally accepted, much to the consternation of the community.

Unwilling to accept the high court's ruling, a mob of about seventy-five masked men arrived at the jail on the morning of May 28, 1879.[99] In keeping with literally dozens of other accounts, some childish ruse was used to get the jailer to open the door, at which point the sheriff's men were overpowered. After a brief search for the keys, the mob proceeded to William's cell and hanged him to the rafters. Thomas was hanged in the same fashion. An editorial at the time explained that contrary to the popular image of an unruly mob, many of the best citizens in the county had participated in the lynching. Intended to justify, or at least normalize the mob's actions, it also suggests that the reporter knew more about the case than he reported. After all, if the mob was masked, how did he know it was composed of the best citizens? Other reports bluntly stated, given the failure of the legal system, particularly with regard to the first trial, that justice was inevitably served even if the law wasn't. Still another asserted, "They were desperadoes of a type which cannot die out too soon for the good of society, and if the law has not had its course in the case, justice has."[100]

After a few weeks had passed, as was often the case, an editorial suddenly appeared condemning the lynching. In this particular case the editorial went so far as to argue that lynching was a danger to society and to the public at large. More importantly for this study, it went on to make one rather telling observation when it argued, "No one of those who acted the part of executioners would probably be pleased to be charged with seizing an unarmed man, manacled and chained to the floor, beating and shooting him to death, and then hanging his dead body to the roof of his dungeon."[101] The sheriff's men had manacled the men to their cells for their own safety, the assumption being that lynching a manacled man in his cell would be a difficult task, as indeed it was, and yet the mob's insistence that the men be discovered hanged, whether it was the actual cause of death or not, reveals just how deeply coded the practice of lynching had become by the 1870s.

TO THIS JURY UNKNOWN

On December 22, 1875, a murderer was apprehended in Mendocino County and taken to Hopland.[102] It was around six o'clock in the evening and a few days before Christmas. The sun had already gone down, and many residents were probably already busy eating dinner, maybe a few still busied themselves by wrapping Christmas presents or were getting a head start on the their holiday cooking, and Judge Dooley wanted to be home. The court had been busy and he was still in his courtroom. In fact, there was some degree of urgency in the matter. He was to examine a man by the name of José Antonio Ygarra. Ygarra was 35-year-old California native who was to be questioned on murder charges.[103] The murder had occurred at a dance on the previous night, and emotions ran high in the community. As if that weren't enough, Ygarra was widely believed to have been a member of the notorious Vasquez Band.[104]

On the night of December 21, 1875, a local resident by the name of William Granjean had attended a local dance. One account suggested that he was dancing on a table when a bullet came through the window and struck a fatal blow.[105] According to witnesses Ygarra had been seen in the vicinity just before the shooting and was a natural suspect. Furthermore, local hearsay suggested that Granjean had been a witness in several cases involving Ygarra, which added a motive to the crime. At approximately 6 P.M. a mob of twenty men stormed into the courtroom and took Ygarra from the building. They were armed and wore no masks. He was taken several hundred yards from the courthouse and hanged to an oak near the road. His body was found the next morning.[106]

When asked what they had done with Ygarra, members of the group, probably with a wink and a nod, stated that Ygarra had run away. No one was prosecuted. No one followed the group after the abduction, and no law enforcement officers were available within the courthouse to stop them. This illusion of spontaneity was an essential and reoccurring element in nearly all lynching cases, and yet it is impossible to believe that so many men, without some planning, some premeditation, could have found each other in the dark of night or found a single tree located on the outskirts of town—somewhere between Hopland and Senel.

As guilty as Ygarra may have been, the case reveals the willful disregard for the criminal justice system; after all, the judge was working late, and still Ygarra was willfully denied due process. Like so many cases nationwide, the only official record of his death would be the coroner's jury report, which like so many thousands of cases nationwide, read "death by some person or persons to this jury unknown."[107]

WITHOUT JUSTICE

In considering Beccaria, Baudelaire, and the history of both legal and extra-legal forms of execution in California, this chapter rests on a singular assertion: in a representative democracy, justice must be more than majority opinion alone. The judiciary was established as the third branch of government to establish equality under the law, and while its boundaries have expanded beyond those individuals it initially sought to protect, its reliance on legal precedence has helped to ensure that no ruling can completely disregard past rulings. As trying as it may be to the patience of any community, the right to due process remains the defining principle of the U.S. judicial system.

The history of lynching demonstrates that without a legal code of law, justice is little more than fleeting passion—mob rule. Indeed, many individuals today may share the sense of anxiety and frustration felt by those first waves of "American" settlers, who regularly bemoaned the length and cost of capital punishment in editorials and published letters. In one such letter, addressing a posse that had set out in search of a band of Latino robbers, an unnamed author echoed the dominant view of the Anglo-American community at the time: "We hope the companies will shoot down the ruffians, should they find them. We want no prisoners, to saddle the county with their support for months, winding up with the farce of trial and acquittal."[108]

In an unrelated case that took place seven years later, another editorial blankly asserted, "We are not disposed to question the mode or manner of punishment, provided it be effectual."[109] In 1881, still another argued, "We are not quick to advise a resort to unlawful methods even to obtain justice. But there are times in the history of nations, states, communities, and individuals when revolution is necessary."[110] The invocation of a necessary "revolution" in the once-thriving mining town of Bodie is ridiculous because it asserts the complete disavowal of a code of law that had been consciously disregarded hundreds of times since statehood.

Was this rejection because justice could not be served by the law? Or simply because lynching had become so accepted in the American West— and elsewhere—that its rituals of cruelty were no longer even questioned? As the NAACP records make clear, reports of lynching increased through the last decades of the nineteenth century, and in some states, continued to grow well into the 1920s. Less concerned with justice than with the selfish desire to deny justice, the semantic blurring of the lines between lynching, committees of vigilance, and legally constituted executions in the West helped to ensure that the practice of lynching would go unrecognized in the West.

17. "Seal of The San
Francisco Vigilance
Committee," 1856–57, 2.25
by 2.25 inches. Collection
of the author.

THE VIGILANT EYE

The second San Francisco Committee of Vigilance created a logo for itself
that incorporated a floating eye in the center of its design, and this image was
circled by the words, "No Creed, No Party, No Sectional Issues." This disembodied eye was not unlike the one found on a $1 bill and was a recurring
symbol that could be found in the seals of fraternal societies throughout the
West. The eye's presence was meant to suggest that God looked over and approved of the actions of the vigilance committee. But in American jurispru-
dence, justice is symbolized by the idealized image of a woman who stands
blindfolded with the scales of justice in her hand. Unlike the vigilant eye, her
symbolism is intended to assure us all that justice will be blind to the wants
of men and women and not simply to mirror their desires (figure 17).

The press would repeatedly emphasize how a given vigilante committee
displayed military-like organization and discipline; or, in the case of a lynching, they would regularly note the presence and participation of the town's
leading citizens.[111] Such efforts represented an attempt by the press and the
community to steer readers, whether from nearby townships or from across
the nation, toward the idea that the committee of vigilance and the lynch
mob represented something other than the complete rejection of legal authority. After the great success of San Francisco's first vigilance committee,
lesser committees would continue to erupt in nearly every region of the state,
and they would remain in existence for the next seven decades. In one case,
occurring near the Nevada border in Bodie, it was noted that the officers of
the law did not even attempt to interfere with the actions of the vigilantes.[112]

18. Unidentified artist, "Man with Top Hat at Summary Execution," n.d. Courtesy of California History Room, California State Library, Sacramento, California.

Such claims were intended to suggest that no laws had really been broken because such highly valued members of the community appeared to have supported the decision; therefore, the actions of the vigilance committee or lynch mob should not be seen as criminal (figure 18).

A reoccurring, if equally deceptive, claim argued: "The vigilance committees were organized, not because there were no established institutions of law enforcement and justice, but because those institutions had failed, in the eyes of the vigilantes, to provide justice."[113] Even as the right of citizenship expanded and contracted throughout the nineteenth century, the principals of justice established by the framers of the U.S. Constitution, reflected in both the nation's and the state's constitutions, continued to demand that justice be more than a majority opinion; each person was promised the right to trial by a jury of one's peers, a concept that was intended to ensure that the right to due process would be guaranteed to all. In exchanging individual (or group) morality with a secular code of law, the committee of vigilance and the lynch mob consciously undermined the very constitution they claimed to protect. Without a code of law, the concept of justice shifts its emphasis from the means to the ends. This is one of the differences between a legal and a moral code. As the history of lynching in United States makes clear, once due process becomes a choice and not a right, it is increasingly difficult, if not impossible, to distinguish between the best intentions of those first vigilante committees, which assembled in the light of day, and the bloodshot vision of the lynch mob, assembled in the dark of night, to give the rope one last tug. The disembodied eye of the vigilance committee seems to insist that impartiality is not necessary for the application of justice, only consensus among property owners and taxpayers, but as this book makes clear, this misrecognition of the past continues to haunt the present. As early as 1857, skeptics specifically rejected claims by the Mexican community that they were treated unfairly in Los Angeles: "The whole is a tissue of groundless accusations against the Americans, who are made to appear as very demons of ferocity, in comparison with the citizens of other descent."[114] However, as the case list reveals, even though many communities were touched by the history of lynching in California, Americans can no longer turn a blind eye to the fact that a disproportionate number of persons of color (including "Mexicans") died at the hands of the lynch mob, a fact that provides some historical ballast to the lingering romanticization of frontier justice in the American West. Some have argued that lynch mobs and vigilance committees only formed when the guilt of the accused was unquestioned by the community, for example, when a saloon brawl or botched robbery ended in a fatality, but the case records reveal that there were just as many situations in which the "evidence" was completely circumstantial or in which the crime would not have resulted in a death penalty under the law, as in the killing of the doctor and the young boy in the Chinese massacre of 1872.

Trying to unmask the faceless mob is a difficult task, so one must also wonder how, or why, these histories have remained unseen and unseeable to so many, for so long? Whether traced through a thousand documents or a handful of scraps, the fact that African Americans, American Indians, Asians, and Latinos, alleged or convicted, figured so prominently in this history only complicates an already difficult task. Were they victims? Or was justice served?

CHAPTER THREE

In the Shadow of Photography:
Copy Prints in the Archive

The circus came to Santa Cruz in the spring of 1877 and at least two men were anxious to see it. Unfortunately they were also unemployed and quite short on cash. They decided that robbery would be the surest means of gaining the admission fee and quickly set upon a plan. They would hide themselves in an overgrown tangle of willows along the side of the road and wait for an unsuspecting victim to pass by. In short order, a man appeared in the distance and the two men were careful not to be seen. One of them fired a shot and missed. The unarmed man had nowhere to run when the second bullet pierced his chest and he fell dead in the middle of the road. They then dragged the body of their sixty-year-old victim some fifty yards, into the grassy shade, where they preceded to ransack his pockets for whatever money he had. With cash in hand, the two men went to the circus and left his dusty body where it lay. After having thoroughly enjoyed the spectacle of the circus they went home.

The newspapers would later report that the men had collected somewhere between $8 and $20.[1]

On the following day the body of Henry De Forest was discovered where they had left it, and word of the murder swept through town. The sheriff began the investigation by asking nearby residents if they had seen any men in the area. Fortunately, one witness was able to place the two men at the scene of the crime shortly before De Forest was killed. Accounts vary slightly, but this unknown witness appears to have been the mother of the youngest of the two suspects.[2] The men were quickly apprehended and deposited in the San Lorenzo jail where they were questioned. While being held in separate cells, the younger man was reported to have fingered his partner in front of witnesses, but before a trial could be mounted and their guilt or innocence determined before a jury of their peers, the jailer and undersheriff were over-powered, and the prisoners were taken by the mob or vigilance committee sometime before 2 A.M. on May 3.[3]

They were transported to the Water Street Bridge where they were questioned and were later reported to have admitted their guilt.[4] Having gathered all the information they desired, the mob concluded their investigation and hanged the two men to the crossbeams of the bridge.[5] On the following morning, the town residents discovered a different kind of spectacle than the one encountered at the circus; this time it was the lifeless bodies of Francisco Arias and José Chamales as they swung from the crossbeams of the bridge. If she walked to town that morning, one can't help but wonder if Chamales's mother would have retained her faith in the judicial system or given in to her passions, as the mob had done the night before.

Chamales was twenty-one or twenty-two years of age, and he had only recently been released from San Quentin where he served three years for robbery. The majority of reports surrounding the case identified both men as "Mexican," but as previously noted, nineteenth-century Anglo-Americans had a tendency to call all Spanish-speaking persons "Mexicans," no matter where they were born. It was widely reported that Chamales had been born a mere three hundred yards from the place where he was hanged.[6] Even at twenty-two years of age, Chamales would have been born a full five years after California had become a state, and so while calling him a "Mexican" may have been ethnically true, it bore no relationship to his nation of birth. Arias was thirty-eight years old and from nearby Pescadero; he had just been released from San Quentin where he served three years for manslaughter.[7] There is no mention of whether Arias was actually born in Pescadero but it seems possible since several accounts noted that he had many relatives in the area.

The Arias and Chamales case shares many aspects found in other cases of lynching, and after they were hanged, there were no attempts to identify or prosecute any member of the lynch mob by law officials. Local newspaper accounts generally supported the mob's actions and, in one case, even remarked that the citizens could breath a sigh of relief now that the town was no longer "endangered by the existence of two as desperate assassins as ever stretched hemp."[8] Another newspaper account would justify the killing based on the familiar claim that the mob was composed of "no common rabble," insisting that the lynchers were primarily property owners and tax payers.[9] One might wonder how the correspondent was able to divine which members of the mob paid their taxes or not unless he knew who was there, which would have been no small challenge considering that most accounts reported that the men's faces were either blackened or masked.[10] One possible explanation might have been that the reporter simply claimed that the mob was masked. This scenario might also explain why so many versions of the story have come down to us; some claim the mob was masked, others assert that the men had blackened their faces, and still others make no mention of any disguises whatsoever.

The cold-blooded murder of an unarmed man is inexcusable in any civilized society and doubly so under such villainous circumstances, but of all the details known in the Arias and Chamales case, the most interesting fact is that it was also the subject of one of the earliest photographic documents of a lynching in the United States, and provides a unique opportunity to consider the lynching photograph.

Lynching photographs, view cards, and postcards are scattered throughout regional, institutional, and national archives. I was surprised to discover that after presidents and celebrities, postcards and view cards of those lynched or condemned to be legally executed were among the earliest mass-produced photographic images in the West.[11] In recent years, there has been an expanding interest in exploring the relationship between photography and historical, institutional, and subject-based archives, but to date, there has been no significant study addressing the impact of such archives on the history of lynching in the West.[12]

This chapter extends the underlying theme of erasure to the historical, institutional, or subject archive in order to ask how so many deaths could have garnered so little attention. Using the lynching photograph as a point of departure, the chapter begins by considering the impact of the archive on the photographic image and then alters course by asking the reader to consider how such photographic images may have impacted the history of lynching itself. In order to do this, it is necessary to address a number of photographic images ranging from the lynching photograph of Arias and Chamales to later view cards and photographic postcards of lynchings and those condemned in court of law; in doing so, this chapter considers the impact of the institutional copy print to the history of lynching.

In examining hundreds of images produced in California, I was unable to find a single photographic image that documented the lynching of African Americans, American Indians, Asians, or Asian Americans in the many regional archives visited in researching this book. This is not to say that such images may not one day be uncovered, but it begins to suggest the challenge of working within the archive.

THE LYNCHING PHOTOGRAPH

In the United States, lynching usually included a period of public display after the suspects were killed, and as one might expect, the photographic image of Arias and Chamales was only possible because the bodies had been left hanging through the night. The following morning, local residents, journalists, and at least one photographer were able to fully appreciate the mob's handiwork. The usual justification for leaving the bodies hanging through the night was that it served as a warning to other would-be criminals, but the reality seems to be that such public spectacles were an integral part of lynching itself.

Even beyond the public display of the bodies, the details of the Arias and Chamales case are nearly identical to cases that occurred across the nation. To give an example from the history of lynching in the South, the jail in Barnwell, South Carolina, was broken into by a mob at 4 A.M. on December 28, 1890, and eight African American men accused of murder, who similarly had not been tried, were taken from the jail and hanged by a masked mob.[13] The comparison is significant because many have tried to argue that "Mexicans" hadn't been lynched but were hanged by vigilantes and sheriff's posses, which was somehow more acceptable. Such arguments are racist, not simply because they devalue the killing of American Indians, Asians, and Mexicans, but because they racialize the term "lynching" so that African Americans killed in the American West are included on the national statistics on lynching but other communities are excluded. One element that often confuses those unfamiliar with the history of lynching in the West is the fact that the accused were often held in a jail cell for a period of time before they were lynched, but as the Barnwell case demonstrates, this particular aspect of frontier justice was neither unique to California nor restricted by race.

THE PHOTOGRAPH

After the sun rose on May 3, Anglo men and boys slowly began to assemble at the edge of town as they struggled to get a closer look at the broken bodies of Arias and Chamales. In looking at the photograph, one can't help but wonder if some of the children depicted in the photograph hadn't been at the same circus that the two men had been so villainously bent on seeing. Those arriving at the scene encountered an added treat; standing just in front of the two lifeless bodies was a strange box on spindly wooden legs—a photographer's camera.

Peering at this curious contraption, and apparently directed to stand behind the two carefully turned bodies, a wall of Anglo men and boys stood four rows deep when the picture was finally taken. Having seen the bodies, they crowded within inches of the dead men in order to have their photograph taken. Probably the only Mexicans they would ever have their pictures taken with, but the obvious appeal wasn't the fact that they were "Mexicans," but they were dead Mexicans, and having your picture taken next to such villainy was proof that you had been there—it was a trophy photograph (color plate 4).

In the space between the suspended bodies, two barefooted children don't even seem to notice the hanging bodies as they eagerly peer into the camera's dark eye. In fact, one might be startled to discover that all eyes are transfixed not on the victim's bodies but on the camera itself. Some viewers may be tempted to interpret this image as a "documentary" photograph, but unlike modern documentary photography which strives to make the camera disappear and to let the viewer experience the world with as little mediation as possible, the Arias and Chamales image doesn't even document the crowd's reactions. If it documents anything, it documents the presence of the photographer and the spectacle of the camera itself. Standing in a cluster and pressing one to the next, the living are posing for an image that not only links this case to the history of lynching nationwide but to the history of portrait photography as well.

Taken in 1877, the photograph of the Arias and Chamales case is one of the earliest images of a lynching taken in the United States. There is at least one earlier photograph taken of another double lynching in Helena, Montana, in 1870, and it is similar to the Santa Cruz image in that the crowd gathered around the two hanged men and stared transfixed into the camera.[14] Standing next to the criminal body, such images were not only testaments to the modern marvels of photography, but given photography's propensity to multiply, they were also destined to become sought-after commodities that would be bought and sold.

Seemingly weighed by an unseen balance, the two bodies have been disfigured by the deadly impact of two coils of rope. Their feet are tied and their elbows have been pinned to their bodies with hay ropes. In the photograph, the two men still wear their hats but one can fairly conclude that the photographer must have placed their hats back upon their heads before the photograph was taken. Their clothes are worn and faded. Their boots are scuffed and covered in dirt. Their complexions are dark and undeniably mestizo.[15]

Photographed a few hours after the lynching, most of the faces in the crowd are discernable, if slightly blurred. Some might interpret these blurry figures as a technical flaw, but the juxtaposition of the living against the dead may actually serve the same symbolic function as the extended display of the lynched body itself; it transforms the photographic instant into something more. It smears time; it acknowledges that time is passing and bodies are moving.[16] It is uncanny, a photographic stutter, that extends that photographic instant to infinity, and reveals the most chilling truth of the lynching photograph—that this scene will never end. It is the unpleasantness of this reality, which cannot be undone.

On a formal level, the Santa Cruz photograph was printed in an oval vignette; a convention that was embraced in studio portraiture of the period precisely because it was able to mask out the external world. As a technique, it continues in studio portraiture today. In the lynching photograph, the vignette serves much the same purpose because the two lifeless Mexicans are literally and metaphorically isolated from their communities, from their families, and from the men who dragged them to the edge of town—a detail that is hinted at by the dust on their clothes. Then there is the angle of their heads—an unnatural one that announces that their necks have been broken.

Writing on the lynching, one newspaper editorial claimed that "Judge

Lynch is a very dangerous magistrate, we know, and should never be called on to preside except as a last resort. But he is the terror of outlaws and desparadoes, and a most able defender of public safety."[17] But just how two prisoners being held in jail could have been seen as a threat to public safety is never explained. In nearby San Francisco, one paper challenged the actions of the mob, admitting that while the two "desparadoes" defied the law, their acts did not justify the lynching and asked, "Why should forty or fifty other men defy the law by the commitment of another crime . . . society is never protected by a mob which avenges one crime by committing another."[18] As a general note, it was not uncommon to find that local papers were consistently less critical of cases occurring in their own town than those occurring in others.

Normally spelled "desperadoes" in English, the term cannot be found in Spanish dictionaries, though *desesperado* is the Spanish adjective for desperate. And if it derived from the Spanish term, one can't help but wonder just why they were so desperate? Spelled "desparadoes" in at least two different sources in connection with the Arias and Chamales case, I would like to argue that such terms became a part of a new vocabulary that evolved to meet specific needs, in this case, to efficiently communicate both the subject's criminality and "Mexican" origin.[19]

The term was sometimes extended to Anglo outlaws, but from its usage in this and other cases, it becomes clear that even when the term is applied to Anglos, its presence is intended to augment their criminality and not diminish it. That the term "desperado" appears in English dictionaries and not in Spanish ones suggests that while it may be based on a Spanish word, its actual origin must be traced to nineteenth-century anti-Mexican sentiments.

Moving from image to text, I would like to introduce a second case that occurred a short distance from San Jose, just two months after the Arias and Chamales double lynching, because its treatment in the newspapers reveals a degree of race hatred that is normally excluded or watered down in discussions of frontier justice.

On July 12, 1877, in nearby Monterey County, a man named Justin Arayo approached and shot another man by the name of Manuel Butron when, according to his testimony, he failed to collect money he was owed.[20] He was immediately incarcerated in the local jail, but despite the fact that an extra detachment of men were sent to guard the jail, on Friday, July 13, at one o'clock in the morning, a mob of masked men overtook the guards and hanged Arayo to a nearby tree.[21]

The newspaper editorials supported the lynching, noting that an inoffensive man was fatally wounded after being attacked without provocation.[22]

Another newspaper treated the episode as a comical skit when it summarized the lynching in the following manner:

> In San Juan one Spaniard in cold blood murdered another. He was arrested and placed in Lockup. During the night he attended a neck tie-party, and the next morning was allowed to tell his story. He said not a word, but his countenance looked volumes. There are speech-making times, and it is assumed that he mounted a platform, that the platform was then taken away, and that he determined to remain in midair till break of day, when he would give way to the candidates of San Benito and Monterey.[23]

The passage emphasized that the only "speech-making" Arayo would be allowed would be the "speech" symbolized in his own dead body.

Those supporting the lynch mob usually argued that the legal system was not yet fully established, or that such criminals might have escaped the prison cell, or worse, that they might have been acquitted in a court of law (perhaps because of the frequent lack of evidence), and the Arayo case was no exception. But as the historian and publisher Hubert Howe Bancroft (1832–1918) stated in the epigraph, in his opinion, lynching was no more necessary in Santa Cruz of 1877 than it was in any other city of comparable size.

THE LYNCHING POSTCARD

Shifting from Santa Cruz to Santa Rosa, I would like to consider a second lynching photograph, on a postcard. It was taken in Franklin cemetery in Santa Rosa on December 10, 1920.[24] Santa Rosa is located about fifty miles due north of San Francisco on the western edge of the Sonoma valley and is a stone's throw from some of California's most celebrated wineries. Newspaper accounts reported that at 12:30 A.M. a mob of between 50 and 200 "masked" men entered the city jail, overpowered the guards, and removed three prisoners from their cells. They proceeded in "fifteen machines" down Fourth Street and stopped at the cemetery just beyond of the city limits. Illuminated by the headlights of three automobiles, the mob worked quickly, and it was reported to have taken them less than fifteen minutes to extract the three men from the jail and to lynch them to what was reported to have been an oak tree.[25] As the cars slowly dispersed and the light bounced off the surrounding trees, three motionless bodies, two Anglos and one Latino, would have been visible for a moment before receding into the black of night. Their names were George Boyd, Terrance Fitts, and Charles Valento, and they had just been lynched by a mob that was rumored to have included members of local law enforcement[26] (color plate 5).

The back of the postcard looked like every other postcard I had ever seen, but as I flipped it over I was startled to see a young Latino man at the center of the image.[27] His hair rose in thick black waves above a slightly tilted head, and though his face was smooth, one could make out the faintest shadow of a mustache above his lips. He was a young man. His arms were draped submissively in a gesture that, in another context, might have been taken for solemn or reverent prayer. It was evident that his shirt had been ripped from off his back, and what little of it remained was draped in loose folds over his joined hands or clung to the curve of his neck. His chest and arms were bare, and the fact that his lower torso was covered in long underwear or long johns, as the old timers called them, was the only clue that it was winter. His legs descended in a straight line, but there was something unexpected about the way his ankles touched, and then I realized that a small length of rope extended beyond his toes and revealed that his legs had been tied together.

Valento was the only man to have his shirt ripped from his body, the only man to have his hands tied, and he would have the ignoble distinction of being the last Latino lynched in California.[28] Though a seemingly gruesome task, to my surprise deciphering such coded displays was the first step in acknowledging a history that had been nearly erased or so mythologized that its legacy remained unknown, unacknowledged, or worst of all, dismissed.

THE DECISIVE MOMENT

The first clue appeared in the faint and nearly unrecognizable glow of a tombstone in the far right of the image, but this ghostly blur revealed more than just the location of the lynching, it revealed the transformative presence of light on the scene itself. Given the sharpness of the shadows cast from the ropes onto the tree branches, it would appear that the image was taken with the help of photographic flash powder or from the directed beams of the automobile headlights that were reported to have illuminated the tree for the lynch mob.

The image bears an uncanny resemblance to a photographic image taken in daylight. It depicts the three men that were lynched, the ropes that were used, and the tree itself, but unlike a daylight image, it also produces a highly detailed record of the moss and lichen that clung to the trees branches, details that would be overlooked by all but the most avid horticulturalist in the light of day. When shot with the assistance of headlights or flash powder, these little dusty gray organisms fluoresce around the three hanging figures. If the effects of the light can transform tree moss into glowing nubs of light, one can't help but wonder what effect this unexpected night vision might have upon the photographic representation of three seemingly lifeless bodies.

Taken hours or perhaps minutes after the lynching, what other subtle acts of distortion go unnoticed? Looking at the three bodies, one quickly recognizes that these are not the lifeless and sunken cadavers found in the Arias and Chamales image. The simple truth is that one can't even be absolutely certain from the photographic image that these three bodies, these three men presumed to be dead, were in fact devoid of all signs of life. Even in a successful hanging the heart can continue to produce a faint pulse from five to twenty minutes.[29] More phenomenological than practical, the angle of the camera's view, the aperture of the lens, the framing of the figures, the tree, the rope, and even the effects of this strange night vision allow this photographic document to exclude as much as it includes. Beyond the technical limitations of the camera and the chemical processes used to produce the photographic postcard, the exclusion of the lynch mob from the scene is not as incidental as it may appear. First, metaphorically, it reinforces the general acceptance of the lynching found in the popular press which depicted the triple lynching as divine retribution rather than the base and brutal actions of human hands. Second, the mob excluded from the picture was rumored to have included local law enforcement.

Most accounts stated that Boyd had shot two, and possibly all three, of the police officers, but in the end, the individual crimes of the gang's members remained largely unknown. This is not to suggest that the men were innocent but simply to emphasize that, in a court of law, their individual guilt may not have resulted in the death penalty—a historical truth that also escaped the camera's view.[30]

Even with all its heightened detail, the Santa Rosa photograph must be recognized as a highly abbreviated record of the event, and aside from the torn shirt, the only other sign of a struggle is revealed in a single piece of fabric that lies haphazardly in the foreground.

That the image captures neither the terror felt by the men as they were led barefoot through the dark of night, nor the outrage of the mob, nor the careful selection of a low hanging branch suggests that the image is not as objective as it might first appear. The interlaced and carefully tied ropes imply that the three men were lynched at nearly the same moment, and yet even with this clue, the taut ropes can only hint at the arched backs and clenched teeth of those in the mob as they pulled the men upward, carefully raising them to the greatest height, and then quickly slackening the ropes so that their bodies could fall fast enough to break their necks, all the while keeping the bodies from touching the ground or becoming entangled in the ropes.

A morality tale on film, the photographic image had but one point to make — that heinous crimes lead to heinous ends — but under different circumstances Valento's closed eyes might suggest the mundane pleasures of sleep. When framed by the end of a rope, these dark crescents suggest the worst; banal and cruel thoughts choked in selfish pleasures from a life filled with crime.

A second glance reveals that Valento's mouth is slightly open and gives the distinct impression that his lower jaw is out of place; a detail that, when taken with the unnatural tilt of the head, inevitably produces some degree of nausea. This state of discomfort derives from more than these two details alone, but suffice it to say that such photographic images are not concerned with beautification but with its phenomenological opposite — abjection. It is precisely this state of abjection that the photographer intends to capture, and it is this liminal presence that may have contributed to the historical erasure of lynching in the West. Whether consciously composed or haphazardly documented, such visceral details resist interpretation. Repelled by the spectacle of death, empathy or identification with the criminal body is all but impossible. Conversely, one of the most fascinating aspects of this case may be the fact that the original coding of the 1920 image may be all but unrecognizable to the contemporary viewer, who, in keeping with much of the scholarship now available surrounding the legacy of violence connected with the history of lynching nationwide, can no longer consider lynching in the American West as a victimless crime. By 1920, California's legal system was undeniably capable of prosecuting three men, no matter how heinous their crime may have been.

The fact that such an image initially symbolized support for the lynching and can subsequently be employed to critique the very history it depicts reveals something about the complexity of the photographic image. The Santa Rosa triple lynching demonstrates that, like the Arias and Chamales case, the spectacle of lynching was inexorably linked to the criminal body and not to the criminal actions of the mob — a mob that was organized and familiar enough to travel in each others' cars as they sped through the center of town.

Boyd, Fitts, and Valento were part of the Howard Street Gang that had plagued San Francisco in the months leading up to the event. The gang, whose total member list remains unknown, was accused of abducting and assaulting young women and girls in their makeshift hideaway.[31] A number of the gang's members had already been arrested and were being held on charges when the three men fled the city and hid in Santa Rosa. Two San Francisco detectives, Lester Dorman and Miles Jackson, had discovered their whereabouts, and with the help of Sheriff Petray of Sonoma County, they went in pursuit of the men.

Once located, there was a shootout, and Boyd may have shot and killed Dorman, Jackson, and Petray before the three gang members were apprehended. Accounts suggest that a lynching was averted on the night of the arrest but that community outrage erupted after the San Francisco detectives were buried. On December 10, a crowd, estimated by later reports to be closer to sixty strong, stormed the jail and overpowered the guards.[32] The lynching was depicted as a spontaneous event in the newspaper reports of the day, but one element seems to challenge such claims. Who took the photograph?

Alerted in the middle of the night, the photographer would have had to travel to Santa Rosa, find the location of the lynching, and set up the photographic equipment. This would have been difficult if not impossible to do without some assistance. Driving in the dark, this person would not only have had to find the location of the lynching but would have encountered the lynch mob or have had to find three bodies in an empty and unlit cemetery on his or her own. If the photographer had encountered the mob, it seems unlikely that no one else would have been captured in the image—a common detail found in many lynching photographs. One explanation for this absence might be that police officers were present at the lynching or that the lynchers knew the photographer and, given the speed of the event, the photographer must have traveled with the members of this mob as they piled into their cars. In return, the photographer would have been careful to keep them out of the image. A difficult hypothesis to prove, but I was encouraged by a second photograph discovered in one of several scrapbooks compiled by Hamilton Henry Dobbin (1856–1930), an avid collector of memorabilia from the theatre and of California history.

The image was of a rather expressionless middle-aged man standing in front of a tree. A handwritten inscription beneath the image identified the tree as the same one on which Boyd, Fitts, and Valento were hanged. Valento is spelled "Valente" on the photograph, but it is spelled "Valento" in newspaper accounts of the event. A fourth name is written beneath the photograph and presumably identified either the model or the photographer as "Borne Miller," though the exact spelling is difficult to make out.[33] Dobbin was a police officer who worked in San Francisco for thirty-five years and certainly must have known the two detectives that were killed, but no matter who is standing in front of the tree, one must wonder why Dobbin chose to memorialize the slain officers with a souvenir photograph of the hang tree in his scrapbook[34] (figure 19).

In the scrapbook there are also other pictures, pictures that are identical to the lynching postcard in every aspect except that they are printed on regular photo paper instead of postcard stock, and one can only conclude that Dobbin knew the photographer. With so many elements pointing back to the San Francisco Police Department, one might be surprised to learn that none of those persons responsible for the triple lynching were ever identified or prosecuted. If police officers were actually connected to the lynching, one can begin to see just how the invocation of frontier justice, maddened mobs, and vigilance committees could have served as a handy cover story for what may have simply been the calculated actions of persons unwilling to put faith in the judicial system they were hired to protect.[35]

HOLMES AND THURMOND

Beyond the Santa Rosa lynching, there are examples of lynching photographs in which the crowd is documented. Illuminated with everything from car headlamps to flares, cases like the 1919 lynching and burning of William Brown in Omaha, Nebraska, or the 1930 lynching of Thomas Shipp and Abram Smith in Marion, Indiana, capture the gawking stares and toothy smiles of the lynch mob with an insidious permanence that was nearly impossible with nineteenth-century photographic technology.[36] These two cases involved the lynching of African Americans in the Midwest, but there are similar examples in California's history of lynching.

John M. Holmes and Thomas H. Thurmond were lynched on November 26, 1933, in San Jose for the kidnapping and murder of a young man named Brooke Hart.[37] Hart, twenty-two years of age and the son of a wealthy storeowner, was kidnapped on November 9, 1933, as he was leaving his father's department store.[38] After the kidnapping, the family received a series of ransom notes and a number of phone calls, but despite the family's willingness to pay the ransom, the kidnappers were unable to decide on a final plan to collect it. Apprehended on November 16, Thurmond made a nearly complete confession, which Holmes would later refute.[39]

While Thurmond and Holmes were being held for trial, Hart's body was discovered in the marshy edges of the San Francisco Bay on the afternoon of November 26, 1933.[40] The newspapers disclosed that the kidnappers had

The tree in Santa Rosa Cemetery on which
Geo. Boyd, Terrance Fitts, Charles Valente
were lynched for the murder of Lester
Dorman and Miles Jackson S.F. Detectives

19. "The tree in Santa Rosa Cemetery . . . ," in Dobbin, *Album of San Francisco*, page 81, gelatin silver print mounted in album. Courtesy of California History Room, California State Library, Sacramento, California.

thrown Hart off the San Mateo Bridge, bound by wire and tied to a "freeway brick," before they even wrote the first ransom note.[41] Their idea was that without a living witness, they wouldn't have to worry about the complications of returning the kidnapped victim.

Divers had been searching the bay since Thurmond's confession, but Hart's body had not been found. After two weeks of searches it finally washed up in a marshy bog where two men on a duck hunting expedition discovered it. The body was reported to have been in an extreme state of decay, a fact that was not lost in the newspaper reports. The two men were being held in the San Jose jail when, some four hours before the lynching, the sheriff's office got an anonymous call suggesting that a hearse be at the police station at 11 P.M.[42] One author has even claimed that the lynching was announced on a local radio station within hours after the body was discovered and that by the evening broadcast the local newscaster was inviting everyone to drive to the Saint James park in San Jose to witness the lynching.[43] Another report claimed that a young boy had taken credit for the lynching, saying that he had brought the rope from his father's farm and that he had announced the lynching at all the local watering holes.[44] At the nearby American Theater, the early show was just ending (around 10 P.M.), and an unconfirmed report claimed that the projectionist flashed a slide on the screen informing the audience the lynching was about to begin.[45] Whatever the origins, the newspapers reported that some 15,000 persons headed to the park to watch the "vigilantes."[46]

At approximately 11 P.M. the crowd went wild when an enormous metal pipe suddenly materialized from the construction site of the new post office building.[47] In one version, a "fur coated blonde goaded the rammers into their final, successful assault."[48] A photograph taken at the time depicts a woman standing alongside of the men at the precise moment they rammed down the front door of the police station, but she doesn't appear to be blonde. The presence of other women at this lynching is also confirmed by the many newspaper reports that included photographs and eyewitness accounts from some of the women who had attended (participated) in the lynching, one of whom told a newspaper reporter that she had been close enough to touch the bodies if she had wanted to.[49]

The police had attempted to disperse the crowd minutes before the lynching by using tear gas, but the gas was no match for the enormous crowd, and the two men were extracted from their cells within a few minutes after the door had been breached.[50] Three unauthored photographic negatives from the archives of the *Oakland Tribune*, now stored at the Oakland Museum of California, document the event. In the first, one senses the carnivalesque mood of the scene as men in three-piece suits and young men, possibly students from Brook Hart's alma mater, stand side by side as they struggle to break down the jail doors. One man wears a handkerchief to cover his face, but the majority didn't even bother with a disguise. In the foreground one can make out rubble, rocks, and broken glass. In the far right of the image, a single unbroken flashbulb lies discarded on the ground in what may be one of the earliest uses of a flashbulb in the history of lynching (figures 20).

According to some reports, the lynching was "more like a Roman holiday, than like a sober crowd inflicting summary punishment. There was dancing in the streets and mothers held up their infant children to see the anger driven mob inflict its sadistic wrath upon the two kidnappers."[51] The photographs reveal that Holmes's face was covered in blood and that the crowd had managed to strip the clothes from off his body as bloodstained souvenirs of the lynching. In one of the photographs Holmes's appears naked except his socks and one shoe. In another, the blurry image of a young woman in a fur-lined coat can be seen as she is escorted past the stripped corpses (figure 21).

Thurmond had also been lynched and photographs document that, at least in his case, his pants were not removed until after he was dead. Apparently someone in the crowd had attempted to light him on fire but the flames kept going out.[52] A number of other images also exist of the lynching, but perhaps one of the most telling was a postcard created to "document" the scene. The image shows both men, but their photographs have been spliced together to make it appear as if they had been lynched to a single tree instead of two separate trees. The postcard also gives the time of the lynching as 11:15 P.M., precisely fifteen minutes after the event was said to have begun, a time frame which makes clear that this double lynching bore no relationship to the best of California's early committees of vigilance.

As the bodies swayed beneath two trees in Saint James Park, reporters made their way to the governor's residence where he triumphantly concluded, "This is a fine lesson to the whole nation . . . there will be less kidnapping now."[53] When asked if the lynchers would be prosecuted for homicide the governor flatly replied, "I don't think they will arrest anyone for the lynching. . . . They made a good job of it. If anyone is arrested for the good job, I'll pardon them all."[54] The next day his statements appeared in newspapers from coast to coast, and in less than seventy-five years of statehood, the vigilance committee had been transformed from a "law-and-order"

20. Unidentified photographer, "Breaking down the Door," 1933, gelatin silver print from original negative, 8 by 10 inches. Photograph courtesy of the Oakland Museum of California.

21. Unidentified photographer, "The Stripped Body of Jack Holmes," 1933, gelatin silver print from negative, 8 by 10 inches. Photograph courtesy of the Oakland Museum of California.

movement to its absolute opposite, a lynch mob sanctioned by the state. That both the governor and the press referred to the mob as a "vigilance committee" was nothing less than a willful misrepresentation of events since there wasn't even the semblance of a trial *by the people*, and like the vast majority of cases recorded in the first appendix of this book, the deaths of Thurmond and Holmes conform to the Tuskegee definition of a lynching in every detail.[55]

DISFIGUREMENT

The stripping of the lynched body was relatively rare in California, and there is almost no mention of bodies being forcibly mutilated. On the East Coast lynched blacks were stripped, chained, burned, shot, mutilated, and blowtorched. Numerous scholars and artists have considered with horror the ways in which the mutilated body of black men became a spectacle for the amusement of their tormenters; a practice, it has been argued, that not only dehumanized the victims but served to instill fear in all blacks.[56]

In the post-Reconstruction South, the lynching of African Americans has been credited with severely reducing the willingness of blacks to demand their legal and civil rights, particularly those promised under the thirteenth, fourteenth, and fifteenth amendments—the most targeted of which was the right to vote. Jacqueline Royster summarized the period when she wrote:

> By the 1870s secret terrorist organizations such as the Ku Klux Klan (first organized in 1866), the Knights of the White Camellia, the Red Shirts, and the White Line gained momentum. These groups specialized in mutilating, humiliating, intimidating, and even murdering African Americans and anyone else whom the terrorist groups viewed as African American sympathizers or whom they perceived to be in opposition in any way to their beliefs and desires. During this period, lynching and other acts of mob violence began to escalate."[57]

In California, there was only one case attributed to the Ku Klux Klan, and it occurred on August 25, 1868, when a man known as B. S. Templeton was lynched in Visalia, Tulare County.[58] While such groups as the Klan had no substantial presence in the West, the lynching of African Americans, American Indians, Asians, and Latinos by vigilantes and lynch mobs must certainly have heightened fear in many of these communities.

Beyond the specific cases of lynching, there are literally dozens of accounts where suspected criminals, of all races, had their heads shaved. There were also ear-croppings, scarification, and branding, practices which recognized the power of marking the criminal body, symbolically and literally marking their difference. Such cases were the most frequently recorded in the early years of statehood, and within the first few months, no less than seven men were whipped or flogged and no less than three had their heads shaved or were branded in February through May 1851.[59] Whipping was not an uncommon punishment for stealing, and whipping and flogging were regularly referred to as "lynching," but even in these cases, the newspapers were careful to specify which punishment had been assigned for which crime. For example, in 1851, William H. Robinson was "lynched" for "using rather freely" the money of his partner, for which he received an undisclosed number of lashes.[60]

Head shaving could be added to flogging for sexual assault, theft, and a wide range of other criminal offenses. Head shaving was not as painless as it might sound because the procedure was usually completed, not with shearing scissors, but with a large knife, and as a result, it was not uncommon for the knife man to take off more than a few layers of skin—occasionally revealing flecks of white bone. In March 1851, an unnamed man was sentenced in Weaverville by "lynch law" for stealing a mule.[61] Found guilty by an impromptu jury of twelve, he was sentenced to have his head shaved and receive fifty lashes. The sentence was promptly executed but as one newspaper explained, "An old razor was employed in the shaving operation, and, being rather dull, large pieces of the cranium were frequently clipped off, whilst he was losing his hair."[62]

Branding was also relatively common for theft and might result in receiving a letter "T" for thief or an "R" for robber, which would usually be burned into the cheek or forehead so that it would be visible to all.[63] But as one might imagine, it was not impossible for a suspected criminal to receive more than one punishment, and in February 1851, a man who gave his name as Robert Fisher from Pennsylvania was "arraigned" at Green Springs. Accused of stealing a horse, he was found guilty and sentenced to be branded with the letter "R" on his cheek.[64] In addition, he was to have his head partly shaved and to receive thirty-nine lashes. The sentence was attributed to "Judge Lynch" in the newspaper.

Another early account noted that the election of a judge in the mining camps was sometimes rather informal, as in the 1851 court of "Judge" Johnson.[65] Johnson, who was also a cook, had called his court into session a little later than expected because he had to complete his dishwashing duties first. Then, with the assistance of a "jury," he sentenced a man named Jackson to be flogged and to have his head shaved. Afterward, poor Jackson was said to "cut rather a grotesque figure, and might have been compared to a half finished man—one half the hair of his head, one half of his moustache, and one half of his whiskers having fallen prey to the vengeance of the jury."[66]

The practice of tar and feathering was reserved for particularly vile offenses, but in 1853 there were at least two cases reported, one near Shasta Lake and the other near Yreka, just south of the Oregon border. The two men were of Anglo-American or European descent; one had been accused of attempted pedophilia, and the other was accused of prostituting his wife in a "house of ill fame."[67]

I could find no drawn or photographed images of these brutal scenes, but I did encounter a number of detailed descriptions in the newspapers, most of which seemed to delight in each ghoulish detail and are as widely reported as the many accounts of lynching, vigilance committees, and legal executions.

With regard to legal and summary executions, I was able to uncover many drawings, etchings, wood block prints, lithographs, and photographic copy prints of some of the most celebrated and reviled cases of both legal and extralegal executions in California history.

DEAD POSSESSIONS AND RUBBISH

Writing on the rise of the souvenir industry in nineteenth-century Europe, Walter Benjamin (1842–1940) linked the industrially produced souvenir to the self-alienation brought on by commodity culture.[68] He argued that the consumer, separated from the means of production and seduced by *la modernité* (symbolized by the industrially produced memento), was no longer able to distinguish between the self and those objects with which one surrounds oneself, but what Benjamin probably never imagined was that this flotsam of the industrial age would also become the primary source material to help recover the history of lynching—for what is the lynching postcard if not the ultimate in "dead possessions."[69]

Consider an undated and unauthored postcard entitled, ". . . der Wild West Show" that can be dated to the first decades of the twentieth century. It depicts four men on horseback aiming their pistols at a man who hangs suspended by a rope, one end of which is tethered to one of the horses. This image was taken from a Wild West show and was intended to depict frontier justice. The angle of the neck confirms that the image is staged, but one of most striking thing about the postcard is that the text was written in German and points to the general fetishization of frontier justice in the twentieth century. The image was created as a souvenir postcard, and the fact that it appeared in German suggests that it may well have been sold in one of the arcade shops of which Benjamin wrote so much (color plate 6).

This curious memento also reveals that while Benjamin may have been able to address the consumer's alienation from the means of production, his analysis couldn't have anticipated the full significance of the lynching postcard. It is the survival of such images, whether real or staged, drawn or photographed, that leads to the uncovering of lynching in the West.

Lynching postcards were often produced anonymously and sold shortly after the lynching had occurred; some were industrially produced by postcard manufacturers and others were produced by local photographers with the help of industrially produced photographic supplies. These supplies included the chemicals, film, preformatted paper, and the die-cut card stock to which the photographs were regularly mounted, not to mention those photographers who made use of the latest innovations in flash photography.

Depending on the process, photographic images are infinitely reproducible, and it was not uncommon for such photographic images to be rephotographed, usually after any photographic credits were removed.[70] Benjamin addressed the reproducibility of photographic images in his canonical essay "The Work of Art in the Age of Mechanical Reproduction," in which he contrasted the relationship between photographic portraits or "the cult of remembrance" to the use of photography for "the purpose of establishing evidence."[71] However, as the Arias and Chamales case demonstrates, the lynching photograph could serve both notions at the same time, because like all photographic images, it has an indexical relationship to the physical world and serves to "document" the aftermath of a lynching, even as Anglo neighbors and townspeople huddled side by side to have their pictures taken and to be remembered and identified with this moment.[72]

Taking the concept of the portrait a little further, the industrial production of the photographic *carte de visite* began as early as 1861 in direct response to an enormous demand for photographic images of Civil War heroes, and it was only a matter of time before this new technology would be extended to lynching and legal executions.[73] The postcard generated for the "Execution of Mexican Murderers" discussed in chapter 1 was produced in New York by the Albert Company and signaled the potential profitability of such mass-produced postcard images. Likewise, after the lynching of Holmes and

PLATE 1. Carl (Charley) Friderich Christendorff, "Execution of Josh the Nigger," 1851–52. *Diary of Adolphus Windeler.* Courtesy of Yale Collection of American Literature, Beinecke Rare Book and Manuscript Library.

PLATE 2. "Adios Amigos! Execution of Mexican Murderers, Prescott, Arizona, 1904," tinted photograph mounted on cardstock, 5.5 by 3.5 inches. Collection of the author.

Lynched by a mob of about 300 people in front of Court house in Yreka, Siskiyou Co., Cal.

[handwritten along left margin, vertical] *between Thursday night & 10 o'clock on a Sunday night.*

Copy-right and fire.

NULL   STEMLER   MORENO   JOHNSON

[handwritten below photograph] *a rail road rail was strung across from one tree to the other to hang them on*

PLATE 3. Edgar Wade Howell, "Lynching of Null, Stemler, Moreno, and Johnson," 1895, photographic print mounted on mat board, 6.5 by 9.25 inches. Courtesy of the California Historical Society, FN-19688.

PLATE 4. Unidentified photographer, "Hanged at the Water Street
Bridge," 1877. Courtesy of Covello and Covello, Santa Cruz, California.

PLATE 5. Unidentified photographer, "1920 Santa Rosa: s.f. gang came to Santa Rosa," 1920, gelatin silver print on preformatted postcard paper with Artura stamp, 5 by 3.5 inches. Collection of the author.

... der Wild West Show.

PLATE 6. Unidentified photographer, ". . . der Wild West Show," n.d., photographic print on preformatted postcard paper, 5 by 3.5 inches. Collection of the author.

PLATE 7. Unidentified photographer, "del Valle family group," n.d. Courtesy of the Seaver Center for Western History Research, Natural History Museum of Los Angeles County.

F. G. Schumacher

Los Angeles.

PLATE 8. F. G. Schumacher, "Rodolfo Silvas," n.d., photographic print
mounted on card stock, 5 by 8.5 inches. Courtesy of the Seaver Center for
Western History Research, Los Angeles County Museum of Natural History.

PLATE 9. Bradley and Rulofson, "Tiburcio Vasquez," 1874, photographic
print mounted on card stock, 4.25 by 6.5 inches. Courtesy of the
California Historical Society, Luke Fay Collection, FN-00947.

PLATE 10. Alexander Gardner, Brady's National Portrait Gallery, "Abraham Lincoln," 1861, 4 by 2.25 inches, albumen print mounted on card stock. Collection of the author.

PLATE 11. Charles Christian Nahl, "Joaquin Murrieta," 1868, oil on canvas, 39.75 by 29.75 inches. Courtesy of California History Room, California State Library, Sacramento, California.

PLATE 12. Unidentified photographer, "La Chola Martina" (Espinoza Martina), n.d. Courtesy of University of Southern California, on behalf of the USC Specialized Libraries and Archival Collections.

PLATE 13. Ken Gonzales-Day, "Santa Rosa Cemetery," 2005, chromogenic
print, 36 by 46 inches. From the series "Searching for California's Hang Trees."
Courtesy of the artist.

PLATE 14. Ken Gonzales-Day, "Next Morning When Jimmy Awoke, the Cowboys Were Gone" (Livermore), 2003, chromogenic print, 36 by 46 inches. From the series "Searching for California's Hang Trees." Courtesy of the artist.

PLATE 15. Ken Gonzales-Day, "Run Up" (Sonoma County), 2002, chromogenic
print, 36 by 46 inches. From the series "Searching for California's Hang Trees."
Courtesy of the artist.

PLATE 16. Ken Gonzales-Day, "With None But the Omnipresent Stars to Witness" (Sonoma), 2002, chromogenic print, 36 by 46 inches. From the series "Searching for California's Hang Trees." Courtesy of the artist.

Thurmond, someone produced a multicard set of images that depicted the journey from the prison cell to the hang tree, and they were sold shortly after the lynching. That there was a ready market for such images can hardly be surprising given that the members of the mob had tried to purchase pieces of the fatal rope and battled over scraps of clothes. One account noted that within minutes of the bodies being cut down, someone had managed to saw off one of the branches with the intention of selling pieces to eager souvenir collectors.[74]

That the lynching postcard was created as a souvenir to document the spectacle of lynching is self-evident, and yet it does not conform to Walter Benjamin's characterization of the souvenir in a number of significant ways. Deposited in the archive by later generations, the psychic alienation and despondence attributed to such objects by Benjamin cannot be fixed. Then there is the quality of the image itself: a discussion that brings us back to the specific role of the copy print in the archive.

Institutional, regional, and subject archives are primarily concerned with gathering and preserving information, and for this reason, many institutions have created copy prints, or "study prints," from which researchers may work. Some archives also allow researchers to purchase copy prints to study on their own, and I certainly purchased many such prints in conducting my research. Beyond the status of the copy print itself, the archives must also categorize these objects so that they can be efficiently retrieved. Such categorizations inevitably reflect social values, and as a result various qualities may be highlighted or diminished. This simple fact has, at least partially, contributed to the misrecognition of Latinos in California's history of lynching for the simple reason that the term "Latino" didn't even emerge until the end of the twentieth century. So where might one even look for such images?

Once acquired, these objects wait in stasis until they are acted upon, categorized, or disintegrate. Actions that celebrate, redeploy, reinterpret, or otherwise draw attention to a particular quality of the object could be said to add value. But value, in this context, signifies far more than monetary value alone.[75]

In *Rubbish Theory*, the anthropologist Michael Thompson observed that the value of possessible objects could be broken down into two fundamental categories: they were of either durable or transient value. For Thompson, durable goods increased in value over time while transient goods decreased in value, until they had zero value, at which point they become rubbish. In between these two regions of "fixed" assumptions he places a third region, which he termed the "region of flexibility." In this region, transient goods could be converted to durable goods and actions could reshape existing paradigms of value, which Thompson characterized as a "world view." Leaving questions of globalism aside, for Thompson, this concept recognized that collectors, historians, and even nations, could enhance the value (monetarily or otherwise defined) of a given object.[76]

Thompson argued that a manufactured good like an automobile is an object of transient value because it begins losing its value the moment it is driven from the lot and continues to decline until it is considered worthless. However, its scarcity, design, or other properties may also cause a certain model to rebound in value, as with the classic car phenomenon in the United States. Thompson argues that such transformations are only possible through innovation and creativity, but he is careful to note that such transformative powers cannot, or are not, extended to every member of society and that differential access is "imposed through the social order."[77] Thus, by extending his analysis to the material artifacts in the archive, whether they are Indian baskets, political ephemera, or lynching postcards, one is able to recognize that such transient goods can potentially be transformed into durable goods or, perhaps more accurately, durable histories. In this respect, *Rubbish Theory* is useful to thinking about lynching in the West, and the lynching postcard in particular, because it allows one to consider the souvenir from another vantage point than the one suggested by the critique of commodity culture offered by Benjamin.

In Benjamin's model, those communities touched by the history of lynching would appear to be subject to the same degree of self-alienation as those communities or individuals responsible for the lynching in the first place, but in Thompson's model of "differential access" one is able to conceptualize the transient value of certain histories, or more precisely, the transient value of the lynching postcard as a historical artifact. Writing on the souvenir, Benjamin foregrounds the alienation of those who inventory their lives through the souvenir, which Benjamin characterized as "dead possessions," but what are we to make of those who must look for their past in the dead possessions of others? By this I mean to suggest that an African American looking at the lynched body of an African American, or a Latino looking at the lynched body of another Latino, cannot possibly generate the same degree of "alienation" as that experienced by an Anglo-American member of a lynch mob looking at, collecting, photographing, or otherwise perpetuating the creation of such souvenirs. Such a comparison is necessary because it directs our gaze back to the relationship between value and social order raised by Thompson.

In this respect, the recovery of California's history of lynching is not driven by the monetary value of objects that reference the practice of lynching but by the lack of *value* placed on the Western history of lynching itself, and it is the devaluation of the Latino, Native American, and Asian body within the social order that has resulted in the near complete erasure of these communities from the historical landscape.

Unlike the museum, which represents "a region of fixed assumptions," the archive can be seen as a "region of flexibility" from which hidden treasures may emerge or into which both reviled or cherished objects can fade from view. Take, for example, the innumerable family portraits that have accumulated in nearly every regional archive; once cherished by family and friends, many of their names have long since been forgotten. In spite of ever growing regional collections, more and more is lost each day as institutional and regional archives earnestly strive to preserve even the frailest of objects. Their exposure to sunlight is limited, their temperature and humidity are carefully monitored, but even the best intending archivist can't stop the inevitable, until finally, too frail to be examined, each object is replaced with a copy print and another clue is lost. It is not alienation from the means of production but the alienation from a social discourse which systemically, and inevitably, reduces complex social histories down to a handful of dominant historical narratives that must then be institutionalized, catalogued, and filed away.

THE COPY PRINT

Art historians are trained to look at the surface of objects—the patina on metal, the varnish on a piece of furniture, the signature of the artist; the fabricator's mark—and each of these elements can alter the value of the object. A copy print can claim few of these merits: it is a photograph of a photograph. Seen as marginal to the history of image making, their status as copies, reproductions, and imitations often parallels the histories they represent.

In the archive, the function of the copy print is primarily an administrative one: it is meant to index or point to the existence of an object in the collection, be it a vintage print, a previous copy print, an original negative, or a copy negative. There is little doubt that the glossy black-and-white paper of the copy print has none of the charm of a vintage print. There are no stains, cracks, or clues to the image's origin; no handwriting, no insightful note, no names scribbled in a loving hand across the back.[78] In fact, the backs are almost never reproduced at all. This wouldn't be so bad except for the fact that many institutional archives tend to position all such objects as supplemental data rather than as primary source material, and in some cases they may be incapable of identifying the source of the copy print. The records may not indicate, particularly in the case of photographic images, whether they possess an original vintage print, a copy print, or a vintage copy print.

For much of the nineteenth century, photography was not considered a fine art, and so even in the best of circumstances, distinguishing between a copy print and a vintage print can be difficult. Seemingly trivial, this distinction regularly disrupts the study of photography for art historians and nonhistorians alike. For example, a copy print is also made when the original negative is no longer available or when the photographic technique did not actually create a negative, as is the case, for example, with daguerreotypes. Likewise, multiple versions often exist in multiple places: an original vintage print in one collection, a modern reprint in another. Vintage postcards, stereoscopic view cards, and *cartes de visite* were all made from negatives, but they could also be retouched, cropped, and rephotographed along the way.

RECONSIDERING THE COPY PRINT

On March 21, 2002, a small and rather innocuous photograph, taken of a seventeenth-century Dutch engraving depicting a man leading a horse, sold for the equivalent of $443,220 (£278,000) at Sotheby's auction house in Paris.[79] The photograph was purchased by the National Library of France. Previously unknown, at least to photographic historians, it is now recognized as the earliest known photograph in existence. Taken by the French inventor Joseph Nicéphore Niépce (1765–1833) in summer 1825, its early date shook the photography world and reminded us all that the study of photography is a relatively new historical field. According to the first newspaper accounts of the sale, the print's owner, André Jammes, had understood the significance of the work but chose to keep its existence a secret.[80] Perhaps the most fascinating aspect of the Niépce photograph is not what it can tell us about early photography in France, but what it reveals about how value works.

Less concerned with the economic principals of supply and demand than with the ways in which the emergence of the Niépce photograph corrected the historical record, his photograph provides a remarkable opportunity to rethink the copy print because as shocking as it may sound, the Niépce photograph is a copy print of an etching. Admittedly, it is the first one ever made and demonstrates that finding merit in a copy print is not as inconceivable as it sounds; it highlights the relationship between value and social order in Thompson's rubbish theory. The Niépce photograph is a stark reminder that even the most instrumental of photographic images can be of great value, in this case not only for its significance to the history of photography but for its significance to a nation. But if photographs can acquire value, the history of lynching in the West reveals that they can also lose it.

The lynching photograph of Chamales and Arias demonstrated how the conventional vignetting of studio portraiture could serve to mask social, racial, and economic distinctions from the very site of their lynching. This decontextualization equated the racialized body with the criminal body and perfectly paralleled the concept of the desperado. In a similar manner, the night image of the Santa Rosa triple lynching served to "vignette" and de-contextualize the illegality of a lynching that may have been conducted by, or included, law enforcement officers. Each of these examples suggests that era-sure works in different ways and serves to clarify, at least on some level, that it was the conflation of the Mexican body with the criminal body that has contributed most to the erasure of the history of lynching in the West. But such erasures need not be permanent, and it is the analysis of such disenfran-chised bodies, and the histories they represent, which reveals that there can be immense value to even the darkest of histories, the most reviled citizenry, and the lowest of objects—the copy print.

TWO PORTRAITS IN THE ARCHIVE

It is at this point that I would like to consider two portraits taken in southern California at the end of the nineteenth century. Each existed as a copy print in the regional history archive where I found them, and in each case I was not allowed to see the original image, if indeed there was one. This is not an experience that one would find in a fine art museum where the ability to experience the work is considered essential. On a formal level, the two por-traits are representative examples of early California photography. The first was taken in an outdoor setting and depicted what appeared to be a rather intimate and playful picnic scene. The second was a formal studio portrait of a man dressed in jacket and vest, as he leaned on a pedestal draped in fur (color plates 7 and 8).

The first image is an intimate and unidentified family portrait of a group of young people, three women, two in long sleeves and high-collared Vic-torian dresses, accompanied by two young men reclining on a knoll beneath some trees and enjoying each other's company on a warm spring day. One can tell it is late in spring because of the height of the grass and the presence of seedpods, visible against the crisp white dresses. Their bodies recline as one leans against the next, elbows on hips, elbows on shoulders, their bodies forming a chain, while their grinning faces try to contain their smiles and playful banter. To the left, a young man in suit and tie patiently holds his hat in hand. Looking at the two women in the center of the image, one can almost hear the photographer pleading with them to sit still while he adjusts his shutter speed and aperture. This is not a studio portrait but a lively plein air depiction (color plate 7).

In the center of the image, a beautiful young woman gazes at the viewer, at the photographer: it is a marvelous gaze. Unflinching, her presence commands the image as she leans her elbow upon the shoulder of the second young man. He, in turn, leans his head on a third woman's shoulder. Her legs are crossed, her hip angles up towards the young man, allowing her body to support the weight of his arm, and to some extent, to carry a portion of the weight of the entire chain of leaning figures. The young man, in a relaxed posture, lets his body conform to the two women's angular forms as his body joins the first two women with the third. He is not embarrassed to be affectionate, nor are they. His mouth is slightly open, in the beginning of a smile that is only hinted at from the corners of his eyes and the curve of his cheek. His hands curl as gently as if in sleep. He shares his body and the women share theirs. This is not the image of machismo; it provides a glimpse of something beyond the conventional studio portrait.

There were no names, no photographer's mark, and no date, and to top it all, the photograph was really a photograph of a photograph, marking it as the lowliest of all photographs—a copy print. It would be two years before I would discover the identity of this young woman at the center of the photograph. It was only after looking though thousands of portraits that, quite unexpectedly, I discovered a second group portrait. This time it was a formal studio portrait (figure 22).

Posed before a highly stylized painted backdrop depicting a palatial, if slightly cartoonish interior, complete with a column, a classical sculpture, and a spiral staircase, it appeared to be what the historian Shawn Michele Smith has referred to as the "self-congratulatory, commercial use of the middle-class photographic portrait."[81] I would later discover that their own home wasn't nearly so European in flavor. To my surprise, this forgotten family was none other than one of the oldest ranching families in southern California, and the young woman's name was Josepha del Valle (figure 23).

22. F. G. Schumacher, "Reginaldo Francisco del Valle and Family," n.d., photographic print mounted on card stock, 5 by 8.5 inches. Courtesy of the California Historical Society, Ms. Henry F. Grady Collection, FN-33893.

23. Morse Studio, "Josepha del Valle," 1880, photographic print mounted on card stock, 4.25 by 6.5 inches. Courtesy of University of Southern California, on behalf of the USC Specialized Libraries and Archival Collections.

THE DEL VALLE FAMILY

The del Valle family was among California's most prominent Latino families. The image is significant to the history of lynching because, after the image of the desperado or the bandit, it reflects one of the most widely accepted stereotypes of Latinos in the American West, a stereotype that has come to be known as the "fantasy heritage" of the "Spanish" ranchero."[82] In the archive, the two photographic images, the studio portrait of the single man mentioned above and the studio portrait of the del Valles, were fundamentally indistinguishable. Questions of class, once central to their placement in California society, disappear in the "middle-class photographic portrait" that masked their economic differences just as it accentuated their Latino identities, a phenomenon which begins to suggest the invisible, or perhaps inevitable, force of the archive.

In researching the del Valle studio portrait, I discovered that it depicted five of the children of Doña Ysabel and Don Ygnacio del Valle. There names were (from left to right) Josepha (1861–1943), Ignacio Ramon (Nachito) (1870–1930), Isabel (1868–1936), Reginaldo (1854–1938), and Ulpiano (1865–1936).[83] To my surprise, the image included at least three of the unidentified figures from the picnic scene. The young Ignacio appeared in both the outdoor and studio portraits, along with a number of other photographs not included here, but it made it possible to date the picnic image to somewhere between 1882 and 1888.[84]

The del Valle family was one of a dozen families at the center of the "fantasy heritage" of the great California ranchero, and their name appears regularly in the early newspapers and many histories of California.[85] In 1853, they planted the first oranges in what is now Ventura County; they had a thriving vineyard and grew other produce from apricots to almonds.[86] So how is it that such an image could have come so close to the brink of complete erasure? The story of Josepha's brother Reginaldo may provide some clues.[87]

Reginaldo studied law and practiced before the California Supreme Court and was elected to the State Assembly at twenty-five.[88] In 1882, he was elected to the California State Senate, and in 1884 he ran for Congress, at which time the San Francisco *Golden Sun* described him glowingly as being "born under a Southern Sun . . . with hair as black as a raven's wing, with eyes dark and piercing, sparkling like an eagles . . . a true child of California. The blood of Spaniards flows in his veins, royal blood, and he is one of the descendants of the native Alta Californians who achieved distinction."[89] However, this description was hardly universally accepted, and his opponent called him a "Mexican" and insisted that "no decent man has ever been born of a Mexican woman."[90] Reginaldo was defeated.

In 1853, a massive vigilante action took place in Los Angeles and Reginaldo's father, Ygnacio del Valle, with another prominent Latino family, donated one hundred horses to help Anglo vigilantes to go in pursuit of a band of Mexican bandits and horse thieves, the details of which will be addressed in the next chapter, but it is worth noting that their actions were characterized as a betrayal of their race in the Spanish language paper at the time.[91]

Known as the "Rangers," the majority of these posses were a voluntary association of men, and it was at their hands that many Mexican bandits were shot, legally executed, and lynched. In August 1853, the Los Angeles Rangers received funding from the county for twelve men and the upkeep of the stables for a year, and by 1854 their numbers had risen to fifty men, half of them mounted.[92] In donating horses to the Rangers, these two highly respected families sought to demonstrate their support for such law-and-order efforts and with good reason; traveling bandits and horse thieves pilfered horses and cattle equally from their ranches as well as from those of Anglos.[93]

If the del Valles could slip so easily from historical memory as to be unidentified in a regional archive, then one may not be surprised to learn that the second photograph, the man in the single studio portrait, was destined to obscurity. In the photograph, the young man's hand rests gently on his hip as his arm leans against an ornately carved wooden object that is partially covered by animal fur: a detail that adds something of a Western flair to the image. A closer examination revealed a handwritten note on the side of the print, which identified him as the last man to be publicly executed in Los Angeles. His name was Rodolfo Silvas (color plate 8).

Born just over a year apart, the paths of Josepha del Valle and Rodolfo Silvas may have never crossed. In the summer of 1884, she traveled in the best circles and attended what would have been one of a long history of Fourth of July celebrations that were thrown by her family on their sprawling ranch located at the most northern edge of Los Angeles County, in what is now Ventura County. Though few ranch families could afford to host such costly gatherings, the del Valles had entertained hundreds of guests over the years, and one 1888 account described them as wearing the latest fashions, enjoying music, and serving roast pig, dessert, claret, white wine, and black coffee.[94]

The ranch was fictionalized in Helen Hunt Jackson's *Ramona*, a best-selling novel about the plight of California's Native Americans. *Ramona* also helped to codify the romanticism of the mission legend in Southern California.[95] Jackson visited their ranch on January 23, 1883, and most accounts now agree that it served as the backdrop to her novel.[96] In reading *Ramona*, there is no doubt that the del Valles' Camulos ranch shared many elements found in Jackson's fictional ranch.[97]

By contrast, Silvas had none of the advantages of the del Valles. He was born in Los Angeles and lived a few blocks from the old Plaza Square, about thirty miles to the southeast of Camulos. Working (occasionally) as a laborer for the city, his evenings would be spent in the oldest and shadiest sections of town; known for its old adobe houses, brothels, and Chinese gambling houses, it was called Sonoratown for its many Mexican inhabitants.[98]

RODOLFO SILVAS

In the image, Silvas's dark wavy hair is parted to one side, and his mustache and beard are thick and nearly obscure the delicately patterned bow tie and crisp white shirt he is wearing. His lips and nose are full; his eyes, dark and almond shaped. A faint pattern is visible on his tightly fitted vest. He sports a tailored corduroy suit as was popular in the period. His name was Rodolfo but his friends called him "Adolfo," and in the summer of 1884 he would attend local dances, or fandangos, that were popular among the working class. These dances would last until the early morning hours, after which he might take a stroll to the nearest saloon where he was known to be a regular. He spoke broken English, but much like today, one can navigate through many parts of Los Angeles without knowing a great deal of English. According to the testimony at his trial, it was on one drunken night in July, just a few weeks after one of the del Valle fiestas, that his fate would be changed forever.

On July 22, 1884, at the age of twenty-two, he was arrested and charged with murder.[99] Charged with a second man by the name of Manuel Higuera, the two were arrested for killing an Anglo-American man.[100] Higuera would be tried separately, and many of the newspaper accounts questioned whether his conviction of murder in the second degree was just.[101]

Rodolfo would be found guilty of murder in the first degree before a jury of his "peers" and was sentenced to be hanged on August 5. As it turns out, the note written on the photograph was incorrect in at least one respect; a man by the name of Francisco Martínez would also be executed on the same day.[102] Based on his age at the time of his execution, Silvas could not have been more than twenty-three when the photograph was taken, which would date the photograph somewhere between 1882 and 1885, approximately the same period as the two group portraits of the del Valles. The fact that Silvas was a part-time laborer and of a very different social class suggests that the photograph was taken after he was arrested, not for his benefit, but for sale during the months leading up to his execution.[103]

THE TRIAL

A mean-spirited push, an accident, a drunken brawl, a case of self-defense, a cold-blooded murder — these were just some of the claims made by each side in the case. A duly sworn interpreter was present throughout the trial, and the court transcript is fascinating because it provides a rare glimpse into the actual workings of a legal trial in nineteenth-century California.

Testimony of Tomas Hickey

Tomas Hickey was described as being a rather stout man. He had accompanied his friend James McIntyre to see a fire that had started in the lower part of the city sometime around 11 P.M.[104] It was a warm summer night and the men had each had a few drinks, according to Hickey, to cool themselves off. He explained how the excitement of the fire had gotten the best of them and that sometime after midnight, they headed up to New High Street in Sonora-town (now Chinatown) for a little distraction.[105] Several witnesses estimated that they had seen them pass the open door of one of the neighborhood bars at around two o'clock in the morning.

Testimony of Alfred Olivier

Alfred Olivier owned the saloon in question and was working at the time of the incident. He explained that Silvas was a regular but noted that he had also seen McIntyre on several occasions. Olivier testified that Silvas was sitting in a chair outside the bar at the time the two men passed by the open door. He testified that Silvas was facing away from the men and was "sick to the stomach and vomiting" in the street.[106] He had seen the two men bump Silvas's chair and had heard Silvas call the two men "son of bitches and bastards."[107] It went quiet outside and so he continued with his work. He then explained that Silvas and a friend (Higuera) entered the bar seven to ten minutes after the ruckus and that Silvas ordered two drinks. Olivier was recorded as saying, "I put the two beers on the counter and I noticed that Silvas had blood on his hand and on his shirt. I asked him about the matter of the blood and he just drank the beer and went out down Short Street."[108]

Testimony of Rodolfo Silvas

Coming from a dance on Buena Vista Street, Silvas had stopped off at the saloon and then, in his own words, said he "went out to vomit; went outside."[109] Silvas claimed he was vomiting in the street when the two men came by and kicked him on the foot and knocked his hat off. He described the incident in the following manner:

> I was pretty well intoxicated . . . I was vomiting, when someone passed by, right close by me . . . They passed by me, and I was just in this position (showing vomiting). Then they struck me with the point of their feet, and knocked my hat off . . . then I raised myself, then I says to him "What is the matter with you? What did you knock my hat off for, you American son of a bitch?" . . . Then we were standing close by each other. We was talking, me and him. Another one was turned right around. I didn't know who he was and he hit me in a blow, struck me a blow, and then he threw me in this position (showing) . . . Then I was a little afraid, because they were two, and I drew out my knife.[110]

Silvas recounted the events with the help of a translator. He continued:

When I drew my knife I made towards the one that struck me. Then I says to him, "What did you hit me that blow for." Then says he, "Its none of your business, you Greaser." Then he began cursing me, and called me a son of a bitch; and I replied back. Then we was close by the gate there. He commence to kick me and I began to throw blows this way (showing) with the knife . . . Higuera was right with me also. Then Higuera says to me, "Let's go!" Then we went off and we left him there. Then, after, we went away. Then after that he said, "I drove it clean into the hilt."[111]

Silvas forgets to mention that they went back into the bar for a beer afterward, but explains that after they had left the scene they went on to Juana Gomez's house, where she bandaged his cut and hid the knife. After a few minutes, they headed to a chop house to eat. As they were passing the scene of the crime Silvas and Higuera were arrested.[112]

The Cross-Examination

Under Stephen M. White's cross-examination, Silvas asserted that after his hat was knocked off, he simply stood at the chair and did not chase after the men or threaten them, but the transcript reveals that the prosecution was able to unravel Silvas's self-defense claim by exploiting his inability to comprehend the subtle implications of his statements. When asked if he jumped up aggressively from his chair, Silvas replied simply, "I wasn't crazy, I think."[113]

To which the prosecution slyly retorted, "Well, I should think you would want to claim you were, but that is not the question."[114]

A (Answer by Silvas): No, sir; I just go up and stood right there at the chair . . .

Q (Question by prosecution): And said, "You American son of a bitch?"

A: Yes, sir because he had knocked my hat off.

Q: Well, did you [not] pull out your knife until after you were struck? You didn't I suppose?

A: Yes, sir, when I was talking with him when he struck me the blows. [Silvas missed the nuance and simply repeated that he had the knife on his waist and didn't pull it out till after he was struck.]

Q: Well, did you have the knife pulled out before the blow was struck? That is what I asked you.

A: No, sir, I had it on my waist.

Q: What did you do with that knife, anyway? . . .

A: I don't know whether I throwed it away or what I done with it. I was drinking . . .

Q: What made you desist? Why did you stop? Why didn't you give him a few more punches?

A: Because Higuera said, "Let's go." [Silvas completely missed what had just happened. The prosecution was suggesting that without Higuera's call he would have kept on stabbing an unarmed man.]

Q: And where was McIntyre when Higuera said, "Let's go[.]" Was he kicking at you yet? [The irony of his question was clearly missed by Silvas, the implication being that McIntyre was already collapsed on the ground.]

A: He was to one side when we went off.

Q: Standing up, was he?

A: Yes, sir.

Q: Calling you names, too, I suppose?

A: Surely.

Q: Kicking at you?

A: Afterwards; yes sir. [Silvas completely misunderstood the time frame referenced by the question, which made his response sound even more cold-blooded.]

Q: Afterwards?

A: After we commenced to quarrel, he says. [Describing the beginning of the incident, and not the end.]

Q: But, now tell him, I want to know just exactly what McIntyre was doing when Higuera said "Let's go," and they both went off and took a drink on the strength of it?

A: We left him standing there and went into the saloon — went back into the saloon . . . [If there was any possibility of claiming self-defense, or having the charges lessened to second-degree murder, Silvas had just sealed his fate without even knowing it.]

Q: McIntyre had no knife?

A: I don't know.

Q: Well, you didn't see any, and he would have been very apt to have got it out under the circumstances wouldn't he?

A: I don't know.

Q: Well, you know you didn't see any, don't you?

A: He might have, or mightn't have; I don't know.

Q: But you didn't see any, did you?

A: I think not, surely not. [Silvas struck another blow to his own case.]

A: Surely not. Seguro que no . . . [Interjected the interpreter at Mr. White's request—for emphasis; Silvas had put the final nail in his coffin.]

Q: Why did you and Higuera go out with that woman? What object had you in going out?

A: Higuera invited her to a chop house.

Q: Higuera did?

A: Yes, sir . . . [An answer that was slightly better than saying it was his idea, that stabbing a man gave him a good appetite, but the implication was there.]

Q: You had taken a drink and you wanted some chops, something to eat?

A: Exactly. We was going to the chop-house we was going to have some supper . . . [Silvas had no idea what the implications were to what he had just said. With all the facts established, the prosecution could make its final assault on the man.]

Q: How old are you?

A: Twenty-two years of age.

Q: What year were you born in?

A: I don't know, sir . . .

Q: What year is this?

A: The one we are in? [The subtext here is that his ignorance verges on the primitive.]

Q: Yes, sir; but what one are we in?

A: I don't know.

Q: Do you talk English?

A: Not much.

Q: But he talks pretty well in English doesn't he? So as to get on in a conversation? Ask him if I haven't heard him talk English frequently? [to the translator]

A: Perhaps so, I don't know.

Q: Well, he can talk English, and understand it pretty well, don't he? [to the translator]

A: Very little, I understand it not much, I speak it, but I don't speak it very well. [The prosecution hopes to show that he is simply a criminal caught in a lie, and not a man confused by the subtleties of the English language, or the judicial system.]

Q: That is true. Now did you talk to these men, McIntyre and Hickey, in English or Spanish? [A question that was both an insult and an accusation.]

A: I talked to them in English.

Q: You called them "son of a bitch." You understand that very well, I expect, "American sons of bitches." He used that expression in English; he hasn't translated what he said?

A: I told him so in English. [Are a few curse words a sign of fluency in a language?][115]

The prosecution ended its case on August 1; the defense on August 2. The jury found Silvas guilty of murder in the first degree. On August 5 Silvas was sentenced to hang by the neck until dead, and the date of the execution was set for, and executed on, Friday, March 20, 1885.[116]

In keeping with California law, letters of appeal were sent to the California Supreme Court and to the governor. On March 10, 1885, John S. Griffith, a resident of Los Angeles, wrote a letter to his "old friend," the governor, asking him to examine the evidence in the Silvas case.[117] Griffin argued that it was not a case of deliberate murder but rather an unfortunate incident, due in part to the "influence of liquor" and to the fact that Silvas was "surely and wantonly insulted and provoked."[118] He adds that he doubts "if the case were reversed and Silvas had been killed—if the jury would have found the man guilty of murder. It seems to me that prejudice entered into the finding. I have spoken to many people on this subject, and I find that the greatest number agree with me that this man should not be hung."[119]

A second letter, written on March 17 from another Los Angeles resident, argued that Silvas "was insane with drink, maddened by insult and blows before he did the dreadful deed. If he were an American instead of being only a poor Spaniard, or if he had wealth or influence his sentence would undoubtedly not have been so heavy."[120]

A third letter was sent to the governor on March 13, written on letterhead from Bickness and White, attorneys-at-law. In the top left-hand corner one could read the name, Stephen M. White. Mr. White was the prosecutor in the case, and as one might expect, he did not argue for leniency. He writes, "The fact is Silvas is a great scoundrel. I have had him up two or three times and he ought to have been sent to the penitentiary for past offences, but he was able to slip out . . . he was not drunk . . . he followed McIntyre stabbing him for 135 feet when McIntyre fell dead."[121] The claim that Silvas was not drunk does not match with the testimony given at the trial in which at least two other persons confirmed that Silvas was intoxicated and vomiting.

From the scaffold, Silvas addressed the many that had gathered to witness his demise (some of whom may have purchased copies of his portrait) and proclaimed, "I am innocent, as innocent as the day I was born."[122] Newspapers reported that between six and eight thousand spectators "blackened the hills" or climbed onto rooftops to catch a glimpse of the execution, a detail that stands in direct conflict with California law regarding the "private" execution of convicted criminals.[123] Conducted within the low-walled jail yard, the crowd was said to have included men and women of all ages.

Gleaned from the archive, these images, this transcript, reveal the presence of a fully working judicial system while at the same time demonstrating the leveling force of the archive, a place within which it would seem that only Thompson's rubbish theory could adequately explain how one of the most significant families of the region could have become indistinguishable from a drunken laborer whose bitter rage against Anglo bias led to his own demise.

The Josepha and Rodolfo photographs reveal how studio portrait conventions specifically evolved to mask class distinctions by transporting its subjects from real world spaces and placing them in a vignetted world of fictive spaces, carved wooden columns, and painted backdrops. This decontextualization allows the viewer to focus on the physical appearance of the sitters: their clothes, hairstyle, expression, and skin color. Deposited in the archive, such portraits offer few clues to the sitters past and thus must be placed within existing racial, ethnic, or subject categories. This is a clear example of how erasure works because information that was once widely known has fallen away or has been lost, reducing complexities and differences to a single unifying thread—they were both of Mexican descent. However, as this comparison has made clear, such erasures need not be permanent.

Like a cabinet of curiosities, where fossils, seashells, dinosaur bones, and shrunken heads might be found side by side, in the modern-day archive, nameless family portraits may lie shuffled between oil wells and adobes or be organized by some other feature of interest, such as "women with hats," and so on. However, at most of the archives I went to, the racial and ethnic files didn't tell the whole story; many institutional archives suffer from the same general confusion about where to put "Latinos" encountered in society at large. This is not an indictment of the institutional archive; systems of categorization are constantly changing and before there were terms like Latino or Hispanic, the Spanish had their own fantastic set of categories for the people of the Americas. *Mestizo, castizo, coyote, lobo, vorsino*, and a half-dozen others were intended to keep track of the myriad racial combinations that had manifested themselves throughout New Spain.[124] In the archive, one is reminded that institutional legacies are symptomatic of social ones. This comparison also demonstrates that the racial, ethnic, multiracial, or multiethnic body has been romanticized, vilified, and pathologized for centuries, so perhaps the only question really left to ask is when, or perhaps where, did Western racial formation begin?

The foreign miners, being
civilized men, generally
received "fair trials," as I said,
whenever they were accused.
It was, however, considered
safe by an average lynching
jury in those days to convict
a "greaser" on very moderate
evidence if none better could
be had. One could see his
guilt so plainly written, we
know, in his ugly swarthy
face, before the trial began.

—Josiah Royce, *California*

CHAPTER FOUR

Signifying Bodies:
Unblushing and Monstrous

The discovery of racial bias in the history of lynching in the United States
is not new, yet no one has acknowledged the full impact of lynching on
the many different racial and ethnic communities in the American West or
considered how nineteenth-century anti-Mexican and anti–Latin American
sentiments may have contributed to this erasure. In recovering California's
history of lynching, I was struck by the overwhelming number of cases that
were identified as "Mexican," "Californian," or "Sonoran"—132 of the 352
cases included in the appendix to this publication, with an additional 41 and
29 cases being identified, respectively, as American Indian and Chinese.[1]

Upon reflection, the presence of anti-Mexican sentiments in the nineteenth century hardly seems surprising given the history of U.S. expansionism, the war with Mexico, and a century and a half of debate about the U.S.-
Mexican border that has repeatedly been used to villainize those Americans

(Mexicans, Central and South Americans) living beyond the U.S. border. Initially driven by the fear of racial mixing, anti-Mexican sentiments would later spread to labor issues and questions of entitlement; now, such debates have been reinvigorated by contemporary fears about terrorism.

Without entering into the current debate, it seems reasonable to conclude that the actions of Mexican bandits and outlaws in the nineteenth century fueled racial and ethnic bias. But to varying degrees, bias against Mexicans, Mexican Americans, and persons of Latin American or Mexican descent were openly acknowledged in the second half of the nineteenth century. Why did twentieth-century historians have such a hard time recording, recognizing, or responding to this history? One of the greatest contributing factors was (and still is) bound to the social, political, and scientific debates about racial, national, and ethnic identity.

Who can immigrate? Who can vote? Who can own land? Who can marry? Many of these questions are as heated today as they were a century and a half ago. Ideologically loaded, such questions would have guided historians as much as the reporters and politicians who embraced, encouraged, or criticized the vigilantes, actions which ultimately led to the near total absence of this history from the national statistics on lynching.

In order to reconstruct this history, it will be essential to recognize the impact of physiognomy, racial positivism, and social Darwinism in the nineteenth-century understanding of the Mexican, Latin American, and Spanish "races." This is not to claim that eighteenth-century texts such as Johann Caspar Lavater's *Essays on Physiognomy* (1789–1798) were being read in the gold mines of California but rather that many of these ideas circulated throughout Europe and the "States" before they made their way to the West Coast. Lavater was an eighteenth-century scholar, minister, and "scientist" who believed that he had refined the reading of moral character from the outward appearance of a person to a science.

Moreover, Lavater's *Essays on Physiognomy* were published a total of fifty-five times in separate translations and editions in less than a forty-year period.[2] According to one author, "The book was reprinted, abridged, summarized, pirated, quoted, parodied, imitated, and reviewed so often that it is difficult to image how a literate person of the last decade of the eighteenth century could have escaped acquiring some general knowledge of the man and his theories."[3]

However, for incredulous readers, I would direct their attention to a newspaper article published in San Francisco in 1853 that poked fun at the "science" of physiognomy, if only to show that a basic knowledge of physiognomy was familiar enough to ridicule. The article directly referenced Lavater's *Essays on Physiognomy* and even summarizes one of his basic tenets, that the "characteristics of a man's heart and mind" are bound to leave an impression on the face.[4]

The story itself involved two men, one an amateur physiognomist and the other a professional skeptic. When, as one might expect, the skeptic asked the other man to identify a known criminal from among the group of men who were escorting him to the jail, the physiognomist picked the wrong man. Given the humorous nature of the tale, one must conclude that a chuckle was had by all.

Eighteenth- and nineteenth-century authors regularly traced the origins of physiognomy back to Aristotle, but recent scholarship has revealed that someone other than Aristotle probably wrote his seminal treatise, entitled *Physiognomics*. For lack of a proper name, this author has come to be known as "pseudo-Aristotle."[5] In the text, the author defined physiognomy and the principles of positivism more generally, as the ability to "infer from bodily signs the character of this or that particular person," a definition which comes remarkably close to the 1853 version.[6]

In examining the case records of summary and legal executions, it becomes clear that much of the confusion about what was meant by the term "Mexican" had to do with the fact that it could be used alone or in combination with other words to emphasize nationality, ethnicity, class, type, race, or the mixed racial origins of its subject. For example, it could be used alone or in combination with "Sonoran" (Sonoranian) to signify Mexican nationals, or it could be used in combination with "Californian," "Californio," or "native Californian" to emphasize ethnicity and class in those cases involving Latinos born in California before or after it was annexed by the United States. When used in combination with "greaser," it emphasized racial mixing and often suggested criminality. This chapter attempts to demonstrate that nineteenth-century attitudes about race, racial mixing, and the moral character of the racialized body were guided by racial positivism and the principles of physiognomy, and these concepts had a direct impact on lynching in the West.

By the latter half of the twentieth century, "Mexican" had primarily come to refer to national identity, though it was sometimes used as a ethnic slur against those perceived to be of Mexican descent. Given the divisiveness of both racial and national stigmatization, many Latino communities began to seek more empowering terms. This period saw the emergence of Chicano, Hispanic, Hispano, Latino, Nuyorican, and other terms, each of which placed varying degrees of emphasis on ethnicity, culture, language, and race. In this same period, the United States government acknowledged the ambiguity of "Mexican" and adopted "Hispanic" and later "Latino" as terms capable of representing communities from different regions and cultural traditions. Rather than concerning ourselves with the specific origins and uses of these terms, the point here is to recognize that naming these elusive differences has been tied to questions of race, racial mixing, ethnicity, and national identity since the signing of the Treaty of Guadalupe Hidalgo.

To fully understand lynching in the West, it is necessary to understand what was meant by the term "Mexican." One must unpack the conflation of ideas underlying the term, and, consider the sometimes-deadly consequences of nineteenth-century racial formations. To do this it will be necessary to acknowledge the impact of physiognomy and the pseudosciences in the latter half of the nineteenth century, not only on scientists, artists, and writers but in popular representations of the Latino body, as exemplified by the racialized image of the bandito, the desperado, and the greaser.

This chapter tracks the origins and intersections of nineteenth-century anthropological and criminal typologies in the Southwest which placed emphasis upon physical appearance, a phenomenon which Royce drew particular attention to in the epigraph through his own deeply ironic invocation of racial positivism. He satirizes the disparity between the treatment received by European born "foreign miners" and "greasers" when brought before the lynch mob or "lynching jury," but his emphasis on the "swarthy face" of the accused hints at something more than ethnicity alone.

UNBLUSHING

In 1873, Charles Darwin published *The Expression of the Emotions in Man and Animals*. In it he attempted to establish emotion on a physiological and not a physiognomical level—that is to say, as part of a biological system and not solely based on the outward appearance or semblance between men and animals.[7] Darwin explains this approach by asserting that the "agony of pain is expressed by dogs in nearly the same way as by many other animals, namely, by howling, writhing, and contortions of the whole body."[8] But even in such a physiologically driven project, a number of Darwin's conclusions would have satisfied the physiognomist's desire to read the moral character of their subjects from appearance alone. Though Darwin was a stanch critic of physiognomy, his conclusions are not as dissimilar as he might have us believe. This is nowhere more true than is his treatment of Latin Americans. In the final chapter of the book, Darwin insists that "blushing is the most peculiar and the most human of all expressions" and that it would require an "overwhelming amount of evidence to make us believe that any animal could blush."[9] His argument suggests that the capacity to blush, and the moral sensitivity it implies, establishes a fundamental difference between humans and animals; between man and beast. He then states that "Spaniards" in "South America" are unable to blush. In asserting that these "Spaniards" live in South America and not in Spain as well, one must conclude that he is speaking of, but lacks the precise terminology for, those racially mixed persons who could claim both "Spanish" and "South American" ancestry: an assertion that requires the recognition of the intermarriage of Spanish colonists with the indigenous peoples of Latin America.

Couching his views in the words of another author, his text then asks, "How can those be trusted, who know not how to blush?"[10] Given his earlier insistence that blushing was a distinctly human characteristic, Darwin seems to be insisting that persons of mixed racial origin cannot be seen as fully human because they cannot blush (which, by the way, they can). Citing Lavater and others, Darwin goes even further when he compares blacks to these unblushing "Spaniards," arguing that, at least the "negro" can show signs of blushing, even if unlike the Anglo-Saxon, they appears "blacker" instead of redder when blushing.[11] The ridiculousness of such claims in the 1870s shouldn't even merit commentary, except that they come from one of Europe's leading scientific minds. Given Darwin's stature, one must presume that the presence of bias against California's indigenous and mixed-race communities was informed by far less "sophisticated" theories of race. In fact, it was the presumed racial inferiority of "Mexicans" and American Indians that helped to accelerate and drive U.S. expansionism westward.

GREASER

As previously noted, the term greaser was intended as an insult because, among other things, it asserted the racial impurity of the recipient (the presence of indigenous Mexican bloodlines). The term was directed at Spanish-speaking persons in the nineteenth and early twentieth centuries across the West, whether they were born in the United States, Mexico, Latin America, and sometimes the term was given to those from Spain. To better understand the insult, one must remember that calling a Spaniard a greaser was, at least in some circles, the equivalent of calling him (or her), a degenerate.[12] The implied degeneracy derived from the fact that the "Mexican" was born from the union of the Spaniard who, as one author put it, was "a second-rate type of European" with the "substandard Indian of Mexico," who, the same author insists, "must not be confused with the Noble Savages of North America."[13]

PHRENOLOGY

Phrenology was short lived, but it had many supporters in its day. It was initially developed in the late eighteenth century by Francis Joseph Gall (1758–1828) but was largely discredited in scientific circles by the middle of the nineteenth century. Using "scientific" methods, the phrenologist claimed to have discovered a direct correlation between specific parts of the brain and human actions, insisting that "a particular talent, propensity, or behavior resides in or is caused by a faculty within the cortical organ."[14] But the argument went even further because it maintained that the skull or cranium was directly affected by these skills as they developed, so much so that the "scientist" could "determine a person's mental, psychological, and moral capacities and tendencies by carefully measuring or 'reading' his skull."[15]

In October 1851, less than a year after California's admission to the Union, an itinerant lecturer on phrenology was "endeavoring to make money by head-work" in Placerville or Hangtown, but the lecture was so poorly attended that the event was cancelled and the money returned.[16] The newspaper presented the "lecturer" as nothing less than a charlatan out to make a quick buck when he, like so many thousands of fortune seekers, realized that "the dry diggings did not yield much to the pan, and 'vamosed.'"[17]

By the turn of the century, the editors at the *New York Times* saw phrenology as little more than a joke. Under the heading "Proof Positive," they ran a short comic dialogue which began, "Do you believe there is really anything in phrenology?" To which a second character replied, "I do. I had my head examined by a phrenologist once, and the moment he came to my first bump he told me that my wife used an old fashioned rolling pin."[18] In another paper, the same year, one author spoofed the old image of phrenologist placing his hand upon the head of his subject, when he wrote:

Just here the bump appears
Of Innocent Hillarity,
And right behind the ears
Are Faith and Hope and Charity.[19]

By the end of the nineteenth century, physiognomy, phrenology, and social Darwinism could each be said to have embraced a broad array of pseudosciences, and though many of these approaches came to be discredited, there were scores of popular texts that continued to be published, revised, and re-published well into the first decades of the twentieth century.

Turning the discussion from the racialized body to the criminal body requires only a slight shift because, as the statistics on lynching make clear, the most reviled criminal bodies were often racialized bodies. In looking to the West, it is hard to imagine what more criminal birth could have been imagined by Anglo-Americans than those tainted by the mixing of the races and signified by terms like "Mexican" or "South American" or those that, like the Southern lynch mob, played off the fear of racial mixing, as found in the frequent invocation of the black male as a sexual aggressor and a threat to Anglo-American women and, by extension, the "white" race itself. In California, this same excuse would be extended to Chinese men, as in the case of Hong Di discussed at the end of this chapter.

THE PHOTOGRAPHIC SIGN

Acquired by community members and pasted into photo albums or kept in a drawer, the lynching photograph was created as a memorial to those who suffered at the hands of criminals and to the community that chose to do something about it. Someone looking through these images today understands that those who purchased the lynching postcard did not intend to memorialize the criminals hanging from its branches but sought to remember those victims who are not pictured. Therefore, the lynching photograph points to subjects that existed outside of the frame. In the case of the criminal's victim, it was intended to direct the viewer to the unseen site of the original crime, and as a practice, it was not uncommon for the criminal to be taken to the original scene of the crime to be summarily executed; this was particularly true in many of the earliest cases of lynching in California. The other subject of the lynching photograph is the mob itself, and whether pictured or not, it was the specific actions of the mob that were being documented, recorded, and witnessed.

The lynching photographs then traveled beyond the communities in which they were generated, across time and space, sometimes arriving in other communities (as is the case when something is donated to local, regional, or subject archives) where they could be subject to new interpretations, as suggested by my treatment of these images.

This displacement often empties out all, or at least some, of the stylistic codes and conventions, and even the mechanical traces or clues can become illegible, as noted with night photography, where the precise source of light often remains a matter of conjecture. This is not to suggest that that photographic images are as arbitrary as the linguistic sign or, as Barthes argued, that the photograph is simply a message without a code; rather, while photographs may have some innate (or indexical) resemblance to the things they depict, their translation into concepts is limited or expanded by factors external to the image. Thus, calling the photograph of a lynching an example of "frontier justice" has, at least historically, been sufficient to keep anyone from really noticing that beyond the possible question of race, there may be no discernable difference between a photograph of a "lynching" and a photograph of "frontier justice."[20]

The public fascination with the condemned body is hardly new, and the public display of the conquered, the criminal, and the condemned can be found on nearly every continent. As discussed in the previous chapter, mass-produced studio portraits of those condemned to be legally executed and the widespread existence of the lynching postcard served to expand the audience for such spectacles. At their simplest, the studio portraits functioned as an advertisement for legal execution, and lynching postcards served as a souvenir asserting that the community had chosen to administer justice on its own.

In "Rhetoric of the Image," Barthes broke new ground when he argued that in mass culture, the photographic image was little more than a courier of the linguistic message, recognizable in every image of mass culture via a title, caption, or, as in the case of a postcard, a note across the back.[21]

Extending his analysis, Barthes insisted that photographic images were polysemous (i.e., arbitrary as to any one meaning) and thus constituted a floating chain of signifieds that the reader was forced to fix, choosing one meaning over another with the help of a textual or contextual supplement.[22] Extending Saussure's use of the sign, Barthes writes, "In every society, various techniques are developed intended to *fix* the floating chain of signifieds in such a way as to counter the terror of uncertain signs; the linguistic message is one of these techniques."[23] In exploring the history of lynching and the photographic images of those lynched or condemned to die, I have sought to share the terror of these contested signs and embrace Barthes's observation that "the text *directs* the reader through the signifieds of the image, causing him to avoid some and receive others; by means of an often subtle *dispatching*, it remote-controls him towards a meaning chosen in advance."[24] I must add, however, that the only textual supplement in a lynching postcard might be "and this is what he got," but when combined with a "swarthy" face, in a culture in which images of brown-skinned Latinos (blushing or not) are remarkably rare, an explicit textual supplement may not even be necessary.[25]

In *Camera Lucida*, Barthes acknowledged that it was possible to perceive the *photographic signifier*, but he argued that such perceptions would require a secondary action of knowledge, that is to say, that it required reflection.[26] But even when the response to a photographic image is initially physiological, as might be the case with a lynching photograph, the popularity of such images seems to suggest that such responses are neither constant nor universal. Therefore, one must conclude that the photographic signifier is modified through repeated exposure—just as language is modified through speech. For this reason, it is the textual descriptions associated with lynching images and those condemned to die that have been explicitly and rather extensively noted in this text. Perhaps of all the cases encountered in researching this book, the legal execution of Tiburcio Vasquez provides one of the most fascinating examples of how text and image came to shape the Latino image in the West.

TIBURCIO VASQUEZ

In 1874, the Bradley and Rulofson studio was one of the largest photographic studios on the West Coast, and today one can still find hundreds of studio portraits they had taken during the second half of the nineteenth century. Scattered across the state in regional and historical archives, there are countless images of fuzzy-chinned young men in ill-fitting Civil War uniforms and elegant young women seemingly floating atop carefully arranged pyramids of crinoline and lace. Among these many images, I came across a portrait of a man condemned to die, and while one could argue this is true of all photographic portraits, in this case, the photograph was specifically taken to commemorate the spectacle of his death—in advance of it having occurred (color plate 9).

The studio portrait was of one of California's most notorious bandits, José Tiburcio Vasquez (1835–75), and it was taken at the Montgomery Street studio in San Francisco on May 28, 1874.[27] In order to take the picture, Vasquez had to be removed from his cell, transported to the studio, and then returned to his cell to wait for the day of execution. By why was the photograph taken? Like the souvenir postcard of a lynching, or the *carte de visite* of a Civil War hero, the image of outlaws like Silvas and Vasquez held considerable appeal to the general public and were viable commodities.

The photographic image was produced and sold as a souvenir for something that had not yet transpired; in fact, several images from the sitting were produced and sold for nearly a year before he was legally executed on

March 19, 1875.[28] A celebrity portrait of sorts, when the fateful day arrived, a crowd that was estimated to be somewhere between five and ten thousand men, women, and children came to bid farewell to California's notorious "Greaser Thief."[29]

"I HAD NUMEROUS FIGHTS IN DEFENSE OF
WHAT I BELIEVED TO BE MY RIGHTS"

The first accounts of Vasquez's criminal conduct can be found as early as July 1857 when he was alleged to have stolen at least ten horses and mules from the San Buenaventura area.[30] Arrested, charged, and convicted of the crime, he was sentenced to five years at the state penitentiary in San Quentin.[31] In and out of prison until 1874 when he was captured, for the last time, by a man by the name of Emil Harris in what is now West Hollywood, Vasquez characterized his career in the following manner:

> My Career grew out of circumstances by which I was surrounded. As I grew up to manhood I was in the habit of attending balls and parties given by the native Californians, into which the Americans, then beginning to become numerous, would force themselves and shove the native born men aside, monopolizing the dance and the women. This was about 1852. A Spirit of hatred and revenge took possession of me. I had numerous fights in defense of what I believed to be my rights and those of my country-men . . . I believed we were unjustly and wrongly deprived of the social rights that belonged to us . . . I went to my mother and told her I intended to commence a different life. I asked for and obtained her blessing, and at once commenced the career of a robber.[32]

The passage has been widely cited and has contributed to Vasquez's image as a rebellious antihero for many Mexican Americans, much to the chagrin of Anglo historians who have expressed their profound befuddlement over his continued invocation as a "social bandit" and have repeatedly noted that his crimes made victims of Latinos as well as Anglos.[33] In fact, Vasquez has at least one regional park and one community medical center named after him.[34] These curious honors attest to the fact that he continues to be seen as a significant historical figure for many Latinos and Hispanics. Even though scholars have demonstrated that he killed and robbed both Anglos and Latinos, I would like to suggest that his significance has been largely misunderstood.[35]

Reading his statement, I am repeatedly draw to the passage in which he states, "I had numerous fights in defense of what I believed to be my rights and those of my countrymen . . . I believed we were unjustly and wrongly deprived of the social rights that belonged to us . . ."[36] Nowhere, does he claim that these injustices drove him to specific crimes, but rather, he attributes his life of crime, more generally, to the denial of social rights and as such, the passage is notable, because he specifically calls attention to the injustices experienced by his countrymen.

Vasquez was born José Jesús López in Monterey in 1835 while California was still under Mexican rule, and so his countrymen were both Mexican Nationals and Mexican Americans.[37] The passage is also significant because it demonstrates that Latinos as well as Anglos conflated racial and nation identity, which supports my claim that the absence of clear distinctions had less to do with identity politics than it did with the total rupture of previously accepted definitions of racial, ethnic, or national identity, in reframing this "new" U. S. population.

After Tiburcio was placed in the custody of the legal authorities, another newspaper further conflated his identity when it published an article on his arrest entitled "The Bandit: Arrival of the Greaser Horse Thief," which literally equated the criminal identity of the "bandit" with the racial impurity signaled by the term "greaser."

What is most significant about Vasquez for many Mexican Americans is the fact that he was able to parley the impending spectacle of his own death, signified by the photographic image, into a forum from which to address the Mexican American experience—transforming his infamy into what may be among the most overtly race conscious statements to be credited to a Mexican American in the English language press of the nineteenth century.

Like a flash of light in nearly a century of darkness, his interviews, published in newspapers and pamphlets, transformed his celebrity from that of a phantom threat lurking along California's foothills to a media spectacle that brought him scores of visitors up to the day of his execution and supplied Vasquez with a very different kind of opportunity for speech making that the Western lynch mob had so successfully denied to better men.[38]

Like the Silvas case, Tiburcio's execution conformed to the legal code in all but one respect: after February 14, 1872, state law required that all executions were to be held in a "private place," that "no one under age" be allowed to witness the execution, and aside from the necessary peace officers, that no more than twenty-two persons be allowed in total.[39] With over five thousand witnesses, it would seem that at least one of the state's restrictions was overlooked.

The passage quoted in the epigraph references the impact of race or ethnicity on lynch law, but as Tiburcio's case demonstrates, the impact of bias did not restrict itself to popular tribunals. Indeed, while most contemporary Americans readily acknowledge that racial bias motivated Southern lynch mobs and can even accept that American Indians, African Americans, and Chinese immigrants were victims of Western racism, many continue to have trouble accepting the idea that "Mexican" should be used as a racial category. However, as my case lists demonstrates, and as the many details found within the case records support, the majority of Latinos who were killed by lynch mobs—or who were executed by legal means—were recorded as "Mexican," pathologized as "greasers," and consistently distinguished from Anglos, Asians, blacks, and Indians in nearly every case examined. While ethnicity may be recognizable as a unifying classification by contemporary standards, the term does not appear in the case records, and its absence supports the claim that the terms "Mexican," "Sonoran," "Californio," and "Chilean" specifically sought to point to the mixed racial origins of its recipient.

It is only by acknowledging the fact that nineteenth-century racial categories were unable to fully contain, to fix, the Latino body as a singularly distinct class, ethnicity, or national identity that we can begin to unravel the curious system of judgment that was brought to bear upon this chimerical body, and in more than one case, journalists, scholars, and lynch mobs chose to rely upon the principles of physiognomy to degrade these and other communities.

At the same time, they extended these principles to their own bodies as they struggled to distinguish themselves and "their" nation from their black, Chinese, Indian, "Mexican" and mixed-race neighbors, not to mention the many new waves of ethnic immigrants who sought to make a home for themselves in this nation.

A MADAGASCAR CAT WOULD BE ASHAMED

In order to extend my claim that physiognomy impacted racial formation in the West, I would like to begin by considering a description of Vasquez that appeared in one of the newspapers of the day. It read:

> A low forehead, and a head of coarse black hair are little indications of intelligence and from beneath a coarse, overhanging brow gleam two deep-set, treacherous, cunning eyes of which even a Madagascar cat would be ashamed. The whole contour of his face suggests Indian blood; his cheek bones are high, his mouth large and coarse, his beard and mustache

24. Executed by, or under the inspection of, Thomas Holloway, "Boy with Monkey," ca. 1789–98, 2.25 by 3.5 inches. Collection of the author.

(and the latter extends far on either side the upper lip) are of straight, black hair, and . . . serve to render more repulsive his ugly continence. He stands 5 feet 5 ¾ inches high, and is of good figure, proportionately, but with large hands—an unusual feature in those of Spanish blood. Like all of his class, he is fond of finery and ostentatious display; vain to an extreme, and a thorough bully."[40]

In this text, one can detect the presence of two of the most recurrent methods of physiognomic analysis. For those unfamiliar with physiognomics, let me begin by summarizing the three primary methods of analysis outlined in "Aristotle's" *Physiognomics*. The first was the zoological method, and it referred to the comparison between men and animals. The second was the ethnological method, and it reduces the body and character of a person down to a singular expression of racial and national origin. The third was called the pathognomical method (pathognomy), and it was concerned with the study of passing emotions upon the face, but could include gesture or stance as well[41] (figure 24).

In the passage on Vasquez, one can locate the presence of the zoological approach in the comparison between his eyes and those of a Madagascar cat. The ethnological can be found in the emphasis on his overhanging brow, the contours of his face, and the sentence citing the presence of both Indian and Spanish blood. That the racial impurity of the "Mexican" was seen as an essential character flaw was hardly new, and as early as 1845 Lansford Hastings (1818–68), author of *The Emigrant's Guide to Oregon and California*, had written on what he referred to as the two classes of persons to be encountered in California: the Indian and the Mexican. Describing the latter, he asserted, "Many of the lower order of them, have intermarried with the various tribes, and have resided with them so long . . . that it has become almost impossible, to trace the least distinction between them, either in reference to intelligence, or complexion." [42] Should there be any doubt about his estimation of the Mexican people he concluded, "Ignorance and its concomitant, superstition, together with suspicion and superciliousness, constitute the chief ingredients, of the Mexican character." [43]

Nearly thirty years later, another author approached the question of character from a slightly different perspective, arguing that "even Mr. Darwin's theory of evolution could not, if practically applied, evolve a soul from the mass of selfish brutishness with which he [Tiburcio] is endowed." [44] As obvious as it may be, Darwin's theory of evolution did not specifically concern itself with the evolution of the soul, but such questions were not beyond the reach of Lavater, Spencer, and the social Darwinists. [45]

Furthermore, the reference to class at the end of the passage on Vasquez has far less to do with a Marxist critique of labor conditions than it does with eighteenth- and nineteenth-century wranglings around questions of difference. In the American West, as in many parts of the United States, racial or ethnic identity was often collapsed into class, but such invocations were far closer to a racialized caste system than they were to Marxist economic theory. In such a model, trade, profession, ethnicity, nationality, race, economics, education, and gender could restrict individuals, families, and communities from certain social and economic opportunities. To give one example from the gold mining region, Chinese men were often discouraged and sometimes even restricted from mining for gold, but they were allowed to open laundry services or to serve as camp cooks.

In revisiting the Vasquez passage, one might be surprised to find that the signs of difference upon which the analysis relied could have been taken straight out of Lavater's *Essays on Physiognomy*. As the description makes clear, he was not only a criminal type, a greaser, but his physiognomy—the curve of his brow, the look of his eyes, the shape of his head, the size of his hands, and even the clothes he wore—were essential characteristics for eighteenth-century physiognomic analysis.

In Tiburcio's case, moral failings were even read into his habit of dress, an observation that Lavater would have certainly approved of. Of all the telling phrases captured in this passage, the suggestion that his facial hair renders "more repulsive his ugly continence" strikes the hardest blow because it suggests that greasers—the Mexican, all "Mexicans"—were little more than a shave away from becoming hardened criminals. That his manner of dress, the animal to which he is compared, and the shape of his brow and the whiskers on his face were all represented as emblematic of his class demonstrated that, at least in this case, class was intended as a racial marker and as a standing indictment of his countrymen. That this description sought to read his moral character from his physiognomy is made explicit when compared against another contemporaneous description which presented Vasquez in a very different light: "His complexion is much lighter than the ordinary Mexican. His features are clear-cut, with an intelligent expression. His eyes are rather large and a light grey or blue in color. His forehead is high and well shaped . . . but for his calm, steady eye . . . no one would take him for the terrible Tiburcio Vasquez."[46]

In trying to reconcile the subtle and not so subtle distinctions between the two descriptions I found the existence of the souvenir view card to be invaluable. This is not to suggest that we can glean any truth to his character from the photographic image but rather that, unlike the textual prompt, one can at least recognize that his eyes were not those of a Madagascar cat. Furthermore, the eyes, forehead, and general physiognomy that figured so prominently in both descriptions reveal that bodily signs, perhaps even over his criminal exploits, shaped the public image of the terrible greaser thief.

In Italy, Cesare Lombroso (1836–1909) had extended the principles of physiognomy to something he called criminal anthropology in *L'uomo delinquente* (1870) and *La donna delinquente* (1893), which basically argued for the existence of the born criminal as a distinct type.[47] If California had a born criminal, Tiburcio was clearly it.

In England, the ideal of a distinctly criminal physiognomy can be found everywhere from Charles Dickens and Havelock Ellis to the paintings of W. P. Frith, but gleaning such clues from such a highly coded representation as a painting demonstrates the degree to which both artist and critic had embraced physiognomy and parallels the emphasis on appearance found in both descriptions of Vasquez. According to one author, the belief in criminal physiognomy continued to persist in England until well after 1913, when Charles Goring is credited with demonstrating once and for all that the notion of a distinct criminal type was nothing more than an "anthropological monster" without scientific merit.[48]

The Vasquez case is of particular significance because unlike the many examples of lynching and capital punishment already cited, his photographic image revealed that in the American West, the racial formation of the greaser was directly impacted by the "science" of physiognomy and was closely linked to the popular image of the bandito, the desperado, and the greaser in the Anglo imagination.[49]

When the fatal day finally arrived, Tiburcio was provided with a seven-foot drop and his life was quickly extinguished. Five doctors (well beyond the number mandated by state law) were reported to have been at the scene, perhaps to ensure that Tiburcio would not cheat death. They dutifully noted the "pulsations of the heart and wrists" from the moment the body dropped and reported that "For the first minute the beats were 69, for the second 68, the third 72, fourth 112, fifth 136, sixth 120, seventh 120, and for the next half minute 85 . . . the stethoscope indicated faint beating at the heart until about twelve minutes had transpired."[50]

GREGORIO CORTEZ

In 1901, another well-known case took place in The Lower Rio Grande Border region of Southern Texas, but this time it was the "sheriff killer" and Mexican folk hero, Gregorio Cortez, whose real life adventures, from his perilous escape from the sheriff's posse to his unjust imprisonment, the failed attempts of the lynch mob, his eventual pardon by the governor, and even the mythologizing rumors of his death by slow poison all became the stuff of legend.[51]

Celebrated in *corridos* or folk songs, his arrest raised passions in a way that had not been seen in the West since Vasquez. Like Vasquez, there were vast manhunts, and like Vasquez, his photograph was offered for sale: An advertisement appeared in a local newspaper announcing the availability of the photographs for 25 cents each just three days after his arrest.[52] By all accounts, nearly every Texan imagined that this "sheriff killer" would be hanged or lynched. Remarkably, he was not. He was released after over twelve years in prison. The saddest part of the story lies in the many accounts of those who had, or who were believed to have, helped him in whatever way they could during his flight from the sheriff's posse.

In San Diego, a Mexican was killed as part of the "Cortez gang," and others were captured or killed. In Belmont, Texas, a Mexican was hanged to death and another shot dead when they refused to disclose information about the "gang." However, the various accounts of the many trials revealed that there was no gang. In this manner, the case provides a new perspective from which to consider the existence, real or imagined, of "Mexican" gangs in California's own history of lynching. While such associations certainly did exist, their numbers were often exaggerated, and those killed along the way often became gang members posthumously. The most telling aspect of the Cortez case is the fact that it demonstrates the degree to which anti-Mexican sentiment continued to contribute to the history of lynching into the twentieth century.

PHYSIOGNOMY AND THE ANGLO-AMERICAN

That physiognomy influenced racial formation in the United States doesn't really tell the whole story. Rather than considering another of the many negative representations of Asians, blacks, Indians, or Latinos in the American West, it may be more productive to turn our attention to the description of another photograph, this time taken of one of the most significant figures from American history—Abraham Lincoln (1809–65). One must remember that racial formation was as much a part of Anglo-American identity as the racial and ethnic identities from which they distinguished themselves. Like the Vasquez case, it may be useful to consider the textual description of the photograph before looking to the photograph itself. The passage in question appeared in the *Los Angeles Star* on June 8, 1861, under a title heading which read, "Photograph of Lincoln—Read and Laugh, and laugh and read—read it again and laugh deeper."[53] It read:

His mouf, His paw and his footzes am the principil feeters, and his strikin pint is the way them air legs ov hisn gets inter his body. They goes inter each aidge sorter like the prongs goes inter a pitch fork. Ov all the darned skeery looking ole casses for a president ever I seed. he am decidedly the durndest. He looks like a yaller ladder with half the rungs knocked out. I knocked a ole bullfrog once and druv a nail through his lips inter a post, tied 2 rocks to his hine toes and stuck a darnin needle inter his to let out the misture, and lef him thar tu dry. I seed him 2 weeks arterwurds, an when I seed ole Abe I thot hit were an orful retribution come onto me, and that hit were the same frog, only stretched a little longer, and had tuk to warin ov close tu keep me from knowin him, an ketchin him an nailin him up agin; an natral born fool es I is, I swar I seed The same watery skeery look in the eyes, and the same sorter knots on the backbone. I'm afeard, George, sumthin's to cum uv my nailin up that air frog, I swar I am ever since I seed ole Abe; same shape, same color, same feel, (cold as ice,) an I'm d'd ef hit aint the same smell!

Sut Lovegood[54]

Credited to a man by the name of Sut Lovegood, the quote is startling from a number of perspectives. Lovegood's accent suggests that he was not a native of California, and as some may have already recognized, Sut was something of a folk hero whose misguided antics were usually restricted to the Appalachian mountains of Tennessee. His folk status is confirmed by the fact that more than one author appears to have used the "Lovegood" character, though with slightly different spelling. In fact, if folk characters can have proper names, then "Sut Lovegood" was really "Sut Lovingood." The fact that these two names represented the same character is confirmed by the existence of two separate books written by two different authors, each of which uses a different spelling for Sut's last name. If that wasn't confusing enough, one of the stories, known as "The Story of a Shirt," appeared in both books. Indeed, Sut's misguided antics appeared in newspapers and periodicals throughout the 1850s.[55]

George Washington Harris (1814–69), now revered as one of the great American humorists, began writing and publishing a series of satiric narratives that took a backwoods character by the name of Sut Lovingood and let him speak on everything from photography to the abolition of slavery. From the 1850s on, Harris wrote, rewrote, and published Sut's antics until he was able to generate enough stories to fill a book entitled, *Sut Lovingood. Yarns Spun by a "Nat'ral Born Durn'd Fool,"* which was published in 1867.

Nine years before Harris's *Yarns Spun* was published, another book entitled *The Harp of a Thousand Strings; or, Laughter for a Lifetime* introduced readers to a character by the name of "Sut Lovegood." Intended as a humorous romp through various regions of the American countryside, this Lovegood character would only make a brief appearance. The author of *The Harp of a Thousand Strings* was Samuel Putnam Avery (1822–1904).

Trained as a copperplate engraver for magazines and periodicals like *Appleton's* and *Harper's Magazine*, *The Harp of a Thousand Strings* included over two hundred drawings that Avery then translated into his "Kurious Kutz." Given Avery's propensity for collecting images, it seems reasonable to assume that some of the stories were gleaned from a wide variety of sources. More significantly, Avery made no effort to erase or even modify his Lovegood passages, and the second character, referred to simply as "George," appears in *The Harp of a Thousand Strings*, *Yarns Spun*, and the *Star* article quoted above. In all three of these texts, Sut is engaged in a conversation with George, who is, of course, none other than George Washington Harris, the creator and author of Sut Lovingood's *Yarns Spun*. In reading the Avery version, one has the impression that he was less interested in claiming Lovegood as his own creation than in trying to cash in on a popular folk character that had, in 1858, appeared in mostly Southern magazines and periodicals.

Shifting the discussion to the *Star* passage, one may be surprised to learn that it does not appear in either the Harris or Avery versions mentioned. Its absence may be explained by the fact that *The Harp of a Thousand Strings* was published before Abraham Lincoln was elected to the office of the presidency, and *Yarns Spun* was published after Lincoln had been assassinated. If Harris wrote the passage in question, and it is likely he did, it is unlikely that it would have been included in the *Yarns Spun* for the simple reason that lampooning Abraham Lincoln in 1868 (after his assassination) would have been deeply offensive—if not to the author, at least to his publishers. The only remaining possibility as to the origin of the *Star* text would be that it was a stylistic parody, but this is improbable given the detailed characterization of Lovegood's speech. As difficult as tracing the origin of the Lovegood text may have been, searching for the photograph to which it referred was even harder.

In the Avery version, the narrator encounters Lovegood after crossing the Hiwassee River. The Hiwassee winds its way through the Appalachian Mountains in Tennessee, which suggests the origins of Sut's accent. The *Star* passage represents a dialogue between George and Sut Lovegood, and given the many parallels between the three texts it seems reasonable to conclude that the *Star* passage was originally published elsewhere and reprinted without citation: a practice that was common with humorous content in newspapers of the period.

Lovegood was intended to signify a regional "type" distilled from a constellation of traits associated with uneducated Southern whites living in the Appalachian Mountains. Throughout the nineteenth century, the type was invoked as a categorizational tool applicable to every member of society from the criminal to the aristocrat. Embraced by European ethnographers, travelers, and enthusiasts alike, regional types were sought out, observed, sketched, and photographed from Africa to the Americas.[56] Photographic examples from the nineteenth century can be found in many countries, and nearby Mexico was no exception. These *Tipos Mexicanos* regularly portrayed Mexican laborers and craftsmen with the tools of their trade, and the same model might be used to represent a variety of trades or types (figure 25).

THE PHANTASMAGORIA OF PHYSIOGNOMY

What are we to make of the well-dressed dandy who encounters Sut? Was George a "naturalist," simply poking fun? Perhaps, he was the South's version of the flâneur. After all, as Benjamin observed, it was part of "the phantasmagoria of the flâneur: to read from faces the profession, the ancestry, the character."[57] But Benjamin made a point of distinguishing the flâneur's desire to observe difference from the goals of the physiognomist and staunchly rejected those who argued that "the flâneur has made a study of the physiognomic appearance of the people in order to discover their nationality and social station, character and destiny, from a perusal of their gait, build, and play of features."[58] Instead, he insisted that the flâneur devoted himself (at times without knowing it) to the city or to some highly abstracted notion of humanity, but whether the actions of the flâneur were driven by the principles of physiognomy isn't really the question. The suggestion here is not that Western lynch mobs were composed of physiognomists, or flâneurs for that matter, but that physiognomical thought permeated the streets and cafes of Paris, seeped into popular culture, and traveled to the New World, where it informed perceptions of the nationalized, racialized, criminalized, or otherwise stigmatized body, from Abraham Lincoln to Tiburcio Vasquez.[59]

Benjamin noted (regarding the use of physiognomy in nineteenth-century literature) that there was an inherent contradiction in a system which sought to identify those traits unique to the individual, but which, in the process of identification, invariably transformed the individual into a completely new type.[60] His observations are useful because they highlight the difficulty of distinguishing the caricature from the stereotype and highlight the ambiguity of the "type."

In returning to the Lovegood passage, one must acknowledge that more than any physical trait, it is the phonetic translation of Lovegood's speech which is the most salient feature of the text, and it was Harris's unique ability to transcribe this regional cadence and tone that would be revered and emulated by generations of Southern writers from Mark Twain to Flannery O'Conner.[61] Indeed, Harris's depiction of Lovingood's speech was nothing less than a revelation to writers, so perfectly did its phonetic spelling demand

25. S. Osuna, "Peon de Ladrillera, Mexico," n.d., gelatin silver print from original negative, 3 by 5.5 inches. Collection of the author.

to be uttered. In reading the passage, one is literally forced to sound out the words before their meaning can be fully grasped.

Illustrated in both the Harris and the Avery editions, Sut's figure is drawn as an extremely thin man of northern European descent who has angular features and bony limbs. Rendered by Harris in a literary shorthand that was admired for its surgical accuracy, Lovegood is described as approaching the narrator "in his usual rambling, uncertain gait," an image which contrasts starkly with the worldly command attributed to the narrator.[62] Lovegood is cast as a simpleton and drunkard whose misguided antics both charm and amuse the gentleman narrator.

Perhaps most importantly, the Lovegood passage is surprisingly informative to both the discussion of the photographic images and the history of lynching, because it appears just three months after Lincoln was inaugurated to the office of the president.[63] Lincoln had won all four of California's electoral votes when the Civil War broke out on April 12, 1861, after Confederate soldiers, under General Pierre Beauregard, opened fire on Fort Sumter in Charleston, South Carolina.[64] The letter, written with a heavy Southern twang, appeared in Los Angeles just two months after the war began. California was not a slave state, but the question of slavery had been a topic of heated debate before statehood, and it should be noted that both California's Latino and Anglo populations had returned escaped slaves to their owners, attempted to restrict black emigration, and debated the merits of slavery.[65] California's gold would also help to fund the war, and many have speculated on the outcome had California joined the Confederates.

By the early 1860s, newspapers had not yet developed the means to reproduce photographic images, and aside from a few small advertising graphics, no illustrations or etchings appeared in the *Star*. It is possible that print images of Lincoln may have been in general circulation prior to his election but few, if any, Los Angeles residents could have ever seen a photographic image of Abraham Lincoln, if for no other reason than so few had been taken. This is one of the reasons that the description of Lincoln's photographic image is so fascinating.

"READ AND LAUGH, AND LAUGH AND READ — READ IT AGAIN AND LAUGH DEEPER"

Did the newspaper editors imagine that the reader would laugh at the uneducated and presumably derelict class of citizenry represented by Lovegood? Or was Lovegood a rhetorical foil from which to express their opposition to the war? One might consider that while these may be the underlying justifications for publishing the piece, the piece itself posits that it is Lincoln's physical appearance that justifies his symbolic lynching. Given the date of publication, the photograph referenced in the Lovegood piece would have been the earliest mass-produced photographic image of a U.S. president.

The photograph in question was taken on February 23, 1861, in Washington, D.C., in Mathew Brady's Washington studio.[66] Alexander Gardner (1821–82) worked for Brady during this period and is credited with taking the picture.[67] In addition, Gardner is also credited with outfitting the Brady's studio with four-tube cameras, the kind that that were used for exposing four *carte de visite* images on a single glass plate negative.[68] It was not unusual for Brady to employ other photographers to take shots for Brady's National Portrait Gallery, and the Brady studio is credited with having photographed Lincoln as many as eleven times[69] (color plate 10).

The image described in the *Star* was one of seven photographs taken on February 23. At least one of the seven photographs can be found in the Frederick Hill Meserve Collection at the National Portrait Gallery in Washington, D.C., and there is a high probability that a number of the other images from the shoot are there as well, but as of the time of publication many of the glass plate negatives had not yet been catalogued.

The photographs were intended to celebrate Lincoln's recent election and were taken less than two weeks before he was sworn in.[70] No other photographic session is recorded as having taken place in the short period between his election and the date of the newspaper article. In addition, no other photographic studio would have had the technical resources to mass-produce such an image, and the description of the photograph matches the description found in the newspaper article in a number of significant ways.

The only question that remained was, of the seven photographs taken, which one had been seen by the passage's author? Each of the known images is similar in form and varies only slightly between shots, but all seven have not been reproduced in any publication.[71] In all of the known images, Lincoln is seated in a chair next to a wooden table.[72] His top hat rests on the table in some; in others it does not. The most significant element in this series, and the one most central to the newspaper description, is the fact that at the time Lincoln's hand was said to have been swollen from having shaken hands with so many of his supporters.[73] In looking at the *carte de visite* images from the 1861 date, it appears as if some effort was made to keep his hands out of sight. Described as nothing less than a "paw" in the *Star*, the photographic image of a hand being held in a fist creates a fingerless lump which would explain the "paw" description. In this shot, Lincoln's leg can also be seen to project to the farthest corner of the frame, a detail that also seems to match the description found in the *Star*. In several other images from the series, his leg appears in a more upright position; a formal change that was obviously intended to reduce the elongation of his legs. It was produced as a *carte de visite*. I believe this to be the image referenced in the *Star*, but the question remains, what is one to make of the violent and sadistic mistreatment of the bullfrog?

Lovegood parallels his experience of seeing the Lincoln photograph with his own acts of violence against an explicitly inhuman victim. This juxtaposition resonates within the discussion of lynching because it suggests that Lincoln's body, distorted before the camera's lens, contributed to the misrecognition of Lincoln's body as something terribly monstrous. The disturbing personification of Lincoln as an oversized reptile, and its subsequent lynching, may be shocking to contemporary readers precisely because the title, "Read and Laugh, and laugh and read—read it again and laugh deeper," is explicitly linked to the tortures described. Cut, bound, impaled, pierced, nailed, and left to die, the lynched body of the bullfrog is reminiscent of so many horrific accounts of blacks who were lynched in the United States. Jeered, whipped, flogged, skinned, burned, defiled—there seems little doubt that the article was a not-so-veiled threat to abolitionists. There also seems to be little doubt that the humor, as difficult as that might be to imagine, must have derived from the comparison between humans and animals—or reptiles to be more specific.

The narrator fuses man and reptile and by the end of the piece assures us that Lincoln and the unlucky beast share one thing more—a foul smell. It is the acrid and abject smell of death. As a case study, the text exemplifies a compounded and compressed layering of distinct representational systems. First of all, the Lincoln image is not discussed as a patriotic symbol of the nation but instead is constructed as the image of an abolitionist—as seen through Confederate eyes. By July 5, 1861, less than a month after the letter was published, fifty-eight thousand volunteer troops were encamped around the nation's capital.[74] To give a clearer sense of the Confederate "humor" in the Lovegood letter, it may be worth briefly considering an article that ran on July 24, 1861, in the *Southern News*, a pro-Confederate newspaper that was published in Los Angeles. In it, the editors issued a series of resolutions which left little room for doubt about their position. It read: "Resolved, That Abe Lincoln is a bloody Abolitionist . . . Resolved, That Abe Lincoln is the devil, and much blacker than he is painted . . . Resolved, That we hope the chivalrous Secessionists will kill all the bloody Abolitionists. Resolved that the Yankees should be exterminated."[75]

In asserting that Lincoln was "blacker than he is painted," it becomes clear that the description of bullfrog-Lincoln is a symbolic lynching—if not of an African American then at least of an abolitionist. This reference to the passage as a lynching may be in conflict with the current understanding of a lynching as a summary execution by hanging, but, as demonstrated in the previous chapter, it would have been in keeping with the popular understanding of lynch law.[76]

The image's outdated political allegory also reveals an underlying message, a phantom presence that reaches back through the discussion of photography, lynching, or even the question of national identity and extends the discussion to the nineteenth century's repeated insistence that the disenfranchised or dysmorphic body (whether transformed by race, ethnicity, class, gender, nationality, criminality, ability, or, in Lincoln's case, by his political views) was at constant risk of being characterized as something monstrous.

LOOK AGAIN AT THIS NOT UNATTRACTIVE FACE

The *Phrenological Journal* published an analysis of Lincoln's face in 1864. The article was accompanied by an engraving that had been drawn from a photographic portrait credited to Mathew Brady. It began its analysis by asking the reader to "look again at this not unattractive face which has been so much caricatured and so often held up in the South as that of a monster to frighten foolish people."[77] The article then goes on to list various features, "a nose that is neither beefy or blunt . . . well-cut lips inclining up rather than down at the corners, indicating affection, wit and playfulness," all in an attempt to counter anti-Lincoln sentiments by arguing the phrenological proof of his good character.[78] As startling as such an approach may be, the text attempts to convince its readers to support Lincoln's candidacy. Noting, rather remarkably, that the editors of the journal were beyond party bias because, after all, they had considered Lincoln's (moral and physical) misrecognition "from a higher stand-point." They had drawn their conclusions from "science."[79] What they missed was that such anti-Lincoln sentiments had nothing to do with the phrenological misreading of his face and everything to do with ideological differences over slavery and the future of the nation.

Lavater's *Essays on Physiognomy* begins by asking the reader, "Is there a relation, a sensible harmony between moral and physical beauty? Between moral turpitude and corporal deformity? Or, is there a real disagreement between moral beauty and physical deformity, between moral deformity and corporal beauty?" And concludes by stating that fundamental goal of the *Essays on Physiognomy* is to answer such questions "by evidence."[80]

Embracing the basic tenets of positivism, he equates morality with appearance and physiognomy with science when he blankly states, "Positive characters of face will always announce positive faculties."[81] His basic argument derives from his assertion that the naturalist "and the huntsman" must have a physiognomy of animals and that the job of the naturalist was to uncover the hand of God.[82] Critics, on the other hand, have argued that Lavater's "science" of physiognomy served as little more than a rhetorical ploy for his theological claims.[83]

I am less interested in Lavater's view of science that I am in his view of monsters. In his text, Lavater insisted, "There are some children born with marks and spots, just as there are monsters, giants, and dwarfs. All these singularities really exist, and are inexplicable."[84] He writes, "A Monster is a living and organized being, who has a conformation contrary to the order of Nature, who is born with one or more members too much or too little, in whom one of the parts is misplaced, or else is too great or too little, in proportion to the whole."[85] Given this description of a monster, the modern reader may be able to understand why the distorted image of Lincoln's body was of so much interest to physiognomists and satirists alike.

In his passages on the "monstrous," Lavater included the image of a young girl who he tells us was exhibited in several cities in Europe. Characterizing her discolored and spotted skin as nothing less than monstrous, he attributes her unfortunate appearance to a quarrel the mother had had during her pregnancy on account of a stag. For this reason, he asserts that hair sprouted from the girl's body in the most unusual fashion. No matter how humorous this reasoning may be it is this concept of the monstrous that reveals the violence of the physiognomic gaze (figure 26).

Lavater even had an explanation for those whose character changed radically over the span of their lifetime, as might happen in persons afflicted with mental illness. Lavater insists that such "Accidental Madness . . . will manifest itself by a want of harmony, by an incoherence of the features of the face."[86] In such a model, monsters, criminals, and madmen represented part

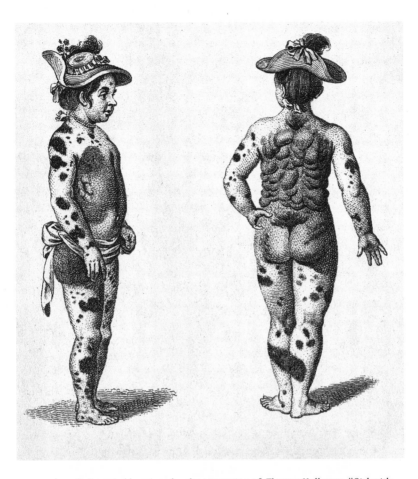

26. Executed by, or under the inspection of, Thomas Holloway, "Girl with Spots," ca. 1789–98, 13.25 by 10 inches. Collection of the author.

of a continuum that saw aberrant behavior and dysmorphic physical features as a direct expression of the moral character of the individual. Difference was synonymous with the monstrous, and its containment served to ensure that existing social, economic, and political relations would remain constant. Lavater was an avid supporter of "diversity" as well, but not in the way contemporary readers might expect; instead, he asserts that "Everyone has his place and his rank, and this very diversity is part of the plan of providence."[87] By contrast, I would argue that it was precisely this notion of the monstrous which held the potential for social change because it threw existing relations into flux and disrupted outmoded chains of signification. A monstrous body was an illegible body; it could not be read.

OF ANIMALS

In a section entitled "of Animals," Lavater links his own reliance upon bodily signs to an excerpt he credits to "Aristotle," which states, "Though there be no resemblance, properly so called, between man and animals, it is possible, nevertheless, that certain traits of the human face may suggest to us the idea of some animal."[88]

As previously noted, this belief in animal comparison, or what Lavater called comparative physiognomy, would be picked up by later physiognomists and nineteenth-century pseudoscientists, and as we have seen in the analysis of the passage on Vasquez, its influence would extend all the way to the West Coast. Later authors would continue to argue that parallels between appearance and behavior were not only to be expected, but were part of the natural order of things. Summarizing this popular view, Samuel R. Wells (1820–75) wrote in his own book entitled *New Physiognomy* that:

> We may state, our bodies, brains, and faces take their shape and are formed by the cultivation they receive, and the state of mind they are in. We may, therefore, take on, to some extent, the character of the goose, the fox, the lion. . . . by associating chiefly with the weak, the crafty, the mulish, or with beasts, birds, and reptiles.[89]

For Lavater, the successful physiognomist must be "endowed with a kind of instinct for perceiving the homogeneity and the harmony of Nature."[90] It is this emphasis on perception, both innate and learned, which opened the floodgates to myriad forms of bias through the insistence that every physical feature could be interpreted through the "divine science" of physiognomy.[91] Among his many claims, Lavater argued that in the absence of any other feature the forehead must be seen as the truest measure of an individual's character, which is reminiscent of the emphasis placed on Tiburcio Vasquez's forehead nearly a century later.[92] Lavater writes, "The form, height, arching, proportion, obliquity, and position of the skull, or bone of the forehead, show the propensity, degree of power, thought and sensibility of man," and goes on to state, "The covering or skin of the forehead, its position, color, wrinkles, and tension, denote the passions and present state of the mind."[93]

Lavater's *Essays on Physiognomy* were only part of a long tradition that argued that the outward appearance of the face and other physical attributes, such as posture or gait, could reveal the inner (moral) character of the individual. Charles Baudelaire would later echo these same sentiments when he wrote in 1863 that "each human being bears the distinctive stamp of his trade."[94] But what makes Lavater's work significant is the overall popularity of his texts and their lingering, if diminished, presence in many nineteenth-century handbooks on physiognomy, phrenology, and a vast array of long-since-forgotten pseudosciences.

Familiar to many, Lavater has been studied in relationship to science, nineteenth-century literature, and even theology, but very little attention has been paid to his particular preference for portraits, paintings, sculptures, and silhouettes rendered by the human hand—as opposed to the living body as rendered "by the hand of Nature." The significance to this study is that Lavater's preference for analyzing representations over actual people is not only surprisingly unscientific but ironic given this book's own reliance upon copy prints which are, after all, representations of representations.

Explaining his preference for observation made from portraits and likenesses he explains:

> The soul is written on the face; it must be perceived in order to be transmitted to the canvas . . . we discern in it the peculiar character of his propensities, of his affections, of his passions, in a word, the good and bad qualities of his heart and mind. And in this respect the portrait is still more expressive than Nature, in which nothing is permanent, where everything is only a succession of movements infinitely varied.[95]

The opening phrase "the soul is written on the face" has been both widely cited and widely misunderstood. Presented in its original context, one can recognize that Lavater places the emphasis on the transcription of the human form and not upon the analysis of the ever-changing living body. While this does little for Lavater's claims for physiognomy as a science, it does much for thinking about how representational systems work, and it touches on one of the basic premises of this book—that even the most detailed photographic image, whether it is a studio portrait of Abraham Lincoln or a lynching postcard, must exclude more than it includes.

Whether considering frontier justice, the antilynching movement, the archive, the mass-produced postcard, flash technology, Vasquez's eyes, or Lincoln's "paw," each must be seen as by-products in a chain of signification which has historically minimized, displaced, and obscured the discussion of race and racial mixing so central to the history of lynching in the West.

In the nineteenth century, "seeing the elephant" was an expression that regularly appeared in accounts from the gold fields and can be found in everything from the tongue-and-cheek image of an elephant wandering through a Gold Rush town in the *Miner's Ten Commandments* to its literary presence in Dame Shirley's *Gold Rush Letters*.[96] Loosely translated as "to have seen everything," the elephant, or at least an elephant, can also be found in Lavater's essays — though with very different implications.

Lavater believed that the silhouette, drawn both frontally and in profile, was of unquestionable physiognomic value for analysis. In his *Essays on Physiognomy*, he provides detailed explanations on how to create the best silhouettes for analysis. He explained that one must place the sitter between a single candle and a prepared piece of paper. Lighting the candle would then project the sitter's shadow onto a specially prepared paper from which the shadow could be traced. In this manner, Lavater's silhouettes were "drawn from shade," a concept that is an eerie complement to photography, which, of course, means to draw with light.[97] The point of intersection between these two approaches finds expression in the development of the mug shot at the end of the nineteenth century. Alphonse Bertillon, one of the fathers of modern criminology, is credited with having invented the photographic mug shot, but the principle of using a frontal and profile view in order to identify individuals (and elephants) appeared in Lavater over a hundred years earlier[98] (figures 27 and 28).

In his analysis of the elephant, Lavater encourages the reader to compare the silhouette of an elephant to that of man and concluded that the silhouette "arrests the attention: by fixing it on the exterior contours alone, it simplifies the observation, which becomes by that more easy and more accurate . . . The silhouette is a positive and incontestable proof of the reality of the Science of Physiognomies."[99] In *Essays on Physiognomy*, he includes two plates from an unfinished project entitled "Physiognomical Lines" which appear as little more than two grids of squiggly lines. Lavater insisted that the attentive observer would recognize in them "a higher value than all the rest of the Work" because they were designed "to demonstrate the importance of the form of the skull and forehead, and consequently, of the exterior contours of the profile. . . ."[100] As unconvincing as his arguments might be to the contemporary reader, they would not be without influence, even in the American West (figure 29).

27. James M. Hutchings, "The Miner's Ten Commandments," 1853.
Courtesy of the Library of Congress.

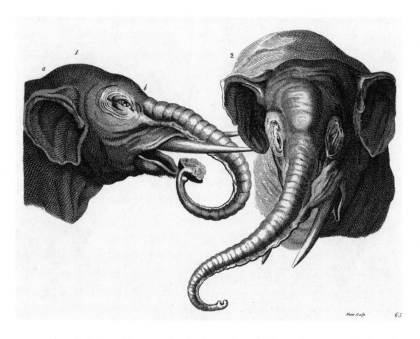

28. Executed by, or under the inspection of, Thomas Holloway, "Elephant," ca. 1789–98, 13.25 by 10 inches. Collection of the author.

THE PICTURE OF INNOCENCE

The first legal execution to take place in San Francisco occurred on the western slopes of Russian Hill when José Forner (also spelled Forne) was hanged before an audience of thousands on December 10, 1852.[101] Depicted in a drawing that appeared shortly after the execution, a small hooded figure can be seen surrounded by an immense crowd of onlookers, including an armed volunteer militia.

The case resulted from the murder of a "Mexican" by the name of José Rodrigues in Happy Valley.[102] On the witness stand Forner testified that the man had stolen a bag of gold dust and explained how he had pursued and overtook the robber when the two men began to struggle. The two men fought but neither man was willing to relent. To passersby it must have looked like a dusty cloud of arms and legs. According to Forner's own testimony, each of the men reached down for his knife in the same moment, and the two men continued to fight until their clothes were black with bloodstains. When it was over, wounded and covered in his own blood, Forner stood wearily above the dying man but was unable to convince his captors that the

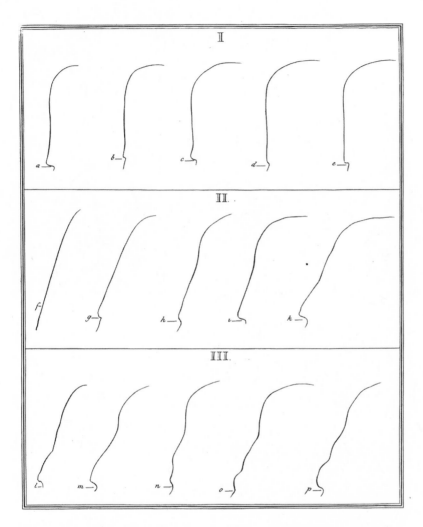

29. Executed by, or under the inspection of, Thomas Holloway, "Contours of Foreheads" or "Physiognomical Lines," ca. 1789–98, 13.25 by 10 inches. Collection of the author.

EXECUTION OF JOSE FORNER, DEC. 10, 1852.
on Russian Hill San Francisco,
FOR THE MURDER OF JOSE RODRIGUES.

30. "Execution of José Forner, Dec. 10, 1852," n.d. Courtesy of California History Room, California State Library, Sacramento, California.

gold was his own. He was arrested, tried, convicted, and hanged, all within two months' time (figure 30).

Four years later, an article appeared on the case when one reporter doing a follow-up story claimed he had uncovered a daguerreotype of Forner. The author used the image to question the justice of the case. Though the image has since been lost, it is his reliance on this photographic "witness" that makes this case notable. Describing the daguerreotype, he writes, "It is that of an educated, kind hearted man, the forehead high and well developed, the whole face agreeable and intellectual."[103] He goes on to explain that Forner declared his innocence from the scaffold and claimed that he had killed the bandit in self-defense. He added that he was from a respectable family in Spain but knew there was no hope for him, as he was a "greaser."[104] The author concluded the article by claiming that nine-tenths of the assembled crowd believed Forner to be innocent.

The term "greaser" drew its strength from the stigma of racial impurity, and so the author's emphasis on Forner's European origins was clearly intended to support his claims of innocence. Drawing directly from the principals of physiognomy, the author also emphasized that Forner's forehead was "high and well developed," qualities Lavater would have approved of—even if they had escaped the notice of the jurors at his trial.

More than any other individual feature, this emphasis on the angle of the forehead and the bridge of the nose remained essential to nineteenth-century physiognomy.[105] That Forner's European physiognomy was being used to argue his innocence would be completely unexpected, if it didn't also serve to insist that the racial impurity of the bloodied "Mexican" was proof of his guilt.

THE NEW BROWN

Retaining elements of Lavater, Darwin, and others, the nineteenth-century physiognomist Samuel R. Wells published *New Physiognomy*. His text is of interest for two reasons, the first being that it was revised, expanded, and reprinted in numerous editions over the next three decades, and the second being that his text reflects the degree of racial anxiety that arose in the aftermath of Darwin's theory of evolution. Wells and others came to believe that Anglo-Americans were themselves undergoing a kind of evolutionary transformation and, in an unattributed passage, Wells quotes the views of one such author who wrote:

> Thus it is that the genuine Yankee, in whatever he differs from his Anglo-Saxon ancestor, does so by a slow, yet very perceptible approximation to the Indian organization. This, or extinction, is indeed the unavoidable fate of all colonial populations widely separated by geographical and climatic intervals from their mother county.[106]

This line of reasoning was clearly, if mistakenly, derived from Darwin's work on evolution, which suggested that environment had a direct impact on the appearance of plants and animals, and so there was obviously some fear among these new "scientists" that Anglo-Americans would one day wake up and find a brown face staring back at them from the mirror. For Wells and others, the actual speed of evolutionary change was largely a matter of speculation, but Wells firmly rejected those who thought that the "Anglo-Saxon" race would begin to darken the longer they inhabited the continent. Instead, Wells took a more proactive view, arguing that whatever the results, only the Yankee would be the "true American of the future."[107] He also made an effort to counter those who argued that the American climate was unsuited to the "pure Caucasian" or those who found refuge in "the blending of the races."[108] Not surprisingly their primary fear was that "white, black, yellow, and red" races would mix and that their offspring would yield the "the future American," whom he sarcastically characterized as the "composite and cosmopolitan *brown man*—the true monarch of the world."[109]

Speaking to the question of racial mixing, and again quoting an unnamed source, Wells describes this future American, stating that, "The purest miscegan [mixed man] will be brown, with reddish cheeks, curly and wavy hair, dark eyes, and a fullness and suppleness of form not now dreamed of by any individual people," a truly *monstrous* creation that he believes would be rejected by "the God-given instincts of every properly constituted white man and woman."[110]

Wells rejected the mixing of races and specifically rejected the union between blacks and whites. Speaking of their progeny, he revealed his own blatant racism when he wrote, "The mulatto, though superior to the negro in intellect, is inferior to both the black and the white man in physical strength and endurance."[111] I have previously argued that the racial mixing signified by the terms "Mexican" and "greaser" reflected elements of the Anglo-American fear of racial mixing, but as the next case demonstrates, this fear was not limited to Mexicans, African Americans, or even Indians.

THE CASE OF HONG DI

> He is a young man, highly regarded by all who know him, tall and slim, but of powerful build. His face would attract attention even in a thousand. Gray-blue eyes light up a face at once intelligent and handsome. A blond mustache ornaments his upper lip, while a mass of dark hair crowns a proudly poised head. He is a picture in repose and a tiger in action.[112]

Reading the newspaper on July 12, 1877, many in the small town of Colusa, California, must have been surprised to see a familiar young man so gloriously described in a San Francisco daily. After all, this "picture in repose" was none other than Bud Welch, a local bartender by trade. Given the newspaper description's exaltation of Welch's good looks and physical prowess, the reader may be surprised to learn that the article detailed how this heroic figure had, just days before, led a mob of citizens in the lynching of a young Chinese boy known as Hong Di.

Hong Di entered public consciousness on July 10, 1887, when a Colusa jury found the seventeen-year-old houseboy guilty of murder in the first degree.[113] He had shot and killed a young woman. Newspaper accounts reduced the murder to three possible motives: "lust," "love of murder," or the actions of "a frightened boy."[114] In a surprising turn of events, the jury recommended the imposition of a life sentence, but at the reading of the verdict there was a riotous uproar. The sheriff had to ask the governor to call out the Colusa Guard, but local merchants refused to sell ammunition to the guardsmen and so the sheriff was forced to disband the men.[115] Around midnight, nearly one hundred and fifty men overran the jail and after a brief search "the quaking Chinaman was discovered."[116] He was taken to the end of town and unceremoniously hanged near the railroad turntable. An editorial published on July 16, 1887, claimed that the mob was two thousand strong and composed of the "best people" in the county.[117] Hong Di was portrayed as an ungrateful employee and, worse yet, in several articles he was presented as a sexual predator and a threat to the racial purity of this predominantly white community. In a rare acknowledgment of the bias against the Chinese, one editorial carried in a New York paper stated, "It is indeed remarkable that a California jury could be found to discriminate in favor of a Chinese criminal; it is even more remarkable, in fact, than the lynching."[118]

In his seminal text *Difference and Pathology*, Sander Gilman writes, "Difference is that which threatens order and control," noting that "various signs of difference can be linked without any recognition of inappropriateness, contradictoriness, or even impossibility."[119] The mob, the spectators, the barkeep, the clerks who refused to sell ammunition to the Colusa guardsmen, the journalists who sexualized Hong Di's otherness, the readers who bought the newspapers, the prosecutors who overlooked the illegality of the mob, and the employers who relied on the low wages of Chinese labor were all symptomatic of the degree of difference that was projected onto the young boy. This difference transformed him in the eyes of the mob into the most monstrous of spectacles; racially and sexually marked, his very existence was seen as an unacceptable blemish in an otherwise homogeneous community— so much so that his lynching scarcely registered as an illegal act in the local papers.

In recording the name and description of the leader of the mob, the *Examiner* gave a face to one of California's, and indeed America's, most anonymous and least recognized traditions—the lynch mob. Once printed in the newspaper, the writer's rhapsodic description of Welch became a powerful force in normalizing, embracing, and even condoning the illegal act, but what may escape perception is the way that Welch's physiognomy is employed as a fundamental proof of his and the mob's innocence, just as Hong Di's racial identity, sexuality, and "heathen" religious practices (all widely noted in the press) announced his guilt. Welch's physical prowess and pleasing appearance provided a justification for the mob's actions, imbuing them with a moral righteousness harkening back to Lavater who boldly asserted, "The morally best, the most beautiful. The morally worst, the most deformed."[120]

Welch was even credited with saving the memory of "the chastity and unimpeachable good character" of a young woman—albeit not in time to save her life.[121] Unlike Welch, the young woman's moral worth was linked not to her actions, but to her passivity. In reading the newspaper accounts of the case it becomes clear that in constructing the historical narrative of the case that there could be no story of unbridled beauty [his] nor pure and modest worth [hers], without a sexual predator [hidden but not unrecognized in the body of a boy]. It is impossible to know what really happened in that room but given the fact that he was found guilty, the heated anti-Chinese sentiments of the day, and the details of the lynching itself, there is little doubt that this seventeen-year-old boy had been transformed in the eyes of the Anglo community into the most monstrous of threats—the threat of racial mixing.

Seemingly inconceivable, it was the fear of racial mixing in the nineteenth century that has long been assigned to the African American experience of lynching. At the close of the nineteenth century, Anglo communities overwhelmingly perceived black men as a predatory threat to white women. This charge was taken up by the antilynching movement which specifically sought to challenge such claims, first in the work of Ida B. Wells and later by historians like Robert Zangrando, who, using the records at the Archives at Tuskegee Institute, was able to confirm that only 25.29 percent of all lynching resulted from either rape or attempted rape charges.[122] Sadly, Wells noted that one black man was lynched for simply asking a woman to marry him; others were lynched for having consensual relations or holding hands.[123]

While such fears were never explicitly associated with the image of frontier justice, the case of Hong Di demonstrates that such suspicions were not restricted to relations between blacks and whites. Or, as in the 1858 case of Joaquín Valenzuela, a "Sonoran" tried by a vigilance committee in San Luis Obispo and convicted of kidnapping and rape; other accounts suggest that the blue-eyed girl was not kidnapped but was being raised by Valenzuela and his wife. His dying wish was that his "step-daughter" be given all his worldly possessions.[124]

On a less literal level, this chapter has also sought to suggest that the question of racial difference is not only laced throughout this history but is further complicated by the question of racial mixing itself and is undeniably linked to the sometimes hazy distinctions between "Spaniard," "Mexican," and "Latino" from the nineteenth century to the twenty-first. In the nineteenth century, the threat of racial mixing was complicated by two interwoven threads. The first is the threat that the newly conceived Anglo-American race might fall prey to the same degeneracy that, in their view, had first lessened the Spanish stock in Europe and then mixed in unchecked passions with the indigenous peoples of the Americas. These views, charted in the many texts and cases cited in this chapter, culminate in the second strain of thought, which spawned the image of the greaser and its progeny, the Greaser Thief, which by 1870s had congealed into a powerful symbol of the inevitable consequences of moral weakness. Tainted by primitive bloodlines, Vasquez was all but seen as a evolutionary throwback in an uncivilized world in which "heathen" Chinese, Mexican half-breeds, and Indian "primitives" threatened Anglo-America's self-proclaimed manifest destiny.

It has just been reported here that
the company of Rangers commanded
by Captain Harry Love, met with
the notorious murderer and robber,
Joaquin, and six of his equally
infamous band, at Panocha Pass, and
after a desperate running fight, Joaquin
and one of his gang were killed and
two taken prisoners; three managed
to make their escape, but one of
their horses were killed and several
captured. Captain Love is now on his
way down with his prisoners and the
head of Joaquin preserved in spirits.

In haste, yours, T. C. A.

Quartzburg, 27th July, 1853

P.S. I have just learned that during
this engagement the Rangers were
commanded by Captain Burns (Love
not being present,) and that the other
one killed was known by the name of
"Three-Fingered Jack."

— *San Francisco Alta California*,
July 31, 1853

CHAPTER FIVE

The Wonder Gaze

NOTORIOUS

The subject of novels, poems, paintings, and even an opera—the head in question had belonged to none other than Joaquín Murrieta.[1] A real historical figure, or perhaps more accurately, a composite of various historical characters, he made his first appearance as a fully developed and highly fictionalized character in *The Life and Adventures of Joaquín Murieta*, published in 1854 by Yellow Bird (John Rollin Ridge).[2] In it, Ridge infused what limited historical facts were available with the familiar dime novel themes of corruption, revenge, cruelty, and malice, but what distinguished this book from the vast majority of "penny dreadfuls" and contributed to the creation of the Murrieta myth was its emphatic critique of social injustice. At the end of the novel, Ridge insists that while Murrieta's life and career were short, the most important lesson to be learned from the story was that "there is nothing so dangerous in its consequences as *injustice to individuals*—whether it arise from prejudice of color or from any other source; that a wrong done to one man is a wrong to society."[3] Ridge was half-Cherokee, and his emphasis on color sought to draw parallels between the social injustice and race.[4]

Part myth, part truth: depending on which account one reads, Joaquín was either named Carrillo or Murrieta, was either Mexican or Chilean, light skinned or dark, blue eyed or brown, fair or raven haired.[5] A master of disguise, he was said to have evaded capture by completely transforming his appearance. Other accounts suggested that he could not be killed because he wore a suit of armor under his clothes, a popular image that would be attributed to other Gold Rush bandits.[6] In the tale, the good-natured young Murrieta was driven to a life of crime only after he had been flogged; his wife was raped; he was driven from his claim, twice; and his half-brother was summarily hanged for a crime he didn't commit, at which point Murrieta decided to revenge himself upon his tormenters, a detail that would also reappear in other Gold Rush tales.[7]

Murrieta's story has been told and retold, and along the way, it has been transformed into one of California's most lasting Gold Rush tales. Credited with brutal crimes against Chinese, Anglos, and Mexicans alike, he and his associates were the subject of the state's first great manhunt. He was reported to have made the Chinese miners he robbed cook for him and his band.[8] Tracked across the state by Captain Love and his men, he was killed in the shootout that ensued. His decapitated head was then transported throughout the state in order to provide proof of his death—and to raise funds for Love and his men. Another member of the Murrieta gang known simply as "Three-Fingered Jack" was also shot down, but his head was too badly damaged to be preserved, so his misshapen hand was taken as proof that he too had been killed. Together these ghoulish relics were displayed across the state in the months following their deaths.

In a possibly unrelated case, in November of the same year, the San Francisco *Alta California* ran an article stating that another company of Rangers had encountered a band of Mexican bandits between the Chowchilla and Fresno Rivers, near where Murrieta's band had been encountered, and that a fight ensued, resulting in the decapitation of fifteen of the bandits. Unfortunately, this account was never confirmed, and so it is probable that it was just one of the many exaggerated accounts of the Murrieta episode, but at the very least, its publication suggests that tensions between Anglos and Mexicans remained high even after Murrieta's death.[9]

THE HEAD PRESERVED IN SPIRITS

The epigraph is from a letter that was published days after Murrieta's gang had met justice at the hands of Love's posse of mercenary Rangers, and the letter raised questions about Love's presence while adding fuel to the debates over what had actually transpired, particularly for those who doubted the veracity of Love's claims.[10] Love was a controversial character in his own right, and questions surrounded the identity of "the head pickled in spirits" from the beginning. Was it really Murrieta's head or someone else's? Had Murrieta escaped back to Mexico or was he hiding in foothills of the Sierras? Many have claimed to have answered these and other questions, but the value of the Murrieta myth to California's history of lynching and extralegal executions must be traced to the ways in which it lived on in the Western imagination, becoming a canon against which all bandits would be measured. Rather than debating his actions in life, this chapter considers the image of Murrieta after his death and looks to the ways in which he was represented, whether in a jar of spirits or in painted and printed images. His story is symptomatic of one of the most turbulent periods in California's history, a period in which more Mexicans, Mexican Americans, and persons of Latin American origin or descent died at the hands of lynch mobs than in any other period. Because of the abundance of textual and visual representations, the Murrieta tale provides another opportunity to explore physiognomy's influence on popular conceptions of frontier justice.

As a side note, in some of the earliest and most contested accounts of Mexican and Latin American bandits, Mexican outlaws and criminals were not yet referred to as "banditos" and "desperados" but were simply known as "banditti," suggesting that the criminal canon of the "Mexican" bandito or desperado had not yet been fully formed. Horace Bell, in describing the period, stated in June 1853 that "the southern counties were overrun by Mexican banditti" and that various companies of Rangers had been raised, one in Calaveras County and the other in Los Angeles.[11]

Chapter 4 specifically addressed a number of European and American texts that both influenced and reflected the nineteenth-century understanding of race, ethnicity, and national identity, not the least of which was Lavater's "science" of physiognomy. In returning to these seemingly distant texts, I have sought to argue that physiognomy and the idea that outward appearances revealed inner truths informed and guided relations between Anglo-Americans and the many peoples they encountered in the American West. Even beyond the West, physiognomy, phrenology, and the pseudosciences repeatedly sought to scrutinize those marked by difference; the dwarf, the giant, the criminal, the prostitute, the racialized body, and the disabled were probed and prodded for physical clues to their moral failings. These physical markers (signifiers) of difference became telling clues in the construction of a vast system of human typologies, a Parthenon of the monstrous.

The criminal, the morally unsound, the butcher, the baker, and the candlestick maker—each became a *type* in a social, political, and economic universe in which human relations were fixed. In terms of social history, it was the very fixity of social relations in Europe that filled ship after ship headed to the gold fields, as countless individuals sought to change their fortune along with their social standing. To mix race was to disrupt what little order existed, and in the American West, new types like the Mexican and the greaser were stigmatized as much by their racial, ethnic, or national identity as they were by the behavior of the banditti.[12]

In the eyes of Yankee and European newcomers, racial mixtures, like prostitution or criminality, were occurrences that should be reduced with the utmost speed, lest they threaten the very fabric of civil society. In the previous chapter the impact of comparative physiognomy was considered in the popular press's treatment of Tiburcio Vasquez; this chapter turns back the clock toward that first turbulent decade of California statehood.

The impact of physiognomy on nineteenth-century poetry, art, and literature in Europe has been extensively studied, but no one has asked whether, or in what manner, physiognomy may have impacted the American West and the history of lynching.[13] How did these views shape the Latino image in the West? Looking at the paintings of Charles Christian Nahl (1818–78) and others who strove to put a face on one of California's most notorious and most mythic of outlaws, Joaquín Murrieta, this chapter turns the discussion of physiognomy back to the painted image from which it began.

The contemporary scholar John Graham detailed the influence of physiognomy in the literary works of the French writer Henri Beyle Stendhal (1783–

1842). Graham was able to identify Stendhal's use of the principles of physiognomy to build his characters, noting that he repeatedly introduces minor characters based on a few detailed descriptions of their facial features and that narrative changes could also be tracked on the faces of the major characters. Perhaps more significant for our purposes are Graham's claims that the characters use the principles of physiognomy to communicate with one another within the narrative and that these principles guide the reader.[14] He argues, "In contrast to its negligible use by earlier writers, physiognomy has become an essential tool for analysis, permitting its organic function in the novels of Stendhal."[15]

Graham provides a second notable example in his analysis of the influence of physiognomy on the work of Honoré de Balzac (1799–1850). Highlighting the profusion of intricate details Balzac employs to describe individuals and their settings, Graham has argued that these details helped to facilitate the reader's interpretation of the scene. Balzac, writes Graham, drew on "Lavater and Gall for both his theory and practice and argued strongly for both men, praising them as pioneer scientists in the study of physiognomy."[16] Not only was Balzac a firm believer in physiognomy but also, in contrast to Benjamin, he felt that "most observant people, students of social nature in Paris, are able to tell the profession of a passerby as they see him approach."[17] Given the broad influence of physiognomy in Europe, the question is, could physiognomy have contributed to shaping Murrieta's image, in either text or image?

On December 12, 1853, the *Sacramento Union* published an article stating that displaying the head would allow the public an opportunity to study the physiognomy of the most celebrated and infamous outlaw of his age.[18] But by the time the *Union* article came out, Murrieta's head and the hand of "Three-Fingered Jack" had already been displayed halfway across the state.

They were first shown at King's Saloon in San Francisco and were said to be in the possession of Nuttall and Black, two of Captain Love's Rangers.[19] A poster created for another such display announced that the head would be on view at the Stockton House (in Stockton) on August 19, 1853.[20] The poster asserted that a man by the name of Ignacio Lisarraga of Sonora had given a sworn statement authenticating the identity of the head; admission was $1.[21] From September 17 to October 22, Love, Henderson, and another member of the Rangers took these drunken relics on a monthlong tour through the mining camps.[22] In February 1854, they were displayed in San Francisco by another former Ranger, John W. Chiles.[23] The reason for displaying these relics may have had less to do with public edification than with raising money for various members of Love's Rangers, but as an added bonus, it continued to fuel the debate about whether the head was in fact that of Joaquín Murrieta, a debate which, as it turned out, brought more visitors (figure 31).

Murrieta's head and the hand of Three-Fingered Jack were sold to a Judge Lyons and a Mr. Plume at a sheriff's sale in 1855.[24] They, in turn, sold them on the following day to a man by the name of Andrew J. Taylor or "Natchez" who placed them on view in his shop.[25] Within a year's time they were purchased again, this time by a Mr. Craigmiles who sold them again in June 1856.[26] By 1865, the head had passed into the possession of Louis J. Jordan, who exhibited it at his Pacific Museum of Anatomy and Natural Sciences in San Francisco (or the Robinson Museum, depending on the source).[27] Jordan's museum was said to have featured an Egyptian mummy, a cyclops child, and of course, Murrieta's head. A modern cabinet of curiosities, some say they remained there until the great earthquake of 1906 while others have argued that both had vanished by 1890.[28]

The contemporary author Richard Rodriguez, who has written and spoken on Murrieta numerous times, described his own journey to see Murrieta's decapitated head, not in the 1890s but nearly a century later. Taken by a Jesuit priest who had tracked the pickled head to a "two-bit museum" in Santa Rosa sometime prior to 1992,[29] Rodriguez described the visage as having open eyes, a cracked lip, and dark hair that floated "like sea grass." One can't help but wonder if this bobbling horror was indeed Murrieta's head or just a new chapter in the Murrieta myth.[30]

CHARLES CHRISTIAN NAHL

In 1868, Charles Christian Nahl painted *Joaquin Murrieta*, and for many years the painting was prominently displayed in the capitol in Sacramento. Nahl, a native of Kassel, Germany, was born in 1818 and later studied at the Kassel Academy.[31] In 1838 he exhibited his work at the Berlin Art Academy, and in 1846 he moved to Paris where, in the following year, he had a painting accepted into one of the prestigious salons of the era. In 1851, he and his family moved to San Francisco.[32] That Nahl was drawn by the lure of quick riches is demonstrated by the fact that once in California, he first settled in the mining town of Rough and Ready before moving to Newtown, where he claimed to have witnessed the "linching" of a man named "Brown" in 1852.[33] However, Nahl was unable to find the riches he had dreamed of and instead began painting portraits for the most successful miners, businessmen, and ranchers. He also exhibited scenes of California life and illustrated pamphlets and books,

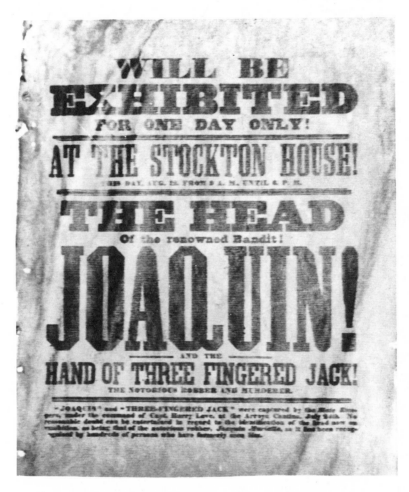

31. "The head of the renowned Bandit! Joaquin!" n.d. Courtesy of
University of Southern California, on behalf of the USC Specialized
Libraries and Archival Collections.

and in 1856 he designed the certificate of membership for San Francisco's most celebrated vigilance committee, of which Nahl was a member and was reported to have served his time on guard duty.[34]

The painting of the famous outlaw shows Murrieta riding horseback up a steep mountain trail — or could his poor beast be a mule? That sterile progeny is descended of the donkey and horse but whatever its ancestry, this undersized member of the Equidae family is rendered with an open mouth and flared nostrils as a single darting eye glares anxiously at its manic passenger.

In keeping with the principles of comparative physiognomy, Nahl has carefully matched Murrieta's expression with the horse's own. As such, the painting is a textbook example of how artists could use the principles of physiognomy to guide the viewer's interpretation (not unlike Stendhal and Balzac's use of physiognomy to guide the reader). Nahl translates the basic principles of comparative physiognomy into the theatrical exuberance of French Romantic painting in an attempt to cash in on the Murrieta craze — and he would also illustrate a pirated version of the Ridge tale for the notoriously sensationalist *Police Gazette*.[35]

In the Murrieta painting, Joaquín is depicted with dark skin, coal black hair, and two seemingly iris-less eyes that are closer to those of a shark than to a human being. His wavy hair and poncho blow horizontally and suggest the reckless speed of an escape, as he raises his knife as both a defiant challenge and a racialized threat to Anglos (and later to those legislators who worked in the capitol in which the painting hung). Nahl, a highly skilled academic painter, had intentionally disregarded his training and drawn Murrieta's eyes out of scale for his face, a point that is made even more explicit when one compares the Murrieta painting to Nahl's other paintings. For those less familiar with the painting conventions he is subverting, I would draw the reader's attention to the fact that the whites of the eyes are visible above the iris (or unnaturally enlarged pupil) in both the Murrieta image and in the rendering of the horse[36] (color plate 11).

Nahl also completed a number of paintings addressing the already much romanticized image of the Spanish past or "Spanish heritage," as it is still known. In these images one can begin to recognize that already unstable racial, ethnic, and national stereotypes begin to break down further once gender enters into the equation. From the fear of racial mixture, a strange fetishization began to occur, and Mexican women could be transformed from Mexicans into "Spanish" senoritas and doe-eyed temptresses in Nahl's paintings, even as their husbands and sons continued to be cast as vaqueros, drunkards, and bug-eyed bandits.

Beyond the overt romanticism of the Murrieta painting, it is clear that Nahl's depiction doesn't quite match Captain Love's description of Murrieta, which described him as being catlike, about 22 years of age, of light complexion and light brown hair, with penetrating blue eyes, a high forehead, a sparse beard, and a scar across his right cheek.[37] A description of Murrieta's head was published in September 1853; it may be the earliest published description of the head and is quite insistent that its physiognomy reveals the character of the man in every detail. It reads as follows:

> The head itself is in complete state of preservation, and bears the impression of his character in every feature and lineament. . . . The forehead is high and well developed, the cheek bones elevated and prominent, and the mouth indicative at once of sensuality, cruelty. . . . The hair, of a beautiful light brown with a golden tint, is long and flowing; the nose high and straight, and the eyebrows, which meet in the middle, dark and heavy — the eyes, now closed in death are said to have been dark blue, with a keen restless glance and when excited a glare of ferocity like that of an infuriated tiger. . . . There is a thin beard like that of a young man who had never shaved. . . . Under his right eye there is a small scar. . . . The death of this monster is an occasion for general rejoicing.[38]

Addressing the use of physiognomy in literature, Graham sarcastically concluded that "a nice problem occurs in the portrayal of the mythical god or unseen historical figure since the idea of the character must be expressed in a recognizable form, leading to a character typology, or, in degeneration, to stereotyping.[39] In extending Graham's observation to the painted image, one must conclude that Nahl was less interested in following the published descriptions of the man than in creating an image, a character typology, that could give form to one of the most mythologized figures in California history. To do this he had to extend his gaze beyond the physical world, generating a stereotypical image steeped in the positivism of eighteenth- and nineteenth-century physiognomy, giving a physical form to what Anglo-Americans imagined to be the most monstrous of Mexicans (figure 32).

THE WONDER GAZE

On February 19, 1854, one newspaper described the summary execution of two "Mexican" men in Mariposa County, explaining that even though the alleged criminals were already in the custody of the sheriff, they were forcibly "liberated" from their cells and taken to the scene of the crime, where they

32. Boeringer, "Head of Joaquin Murrieta," n.d. Courtesy of California History Room, California State Library, Sacramento, California.

were tried and found guilty by a "hanging party." The unnamed journalist then went on to describe the scene: "Their bodies are now swinging to the limb where they were executed, and will probably continue to boast the wonder gaze of the public until time and decomposition shall allow them to fall to pieces."[40]

This invocation of a "wonder gaze" is particularly fascinating, not only because it speaks to the notion of the spectacle or of the scopic pleasure audiences found in looking at or reading about two lynched Mexicans, but because it lays the groundwork for thinking about the lynching postcard and photographic images of those condemned to die. It can even be traced to the continued fascination with, and display of, the head in a jar long after its authenticity had been broadly accepted. Each of these examples can be seen as a part of the wonder gaze, and each required the mandatory presence of the public, as a participant, as a spectator, as a consumer of images, or as a paying audience. The physical presence of a group was central to the Tuskegee definition of a lynching, but in the history of lynching and summary execution this "public" was actually far greater in number than simply those who attended the fatal event. The acceptance of lynching by a relatively small community of participants, and the subsequent dispersal of images, articles, or public displays of support, repeatedly served not only to mask the criminal actions of the mob, posse, or self-appointed vigilance committee but reinforced the image of the criminal body (and by extension the racial body) as different, villainous, and otherwise unworthy of sympathy. Empathy, when it existed, primarily existed between the lynch mob or posse and the communities they claimed to protect. It was this concept of the public that transformed these brutal acts into "popular" justice, a concept that has been lost in the current use of the term frontier justice. So the only real question that remains is, is empathy really possible with the lynch victim, with the criminal, with those marked by difference—real or imagined?

Jacques Lacan (1901–81), the French psychoanalyst, author, and teacher, imagined a very different kind of gaze. Unlike the 1853 appearance of the "wonder gaze," which sought to mark the pleasure of looking, in this case, at the spectacle of two decomposing Mexican bodies, Lacan, in his later essays, went to great efforts to distinguish the eye from the gaze.[41] In Lacan, the gaze is guided by the uncanny feeling of being gazed back at by the very object of our glance. He linked this phenomenon to the mirror stage and the lack which constitutes castration anxiety.[42] For Lacan, the symbolic order upon which the subject relies is undone by the materiality of the "real." In such a model, the gaze must be located in our relationship to things, objects, in so far as this relationship is constituted through vision, and "ordered in the figures of representation."[43] Lacan insists that something is lost in the gap between what we see and what we perceive. He posits recognition as a "transaction" within which the thing, he writes, "slips, passes, is transmitted, from stage to stage, and is always to some degree eluded in it—that is what we call the gaze."[44] In considering the representation of a lynching, this Lacanian "real" must be said to reside in the lynching itself. But in the absence of a temporal representation such as a film or sound recording, describing the act of lynching requires entry into language or culture; put more simply, it requires interpretation. Even something as descriptive as a lynching photograph can only provide the smallest and most circumstantial of experiences. Such photographs may then be pasted into an album, as in the Santa Rosa triple lynching, at which point it enters a new "stage." A copy print can then be made from the album and filed in the archive, which further alters its symbolic order, until finally it is represented in the pages of this book, which brings us back to Barthes's insistence that there can be no direct relationship to a photograph without "reflection" and no reflection without language.

Thus, the experience of the "real" tries to evade us at every turn, and while Lacan might conclude that such images become a screen upon which we project our own narcissist desires, these projections will not be the same for everyone. The idea that the United States of America is Anglo-American has clearly shaped the image of lynching in the popular imagination, which up until now, has effectively downplayed the impact of race, ethnicity, and nation in the history of the West. Thus, the challenge facing us today is not so much about casting all those who died from lynch mobs, vigilance committees, and posses as victims as it is in trying to suggest that while the absence of Latinos, Hispanics, Asians, and American Indians from this history may have been unavoidable, it is not unalterable. To put this idea into perspective, it may be useful to acknowledge the extent of anti-Mexican sentiments during the war with Mexico by using an example that is not included in the final appendix but which may serve to demonstrate that the lynching of Mexicans was not as "unreal" as most Americans believe.

The account details how a party of Mexicans had "murdered" several Americans at a rancho near Cerralvo, just south of the Texas border. The exact circumstances are never explained, but in retaliation, fifteen to twenty Americans descended upon a group of Mexicans. It is unclear if they were in fact the same Mexicans that perpetuated the crime, but the result was that "upward of forty Mexicans" were hanged on the spot.[45] Published in 1847, this account reminds one that the memory of a bloody war must have inflamed racial tensions on both sides, even after the war had ended.

A second and far more recognizable example can be found in a cartoon that was published during the war. The illustrator claimed to have discovered a new rule in algebra when, in the anticipation of chuckles among his readership, he summarized the rule as follows: "Five from three and One remains or The Three Mexican Prisoners, having but one leg between them all." The illustration to which the caption referred showed three Mexican prisoners missing five legs, in what can only be described as degraded caricatures of a people whom most agree had been invaded without provocation and had fought to defend their sovereignty.

Taken collectively, these acts of violence and misrepresentation were not isolated events but systemic of a culture and a nation, which used the spectacle of the fragmented, incomplete, or phantasmic bodies of "Mexicans" to justify westward expansion (figure 33).

Strangely, one of the greatest contradictions to this model can be found in the eroticism extended to the female "Mexican" body. A surprising 1853 newspaper article suggested that the Rangers, upon their return to Los Ange-

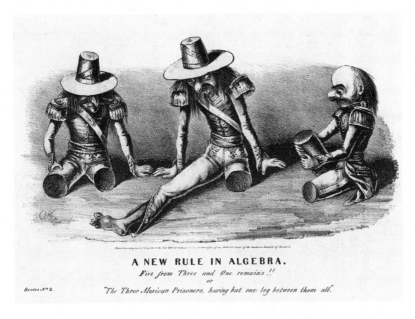

A NEW RULE IN ALGEBRA.

Five from Three and One remains !!

or

"The Three Mexican Prisoners, having but one leg between them all."

33. "A New Rule in Algebra," 1846. Courtesy of the Library of Congress.

les, were reported to have garnered "many approving glances from our dark-eyed senoritas."[46] But here the eroticization of Mexican women was limited to a situation in which they could be defined in relationship to the pleasure of being looking at, in this case, Anglo men being gazed upon by Mexican senoritas at the moment of their return from searching for Mexican bandits. One can't help but wonder if those glances were really as approving as they imagined.

JOSEFA OR JUANITA

On July 5, 1851, Josefa, also referred to as Juanita, entered the historical record when she became the first and only woman to be lynched in California's history.[47] A self-admitted murderer, she was hanged from the Jersey Bridge in Downieville before a crowd estimated to be composed of several hundred to several thousand men[48] (figure 34).

Many historians continue to define the mob's actions in this case as those of a vigilance committee, and not of a lynch mob, because an impromptu jury and judge were included in the proceedings, but it can hardly be said that she was tried by a jury of her peers; the assembled mob of Anglo-American

34. "Hanging of the Mexican Woman," n.d. Courtesy of California History Room, California State Library, Sacramento, California.

and European men were said to have rolled her defense lawyer down the hill on a barrel when he questioned the proceedings. The assembled crowd understood that she had been visited in the middle of the night by a popular Englishman named Fred (or Joe) Cannon, a man twice her size, and that he had either broken down her door or entered her tent (depending on the source) in the middle of the night. The stories all confirm that he returned several hours later; most suggest he went to apologize, but somewhere in the exchange he gives up on the prospect of approving glances and calls her a *puta*—a whore.[49]

The story goes that after calling her a prostitute, she replied by daring him to call her that within her own home, explaining that she would kill him if he did. Incredulous to the threats of a Mexican woman, he entered the house (or tent), and true to her word, she stabbed him in the heart, killing him nearly instantly. There is no doubt that she was a murderer and that she admitted to stabbing an Anglo man, but questions still linger in the details of the case.[50] Would she have been raped? Did he really call her a whore?[51] Was he drunk after one of the biggest celebrations the town had even seen? Was she really pregnant?[52] What did the doctors who examined her really do? Was the legal system sufficiently developed to provide her with a legal trial? Was her skull later dug up and used by a fraternal society?[53] We may never know the answer to these questions but one thing is clear, Josefa was not the "screen" that Cannon had anticipated or imagined, and her refusal to provide him the pleasure of the gaze, whether it was the acceptance of his apology or otherwise manifested, transgressed acceptability and ultimately transformed her into something monstrous before a mob of several hundred men, for whom, a Mexican woman with a knife was no woman at all.

After the murder, she was arrested, tried, sentenced, and hung within several hours' time. Walking up to the scaffold she was said to have exhibited no fear, "first gracefully removing two plaits of raven black hair from her shoulders to make room for the fatal cord" and then "placing the rope round her neck with her own hands."[54] When asked if she had anything to say, she replied, "Nothing; but I would do the same again if I was so provoked."[55]

She was variously described as being in her early twenties, tastefully dressed, neat, plain, or "with the eyes of a devil"; one early resident of Downieville would later say that she was of good character and above the average camp women of the times.[56] Even Bancroft weighed in on the case when he (or one of his researchers) wrote, "The man she murdered offered no violence, and she had no right to kill him. The people were right to hang her, but they were wrong to do it madly and in the heat of passion."[57]

His comments remind me of an 1853 case in which three men condemned to be hung for horse stealing by the citizens of Los Angeles were given a temporary reprieve and sent to San Louis Obispo to stand trial. Traveling by steamer, they landed safely but were greeted by "the people," who were already assembled on the beach and who escorted them to the first tree and hung them. According to the report, the prisoners "uttered no complaints, made no confessions, and scorned the services of the padre, and were game to the last." When asked if they had a request to make, one of the them, a man by the name of Higuerro, replied that "he would die happy if he could be freed long enough to flog one Yankee." The article wryly informed the reader that "his request was not granted."[58] The point is that Josefa undoubtedly understood that a Mexican woman had extremely limited choices, but she chose to take a stand and rejected the narcissism of first her intruder's gaze and then the mob's.

LA CHOLA MARTINA

Nearly completely forgotten, one woman was a witness to Los Angeles's most turbulent period when vigilantes, lynch mobs, and posses scoured southern California. Unfortunately, she left no journal or letters to be read, but I was able to uncover two copies of a photograph taken in the first decades of the twentieth century. Known as "La Chola Martina," according to the hand-written note across the back of one the photographs, she was said to have

aided Juan Flores, the bandit, in killing Sheriff Barton and his posse, two con-
stables and a blacksmith among them.[59] Some accounts suggest that she was
Indian; others simply describe her as one of Flores's many sweethearts who
aided the bandits by tampering with the guns of the sheriff's posse while they
ate breakfast at the rancho of Don José Sepulveda[60] (color plate 12).

According to the handwritten note on the back of the second photograph,
her name was Martina Espinoza.[61] The photograph was in the massive collection of C. C. Pierce, a Los Angeles–based photographer, active from 1886 to
1940, who collected and rephotographed nearly every photograph he could
get his hands on, often selling copy prints and the rights to reproduce them
to newspapers and other print publications, regardless of who actually took
the photograph.[62] He also took many images himself and would go to some
effort to find characters who had a place in early California history. For example, he took many images of Mission Indians, the old land grant families,
and famous locations throughout the southland, selling them whenever possible. As may be familiar to some readers, adding the Spanish "*la Chola*" to
her name marked her as unsavory figure.

Chola, or its masculine form, *cholo*, can be translated as hooligan or scoundrel, and after 1830 in the West, it usually meant a "Mexican scoundrel,"
"Mexican half-breed," or mestizo. In 1860, one newspaper defined *cholos* as
the "lower class of Sonoranians";[63] more than simply a demarcation of class,
it foregrounded skin color and specifically distinguished cholos from those
Spanish-speaking, Spanish-surnamed, land grant–holding California families.[64]

In the photograph, Martina, an old woman, stands before an old two-
story wooden clapboard building. The street is of unpaved earth. There is
no sidewalk but a wooden plank walk can be seen tapering off toward the
right end of the photograph. Flores had been a young man when she knew
him, barely twenty-one when he died, and so she would have been young as
well. In the photograph, she holds a cane in one hand but it is really more of
a stick. The top is wrapped in a rag to cushion her hand. Her other hand is
clutched tightly, its contents, if any, remain a mystery. Her fingers are long
and thin, wrinkled from age and sun. Assuming she was around twenty years
of age in 1857, the same age as Flores, one could date the picture sometime
between 1900 and 1920, well within Pierce's working period. She wears a
well-worn and sun-bleached cotton dress covered in what appears to be a
flower pattern. Her head and neck are covered with a white piece of fabric.
Tied under the chin, the fabric hangs loosely about her chest, the soft curled
ends revealing that it has been laundered many times. A dark cape or piece of

fabric is wrapped around her shoulders and hangs to the ground. The fabric is bunched and drapes in untailored tufts, suggesting that it may be more than one piece of cloth.

Her sun-baked face squints defiantly in the noonday sun, and her mouth is creased into what appears to be a frown. The wrinkles on her brow suggest impatience, frustration, or the sun's glare. An unseen leg presses against the edge of the dress. She waits patiently. Has the photographer given her money to pose? Is there money clutched in her fist? The harsh light and thinly hewn posts in the background, in combination with the angle of the cane, give the image a brittle appearance. Her narrow fingers curve in sharp angles as she forcefully grasps the cane's knotted and slightly soiled end, pressing one shoulder high about the other. Escaping the vengeance of the lynch mob and the posse, she survived one of the most heated moments in California history only to find herself silenced by the camera's lens.

INSURGENTS OR OUTLAWS

> J. E. Johnson, the comic singer returned last week from a professional tour in the southern part of the State. He Says Los Angeles is in every way entitled to the notoriety claimed for it, of being infested with the most reckless set of desperadoes that ever made highway robbery a business and sheriff killing a pastime. He remained a couple of weeks in the place, and saw five men killed and about twice that number stabbed."[65]

The author's characterization of the city is openly challenged by the *Los Angeles Star* in its November 27 issue, calling it a slander, "which is as astonishing as it is degrading and repulsive."[66] Without addressing the accuracy of the charge against the city, it is clear that part of the distaste for southern California had to do with its Mexican, Mexican American, mestizo, and Spanish-speaking populations, signaled by the use of the term desperados and the phrase sheriff killing, which was a direct reference to the murder of Sheriff Barton by the notorious Pancho Daniel and Juan Flores gang the year before.

Some have argued that tensions between Latinos and Anglos began three years earlier in May 1855, when Myron Norton, then judge of the Court of Sessions of Los Angeles County, sentenced two men to the state prison: Juan Gonzales, who had the previous year acted the part of hangman in the summary execution of Dave Brown, and a young man by the name of Juan Flores.[67] Horace Bell, in his much-cited memoir, described Juan Flores in the following manner:

A dark complexioned fellow of medium height slim, lithe and graceful, a most beautiful figure in the fandango or on horseback, and about twenty-two years old. There was nothing peculiar about Juan except his tiger-like walk — always seeming to be in the very act of springing upon his prey. His eyes, neither black, grey, nor blue, greatly resembling those of the owl — always moving, watchful and wary, and the most cruel and vindictive-looking eyes that were ever set in human head.[68]

The use of comparative physiognomy is hinted at in the passage and suggests the subtle influence of physiognomy. Flores, along with Pancho Daniel, an escaped convict from San Quentin and notorious in his own right, would be credited with leading the Daniel-Flores band which was said to include nearly fifty "Spanish Americans" in what may have constituted the largest (if loosely associated) band of robbers and thieves in California's history.[69] The history of their exploits has been widely cited in nearly every account of early California history, but in returning to many of the most prominent historical texts and original newspaper accounts, this chapter attempts to summarize the period, paying particular attention to the means of execution, be it by vigilance committee, sheriff's posse, or volunteer groups of Germans, European Americans, or California's native-born Latinos.

Referred to by Major Horace Bell as an "embryo revolution," members of the Daniel-Flores band made their way to San Juan Capistrano when things began to heat up in January 1957. The gang was reported to have robbed a store and killed a German shopkeeper by the name of George W. Pflugardt.[70] The illusion to an "embryo revolution" is found in several texts and is specifically intended as a reference to the war of reform in Mexico, but for Bell, and given the fact that the bandits had robbed a fellow Latino, his invocation of a revolution is more satiric than literal.[71]

As noted, Sheriff Barton, with six men at his side, five armed and one guide, set out to investigate the murder, and in spite of being warned at the home of José Sepulveda, a prominent Californian of Spanish and Mexican descent, against taking on such a dangerous group with such a small posse, the sheriff set out to find the band when they were ambushed.[72] Martina has been blamed with tampering with the guns, but there is no evidence to support this version of events, and from a narrative perspective, it could be argued that her invocation only serves to shift the focus away from the fact that the sheriff was undermanned and to villainize the young Martina. Barton and all but two of his men were killed, and the bandits were said to have lost three of their number.[73]

News of the sheriff's death traveled fast, and Anglos in Los Angeles feared that the band, now rumored to consist of one hundred well-armed men, "threatened extermination to the Americans," with the added aside that they would surely offer protection to the native Californians.[74] As a result of these rumors, over one hundred volunteer Rangers and Native American guides set out after the outlaws.[75] After a fierce shootout, Flores and Daniel were captured by the El Monte Rangers, but they managed to escape. The El Monte Rangers were a volunteer force largely from "the Monte," a region just east of Los Angeles, and were said to be primarily composed of one-time Texas Rangers, hence their name and, one might add, their heightened severity in dealing with Mexican and Mexican-American bandits.[76] The Rangers, also known as the "El Monte Boys," while traveling to and from their camp in *Los Nietos*, were frustrated by the escape of Flores and Daniel and were desperate to capture outlaws when they lynched Encarnación Berreyesa.[77]

A few days later the *Los Angeles Star* ran an article explaining that four men had been hung at the mission in San Gabriel on January 29; their names were Diego Navarro, Juan Valenzuela, Pedro López, and one unnamed man.[78] There was, of course, no documented proof that any of these men had any connection to the death of Sheriff Barton, and if that wasn't bad enough, one account claims that at least two of the condemned men fell before the job was done, because the ropes were poorly fastened, and had to be shot. The unnamed fourth man was José Santos, and he was later recorded as having died from "the people having taken the administration of justice into their own hands."[79]

The article also reported that another man by the name of Miguel Soto of the Flores band was already dead. Apparently he tried to hide in a reed-filled marsh when the Rangers burned the reeds and shot him; like Murrieta, he was decapitated to prove that he had been killed.[80]

Some historians have argued that Juan Valenzuela, Pedro López, and Diego Navarro were only incidentally connected with the bandits; others argue that their guilt was certain. Speaking of Navarro, one historian summarized the sad event when he states, "They hanged the innocent boy next to three dangling corpses, and, when his torn noose dropped him to the ground alive, they shot him. His wife arrived at the very moment, and Navarro died in her arms"[81] (figure 35).

A posse of native Californians was also organized by Don Tomás Sánchez and (General) Andrés Pico in order to assure the panicked Anglo community of their own desire for law and order. Pico and his men are credited with having captured and hanged to a sycamore tree the Sonoranian Fran-

35. "Execution Scene in Los Angeles by the Vigillance Committee," 1863.
Courtesy of the Department of Special Collections, Charles E. Young
Research Library, UCLA.

cisco Ardillero, alias "Guerro Ardillero," and Juan Catabo, alias "Juan Silvas,"
"Juan Sauripa," and "El Catabo," at the Yorba Ranch in Los Angeles County
on January 30, 1857.[82]

It is at this point that there is an interesting split in the tale. Fearing that
there might be some doubt as to how the two men were disposed of, Don
Andrés spoke to one of his men who galloped up the canyon and returned
wearing a pendant from his neck, something called "shot-pouch fashion,"
which he was said to have described as "a most beautiful necklace made of
human ears strung on a raw-hide string," which was intended to provide con-
clusive evidence that their former owners had been disposed of.[83] However,
two letters detailing the events of the week and published in the local newspaper argued that the men had left the two bodies "when a Monte man resolved upon the trophies" and turned back to get them. This version is wholly
rejected by the *Los Angeles Star*. Whatever their origin, the "trophies" eventually ended up at the Montgomery Saloon, where they satisfied the wonder gaze of a thirsty public. Speaking of the mood in town, the article's author wrote, "The thirst for blood is insatiable with a great many, and a broad
distinction is made between Californians and Americans," suggesting that
Hispanics would not have been well received had they chosen to enter the
establishment.[84] Thus, if Pico's men had acquired the relics, it seems unlikely
they would have been able to deposit them at the Montgomery Saloon since

their own safety would have been threatened; of course, we may never know which version was the most accurate.

Sometime between February 2 and 8, José Jesús Espinosa was captured near present-day Ventura, and after being given the services of a local priest was promptly lynched to a tree.[85] Meanwhile back in Los Angeles over fifty-two Latino men had been arrested since Sheriff Barton's death, but only about twenty remained in jail when, at a town meeting, Judge Scott suggested they be given one more week to clear themselves; the motion was passed by the assembled citizenry, against the protests of the Monte men.[86]

On February 14, 1857, the *Star* reported that two unidentified Mexicans had been discovered hanging from tree, while a third Mexican lay shot nearby; unfortunately the exact location for this "hanging party" was never given.[87] On this same day, the infamous Juan Flores was captured with three of his comrades, after what was nothing less than a spectacular chase.

Once captured, Flores and three of his band were brought into the city and Judge Scott, overseeing what was becoming an ever-increasing band of vigilantes, called for a popular vote. A decision was made to turn the three minor band members over to the law and to immediately hang Flores from the newly erected gallows on Fort Hill in downtown Los Angeles. They proceeded to the new gallows past a "quiet throng of 3,000 observers" and hung him with a noose that was too short to kill him efficiently, causing a protracted death which one newspaper summarized by saying that, "The unfortunate wretch struggled in agony for a considerable time."[88] The English language newspaper suggested that the rope had actually been intended as a bit of poetic justice, because Flores was hanged from a noose made from the *riata*, or lasso, that had belonged to one of the sheriff's slain deputies. Unfortunately, the rope was not long enough, and as a result, once on the gallows, the fall was insufficient to break his neck. Rumors also circulated in the Spanish language newspaper *El Clamor Público* that the rope was intentionally made too short in order to cause as much suffering as possible.[89] If nothing else, the Flores case strongly suggests that being hung by a trained executioner had one distinct advantage over the vigilance committee or lynch mob; it promised a quick death.

Farther north, a "Mexican" named Miguel Blanco was summarily hanged in San Luis Obispo for attempting to stab Sheriff Twist.[90] On the same day two men were legally executed in Los Angeles, one by the name of Thomas King and the other by the name of Luciano Tapia, also known as Leonardo López, and who pleaded his innocence to the end. Many lamented his fate because he was believed to have been a law-abiding citizen before his brief association with the Flores-Daniel gang."[91] Speaking from the gallows, Luciano directed his fellow Sonoranians "to leave the country, as it was no place for them."[92]

In the northern region of the state, two days after Flores's death, another Latino by the name Anastácio García was summarily hanged in Monterey.[93] García had been an acquaintance of the young Tiburcio Vasquez and a man by the name of José Higuera, and they all got into a saloon brawl that resulted in the death of a local constable by the name of Hardmount. Vasquez and García both fled the scene, but Higuera was captured and lynched the following day.[94] Higuera and García were tried and summarily executed for the same murder.

In 1856, García had managed to escape twice from police but was seen in various locales before he was finally captured and sent by ship to Monterey.[95] In 1857 he was indicted for the 1854 murder of constable Hardmount as well as for the murders of five other men: Isaac B. Wall, Thomas Williamson, Joaquín de la Torre, Charles Layton, and an unnamed Indian.[96]

García was followed by two more lynchings, the first of a young Indian boy known only as "Lopez" who was being held in Monterey on murder charges and the second of a black "desperado" by the name of Aaron Bracey who lived in the Gold Rush town of Auburn and was identified in a deathbed testimony by the man whom he had stabbed in the back of the head with a pick ax.[97] Lopez was lynched because the "people" disagreed with the governor's decision to give him a three-week respite due to procedural error by the district court. Further, the newspaper argued, "It was, also, shown that there were men upon the jury that condemned the boy, who had been of the vigilance set that had hung the real murderer; whilst this lad had not been guilty. The whole affair demanded investigation, which mob rule prevented."[98]

In the Bracey case, the mob stormed the jail, overpowered the sheriff, broke down the cell doors with sledgehammers, beat the man, and then so botched the hanging that he had to be lowered back down to adjust the rope which had slipped up around his nose.[99] In this same year, a Chinese bandit was summarily executed by a "committee," and an Anglo man by the name of "Morgan" was hanged in Gold Springs, near Columbia."[100]

Over the next few months, six members of the Pío Linares band, both Mexican and California born, would meet death at the end of a rope. As for Linares himself, he would escape the hangman's noose but not the vigilantes. He was shot. The first of his band to be captured was a young man by the name of Ysidro Silvas, and he would be found hanged from the roof of his cell after he was visited by a group of concerned citizens which included Honorable Judge Murray, whose views on "unwashed" Mexicans were mentioned in chapter 2.[101]

In May, Joaquín Valenzuela was captured and identified as one of five Joaquíns who had initially been named in the hunt for "Joaquín" before he came to be known as Joaquín Murrieta. Valenzuela had been a hunted man ever since the rough and tumble days of Murrieta and met his end when he was summarily hanged in Santa Barbara.[102]

In June, an unnamed Mesteño Indian, José Antonio García, Desiderio Grijalva, Miguel Blanco, and Nieves Robles, Latinos of both Mexican and Californian descent, were all summarily executed in Santa Barbara.[103] In August of the following year, there were two more summary executions in nearby Carpenteria when Francisco Badillo and his sixteen-year-old son were lynched to an oak tree.[104]

There would be even greater excitement when the much-reviled Pancho Daniel was finally captured and brought to Los Angeles to be tried on charges in connection with the murder of Sheriff Barton. On November 27, 1858, the local newspaper had gotten fed up after Daniel had spent months in custody and ran an article on the ongoing and troubled trial. It noted that while the murder of Sheriff Barton had occurred in February of the previous year, there had been numerous delays in the case. The article drew particular attention to the fact that Sheriff Murphy of Santa Clara County had delivered Daniel to Los Angeles on January 19, 1858, after he had been captured in, of all places, a haystack.[105] In February, the grand jury ordered the case to be transferred to the district court, thus postponing the actual arraignment for the murders of Baker, Day, and Pflugardt until March 15.[106] There was a change of counsel due to the retirement of a Col. Kewen, and as a result the trial was reset for March 22.[107] Daniel's counsel then requested that the case be rescheduled for the July term, which it was. In July, due to series of conflicts with regard to jury selection, the jury was dismissed and a new trial was set for August. In August, the new jurors were again discharged and a new date was set for the November term. In November, jury selection continued to be problematic, and the attorney for the defense requested a change of venue to Santa Barbara County, which was granted.[108] Thus, days after various stories of the failings of the legal system ran in the paper, one emphasizing the necessity of "obedience to the law of the land" and the other proclaiming its outrage at a legal system that was both slow and inefficient, a group of citizens assembled at the courthouse just before sunrise to clarify where they stood on the issue.[109] They knew the sheriff would not greet them because he was out of town on business.[110] What transpired next is detailed below:

It appears that at an early hour of the morning, about daylight, a number of persons met the jailer at the door of the prison and demanded the keys of him. These he refused to give up, but the party being numerous and well armed would not be denied, and seeing that resistance would be useless, he handed them the keys. They then went into the yard, bound the prisoner and brought him out; the rope was in readiness, it was put around his neck, he was led to the gate of the jail yard, and assisted to mount an office stool, the rope was fastened to the cross beam, a black handkerchief bound around his face, the stool was knocked from under him and the body of Pancho Daniel swung in the air. . . . After hanging an hour, the body was taken down and conveyed to the upper part of the town by some Californians or Mexicans.

During the day, an inquest was held on the body before Justice Hale. A great number of witnesses were examined; the jury returned a verdict "that deceased came to his death from strangulation, by a crowd of persons to the jury unknown."[111]

On the same day that this account appeared, the newspaper ran a second article that offered a slightly more progressive view, condemning the individuals more on principal than in an actual call for justice. The vigilantes were never identified and the subsequent investigation, a formality. It stated:

On Tuesday morning [November 30], a deed was perpetrated in this city, which we cannot permit to pass without notice. It was the execution, without sanction the sanction or from of law, of a fellow being; one who—even admitting his guilt—was entitled, by the constitution, to the benefit of a fair and impartial trial. The victim of this high handed and criminal proceeding was Pancho Daniel. The crime for which he was executed, was, the perpetration of, or participation in, the murder of the late Sheriff Barton and his assistants. Under this charge he had been confined to jail nearly a year, awaiting trial; term after term passed, and he was not tried. The technicalities of law, as is asserted, may have been taken advantage of, to defeat the ends the ends of justice. But from the many indictments against him, and the testimony to be produced to sustain them, we have no doubt but that justice would have eventually been meted out to him, and the majesty of the law vindicated. Whilst awaiting the hand of the law, he was seized on by a band of men, and led from the prison to instant execution . . . If we are to be governed by the laws enacted under the constitution, then let the action of these laws be general. Let there not be statute law for one man, and lynch law for another. If we are to have anarchy and confusion prevail, let the announcement be made, so that all may take warning . . . The exhibition on Tuesday last,—apart from its criminality—will reflect disgrace upon the community, which years will not obliterate.[112]

The Daniel case is significant in a number of ways, but by far the most important aspect of the case was that the legal system was working. It may not have been working well, but the fact that such a fully developed system was in place certainly challenges one of the main tenets of frontier justice, that the only form of justice available in the West was popular justice.

DISAGREEABLE, MUNDANE, AND POTENTIALLY VIOLENT

The historian Leonard Pitt wrote his now controversial work, *The Decline of the Californios*, in 1966. The attentive reader has undoubtedly noted that I have referenced his text and have included cases of lynchings and summary executions from it. Like Bancroft, it was a valuable source from which to work, and like Bancroft, it does not adequately address the impact of race, ethnicity, or nationality on the history of lynching and summary execution in California.

Today, many Latino, Hispanic, and Chicano scholars take serious issue with Pitt, and for good reason; even in his own day, he appears to have resisted the growing force of the civil rights movements on the West Coast in his insistence on referring to Chicanos and Hispanics as "Spanish-speaking" Californians, because he claimed that "Spanish-speaking" did not "smack of jargon."[113] However, as a term, "Spanish-speaking" can now be recognized as forcibly denying the impact of the indigenous peoples on the "Spanish Heritage" in the West.

In the final chapter of his book, entitled "Schizoid Heritage," Pitt writes that "California" saw the "Spanish-speaking as living at once in two disharmonious worlds, one mythic, the other real. The mythic world emphasizes the 'Spanish' past—carefree, unchanging, and enveloped in a religious aura; the other is a 'Mexican' world—disagreeable, mundane, potentially violent."[114] For Pitt, the "real" is that Mexicans were seen as "disagreeable, mundane, potentially violent"—they were the schizoid in schizoid heritage. As should be clear from this book's extended consideration of the Latino image in the West, it is only by acknowledging the intersection of such characterizations that we can hope to put an end to the pathologizing image of the "Mexican" body. Unlike Pitt's book, this book does not accept that this schizophrenia lies within the Latino experience but is projected upon it, as an extension of the gaze.

Lynching in the West reveals that once stable concepts like type, race, ethnicity, nationality have all been unable to adequately address—to make visible, to fix—the Latino experience, and it is the mutability of these narratives that has contributed to the erasure of Mexican, Mexican American, Chilean, Peruvian, or other Latin American persons and their descendants from the history of lynching nationwide. By extension, the lynching of African Americans, American Indians, and Asians are also isolated from one another and from Latinos, which has only served to further diminish the impact of race on this history.

Pitt's emphatic and even brutal emphasis on the "decline" of California's earliest Latino families implies that there was a time in which dark-skinned Latinos and Hispanics were seen as equal to Anglo-Americans, but as the previous chapters have noted, this was hardly the dominant view. In fact, by the end of the nineteenth century, the lynching of Latinos had declined, even as new waves of Mexican and Latin American immigrants continued to enter California as they strove to create better lives for themselves and their children (which many of them did). The civil rights movement had yet to come, and strategies of self-empowerment (economic, political, and social) were just beginning to take hold in what is actually a great American story.

It has been the contention of this book that in stepping out from beneath the haunted shade of California's past, the history of lynching may actually hold the potential to once again radically shift the understanding of race and ethnicity in this nation, even as racial categories themselves have fallen into question. In revealing his refusal to name the Latino body, Pitt's book reinforced dominant historical narratives and appears to have simply replaced the old stigmas of impurity, racial mixture, and cultural fragmentation with the modern equivalent of the monstrous. Rejecting the hybridization of culture (if not race as well), Pitt has split the Latino body in two through the pathologizing image of a schizoid heritage. In equating the "Mexican world" with the disagreeable, the mundane, and the potentially violent, Pitt has done little more than transform the nineteenth century's emphasis on physical difference, as found in the image of the desperado, the bandito, and the greaser, with a psychoanalytic model which, instead of marking exterior differences, attempts to locate difference within the Latino body itself.

Major Horace Bell, in his colorful account of life in early California, recounts one story that derived from a court case regarding, of all things, the ownership of a mule. However, as his account makes clear, the question of ownership depended upon witness testimony. In this particular case, the defendant's attorney objected to the testimony of two Latino men—two mestizo men, on the grounds that the witnesses were not white men, and according to the law, only whites could testify against other whites. There may be some irony in that, like the mule which is a sterile hybrid, the mestizo was sterile in the eyes of the law.

The plaintiff's counsel maintained that the burden of proof rested with the defendant to prove the witnesses were not white men. As a result, the defendant's attorney called on three experts in "physiology" who, after giving their credentials, were asked if they could by any scientific method determine the difference between "a person of pure white blood and a mongrel."[115] The experts maintained that in comparing the salivary glands of whites and those of mixed-blood they would be able to distinguish the rounded glands of the "mixed breed" from the elongated glands of a white man.[116] But after unsuccessfully attempting to look inside the witness's mouth, the defendant's attorney then asked if there was any other way of determining the racial status of the witness.

"Yes, certainly there is," the doctor answered, and "seizing the upper and lower eyelid of the other witness and turning his eye-ball inside out, and was greatly astonished at the subject springing to his feet, with tears streaming from one eye and sparks of indignation flashing from the other, and yelling *carajo!*"[117]

The court then ordered the interpreter to inquire of the "learned physiologist" what he meant by such unseemly conduct, to which he replied, "Inform his honor that I was about to demonstrate that in a white man the two small orifices called punctalachrimalia, at their intersection with the nasal ducts. . . ."[118] After which, the defendant's attorney asked, "Is there no more practical manner of settling this question?"[119]

"Oh, yes," replied the doctor, drawing a pair of "old pullicans" from his pocket.

"You see, in the white man the wisdom teeth grow straight down into the body of the jaw, and have three strongly developed roots; in the black or mixed breeds the wisdom teeth grow solidly and firmly into the ramus, and have but one root, and to settle this matter definitely I will now proceed to extract a wisdom tooth," explained the doctor. Bell concludes the tale by stating that before the doctor could demonstrate the procedure, the "the birds had flown."[120]

The humor of the scene, whether scientifically meaningful or not, rests in the imagined differences of the Latino body in the nineteenth century. Once believed to be a meaningful biological fact, race is now described in sociocultural and psychological terms. The nineteenth-century view of race as a biological category has been supplanted by the realization that race does not reflect meaningful biological or genetic distinctions.[121] Race, ethnicity, and even notions of nationality are enabled and enforced though social norms, and while they may not be "real," in any absolute sense, they are deeply rooted in the consciousness of individuals and groups. Thus, even though today many Latino communities are defined as ethnic identities, the history of lynching reveals that this was not always the case.

In appendix 1, the reader will see that of the 132 persons of Latin American and Mexican descent that were lynched or summarily executed in California from 1850 to 1935, only 16 were specifically identified as being born in California or Texas. Another 11 were identified as coming from Sonora, Mexico. Ten were identified as being Chilean, and of those, 4 were also identified as being Mexican. Five were identified as being either Spanish or Mexican, but in the vast majority of cases, the victims were identified only as "Mexican." This is not to suggest that they were Mexican nationals or that they had all been born in Mexico (though some of them undoubtedly were), but that in a history of contested acts, the term "Mexican" washed over difference with the same ease rope slides over skin.

CONCLUSION

"I don't recollect the incident," I replied plainly. It happened so long ago. But the truth was, I lied, even now. We heard rumors that there had been an awful fight, and after it was over an American named Taylor lay dead. Word came up river that they had caught a Mexican and there would be a trial, so we made our way to town. By nightfall there must have been a hundred men wandering the streets or at the saloon. It was just before midnight when the men assembled the jury. I guess it wasn't much of a surprise that the Mexican was found guilty. They sent for me and I tied the knot. It wasn't the first time I had been called on. It was just right, thirteen smooth coils around a noose. The greaser didn't say much, and when it was all done the noose slid over his bare neck. Someone yelled "Pull," and his body rose silently from the ground and then stopped with a jerk. Against a dark night sky, I heard a gasp of air escape from his twisted form and it was over.[1]

I read the passage at a small art gallery before these chapters were ever finished. I decided to base the story on the Gold Rush accounts I had been reading, but rather than writing from the perspective of a Mexican who had been lynched, I decided to imagine the story as told by an Anglo-American lyncher. Conceptualized as a performance, or at least a performative act, the reading was intended to expose the audience to the history of lynching in the West. My costume, if one can call it that, was a well-pressed shirt and a pair of trousers. However, there was one other element that the reader may not be able to visualize. As a Latino man, I wondered how my physical presence might play into the reception of the piece. I could not anticipate how my physical presence, the space of the gallery, or the racial or ethnic backgrounds of the audience might influence its reception. In speaking for a character that was imagined to be wholly descended from northern Europeans, I had sought to deflect, or at least to undermine, what I have termed the "wonder gaze." I did not wish to become the greaser. I did not wish to be lynched. And yet, I wanted the audience to have an awareness that historical forces, not of our making, had brought us together. Anticipating the audience's gaze, I sought to head it off at the pass, so to speak, by drawing their attention back to a sequence of actions, the character's, my own, and theirs, and by acknowledging the literal symbolism of my bodily presence—a presence that cannot be isolated from the legacies of Western racial formation, and yet a body whose own *dangerous mixture* might render it illegible.

By the end of the nineteenth century, Manifest Destiny, phrenology, eugenics, physiognomy, and criminology had each sought to draw meaning from physical appearance, a phenomenon which, as I have attempted to suggest, can at least in part be traced back to Lavater's "science" of physiognomy, even as later notions sought to recodify and reconfigure older biases or, like Pitt's *Decline of the Californios*, create new ones. How could I deflect the audience's gaze away from my own body and toward their own, toward a history we all share?

Chapter 1 demonstrated how the image of frontier justice overlooked the presence of persons of color in California's history of lynching and how this absence has contributed to a false binary of black against white in the national consciousness. It is my hope that with the creation of a new case list for the State of California (provided in appendix 1) that this project might one day encourage others to look to other states. It was also my hope that these new statistics might one day be incorporated into the national statistics on lynching. Having laid out what I believe to have been some of the main factors contributing to the historical absence of Western lynching from the national landscape, chapter 2 tried to approach the historical debates surrounding legal executions by tracking their emergence and evolution throughout the latter half of the nineteenth century. The statistics derived from the study of legal executions (appendix 2) also demonstrate that, unlike lynching or vigilantism, the presence of racial bias was diminished in legally sanctioned executions.

Chapter 3 considered the impact of the institutional, regional, and subject archives and their reliance upon the copy print in shaping historical awareness—and this issue is of increasing interest as an expanding number of institutions begin to digitize their material holdings. In practice, the backs of photographic images are almost never reproduced as either copy prints or digital files, a logistical reality that in the case of lynching photographs can also lead to the loss of information, such as a handwritten note across the back. Digital libraries and archives are some of the fastest growing resources in the nation, and questions of metadata coding provide an amazing opportunity to rethink the very categories, or values, traditionally assigned to a given object. Beyond the conventional emphasis on author, subject, title, date, and media, digital technology can also provide new levels of access and potenitally draw attention to new properties of the source object.

Given such opportunities for rethinking objects and the histories they embody, chapter 4 began from the basic question, Where did racism against Latinos and Mexicans really come from? As a racial slur, the greaser may have been one of the first truly Western inventions. The chapter demonstrated that while there had been bias against Latin Americans, American Indians, Africans, and Asians, very few European race theorists had given much serious thought to the peoples of Mexico between the discovery of the New World and the war with Mexico. For this reason, the chapter went back and looked to racial typologies developed in Europe in order to demonstrate that racial bias in the American West was not merely a regionalist construction but that its roots stretched back well beyond Darwin's characterization of the unblushing "Spaniards." Just as physiognomy and racial positivism had played a central role in the creation of a new American type (the Anglo-American), it was also responsible for positioning the image of the bandito, the desperado, and the greaser as its nemesis.

Picking up on this thread, chapter 5 looked at the myth and facts surrounding the life of Joaquín Murrieta, California's most infamous Gold Rush bandit. But rather than addressing the full breath of the Murrieta literature which, needless to say, merits a book of its own, this chapter focused upon the commercial display of his head after his death. This chapter also gave some depth to the horror of lynching by addressing dozens of cases because, it must be argued, knowing that a history of lynching existed and reading the details of the cases can be two very different experiences. The reader was introduced to the wonder gaze, a concept which sought to acknowledge the spectacle of lynching and to reveal that like other forms of violence and bias, the full impact of lynching extends far beyond the lynch victim him or herself and can impact families, communities, and individuals for generations.

Approaching the question of erasure from a slightly different perspective, this book has sought to suggest that unlike the notion of "invisibility," these cases were widely recorded in their own day; they were not so much unseen

as they were displaced.² But *Lynching in the West* is about more than historical correction alone; it is about the ways that racial positivism, criminal anthropology, and anxieties surrounding racial mixing continued to exert their
influence well into the twentieth century as notions like the "born criminal" gave way to new but increasingly pathologizing images, of racial and
racialized communities. Perhaps most importantly, the chapters have also attempted to lay to rest a history which haunts not only me but all Americans
and reminds us that with citizenship comes responsibility and that justice
must be more than mob rule.

In foregrounding the analysis of images, this book has sought to suggest
that even images of terror may hold the potential for social change, in this
case, potentially transforming the Western image of the hang tree from a
nostalgic fantasy of frontier justice into a sight of remembrance for those
now gone.

Having walked the unmarked ground and stood in the wet morning grass,
I have gazed into the haunted shade of California's past and come to the realization that whether dragging my 8 by 10 Deardorff camera under the hot
summer sun or waiting for the morning fog to lift, my actions, like those
who have gone before me, may one day be forgotten—but they can never be
undone.

Case List of Lynchings and
Summary Executions

The case list was compiled by Kenneth R. Gonzales-Day on March 18, 2005, from an extensive number of sources. Some sources are listed in the individual chapter notes, but a full list of sources could not be included in this publication.

Minor variations in the spelling of names or in the date were common among the multiple sources. If the month was known but sources conflicted as to the date, then "oo" is used to signal that the precise date is unknown. If the month and date are both in question, then a question mark is used to signal that the month and date are unknown. As new sources are uncovered, future scholars may be able to expand and improve the list presented here.

The determinations of origin were derived from primary and secondary source materials. As noted in chapter 4, "Mexican" could refer to actual or perceived racial, ethnic, or national origin. Where available, additional information is included; for example, "Sonoran" (Sonoranian) referred to persons born in Sonora, Mexico; Calif/Mex refers to Mexican Americans or native Californians, as they were known throughout the second half of the nineteenth century; Anglo/Euro is used to refer to Anglo-Americans and persons of European descent.

Those cases included in the Tuskegee Institute Archive case files (as of February 2005) and/or the NAACP's *Thirty Years of Lynching* are marked with an "x" in the Date column.

Where possible, errors have been corrected, and major variations in name have been included in parentheses.

The following is a statistical breakdown of the case list:

Total number of persons lynched or summarily hanged in California since it became the thirty-first state in the Union on September 9, 1850: 352
Total number of women: 1

Lynched or summarily hanged by race, nationality, or ethnicity
African American: 8
American Indian: 41
Chinese (not including those shot in 1871 massacre): 29
Anglo-American or person of European descent: 120
    Anglo-American (identified by state of origin): 13
    Europeans, Canadians, and Australians: 28
        Australia (Sydney) and not counted below: 4
        Belgium: 1
        Canada (French): 1
        Denmark: 1
        England: 8
        France: 3
        Germany: 1
        Ireland: 3
        Italy: 2
        Norway: 1
        Scotland: 1
        Spain? "Spaniard" named "Charley the Bull Fighter": 1
        Sweden: 1
        Switzerland: 1
Identified as Latin American or Mexican: 132
    Identified as Chilean: 6
    Identified as Mexican: 126
        Identified as Mexican and/or Spanish: 5
        Identified as Mexican and/or Chilean: 4
        Identified as coming from Sonora, Mexico: 11
        Identified as Mexican national by U.S. government: 1
        Identified as being born in California: 15
        Identified as being born in Texas: 1
Unknown race, nationality, or ethnicity: 22

Date	Name	Town	County	Alleged Crime	Origin
Oct. 00, 1850	Devine	Georgetown	El Dorado	Murder	Unknown
Dec. 25, 1850	Sharp	Auburn	now Placer	Murder	English
Jan. 00, 1851	Unnamed	Nicolaus	Sutter	Horse thief	Unknown
Jan. 00, 1851	Unnamed	Double Springs/ South Fork	Calveras	Murder	Mexican
Jan. 7, 1851	Pablo	Agua Fria	Mariposa	Murder	Mexican
Feb. 00, 1851	Bowen	Curtis's Diggings/Southern Mines	Unknown	Murder	Unknown
Feb. 00, 1851	Unnamed (1 of 2)	Murphy's Diggins	Calaveras	Robbery	Irish
Feb. 00, 1851	Unnamed (2 of 2)	Murphy's Diggins	Calaveras	Robbery	English
Feb. 24, 1851	Frederick J. Roe	Sacramento	Sacramento	Murder	English
March 00, 1851	Easterbrook	Shasta City/ Redding's Spring	Shasta	Murder	Anglo/Euro
March 00, 1851	Evans	Long Bar	Middle fork of the Yuba River	Horse thief	Rhode Island
March 00, 1851	Coyote Joe	Jackson	Calaveras	Murder	American Indian
March 00, 1851	James Knowlton aka Yankee Jim	Bridgeport	Nevada	Horse and cattle thief	Anglo/Euro
March 7, 1851	Unnamed (1 of 2)	Cosumnes River	Unknown	Horse thief	Unknown
March 7, 1851	Unnamed (2 of 2)	Cosumnes River	Unknown	Horse thief	Unknown
April 00, 1851	Unnamed	Sacramento City	Sacramento	Gambling	Unknown
April 12, 1851	Andrew R. Scott	Pinchemtight	El Dorado	Murder	Anglo/Euro

Date	Name	Town	County	Alleged Crime	Origin
May 00, 1851	Hamilton McCauley	Napa	Napa	Governor commuted sentence	Anglo/Euro
May 00, 1851	Unnamed (1 of 5)	Scott's Ferry/ San Joaquin River	Unknown	Horse and cattle thief	Mexican
May 00, 1851	Unnamed (2 of 5)	Scott's Ferry/ San Joaquin River	Unknown	Horse and cattle thief	Mexican
May 00, 1851	Unnamed (3 of 5)	Scott's Ferry/ San Joaquin River	Unknown	Horse and cattle thief	Mexican
May 00, 1851	Unnamed (4 of 5)	Scott's Ferry/ San Joaquin River	Unknown	Horse and cattle thief	Mexican
May 00, 1851	Unnamed (5 of 5)	Scott's Ferry/ San Joaquin River	Unknown	Horse and cattle thief	Mexican
May 12, 1851	Cherokee Bill	Hornitas	Mariposa	Horse thief	American Indian
May 29, 1851	George Baker	Outside Stockton	San Joaquin	Unknown	Anglo/Euro
June 11, 1851	John Jenkins	San Francisco	San Francisco	Larceny	Sydney
June 15, 1851	Antonio Cruz (1 of 2)	Shaw's Flat	Calveras	Murder	Mexican
June 15, 1851	Patricio Janori (2 of 2)	Shaw's Flat	Calveras	Murder	Mexican
July 00, 1851	Jim Hill	Campo Seco	Calaveras	Larceny	Anglo/Euro
July 5, 1851	Josefa aka Juanita	Downieville	Now Sierra	Murder	Mexican
July 11, 1851	James Stuart	San Francisco	San Francisco	Larceny	Sydney
Aug. 10, 1851	William Otis Hall	Monterey	Monterey	Bandit	Anglo/Euro

Date	Name	Town	County	Alleged Crime	Origin
Aug. 22, 1851	William Heppard alias Robinson	Sacramento	Sacramento	Larceny	New York
Aug. 24, 1851	Robert McKenzie	San Francisco	San Francisco	Larceny	Irish (Sydney)
Aug. 24, 1851	Sam Whittaker	San Francisco	San Francisco	Larceny	English (Sydney)
Nov. 8, 1851	Abner J. Dixon	Mud Springs	El Dorado	Murder	Wisconsin
Nov. 12, 1851	Natchez	Mokelumne Hill	Calveras	Larceny, murder	Mexican
Nov. 14, 1851	Domingo	Turnersville	Tuolumne	Murder	Mexican
Dec. 00, 1851	William (David) Brown	Rich Bar	Forks of Feather River	Larceny	Swedish
Dec. 00, 1851	Unnamed	Indian Gulch	Calveras	Murder	Mexican
? 1852	Sam Green	Mokelumne Hill	Calveras	Murder	Texas
? 1852	Joshua Robertson	Rich Bar	Sacramento Valley	Robbery	African American
Feb. 11, 1852	John Bucroft (1 of 2)	Murphys	Calveras	Larceny	Sydney
Feb. 11, 1852	Charley Bucroft? (2 of 2)	Murphys	Calveras	Larceny	Sydney
March 3, 1852	Unnamed	San Gabriel	Los Angeles	Murder	American Indian
March 4, 1852	Brown	Newtown	Nevada County	Larceny	African American
March 30, 1852	Carlos Eslava (Eslaves)	Mokelumne Hill	Calveras	Murder	(Sonora) Mexican
April 00, 1852	James Edmundson aka Jim Ugly	Dry Diggings	El Dorado	Murder	Anglo/Euro
April 12, 1852	Flores	Mokelumne Hill	Calveras	Murder	Mexican

Date	Name	Town	County	Alleged Crime	Origin
April 29, 1852	James Hughlett	White Oak Springs	Unknown	Unknown	Anglo/Euro
May 00, 1852	Joaquín Valenzuela	San Luis Obispo	San Luis Obispo	Kidnapping	(Sonora) Mexican
May 11, 1852	Unnamed (1 of 2)	Mission of San Buenaventura	now Ventura	Murder	American Indian
May 11, 1852	Unnamed (2 of 2)	Mission of San Buenaventura	now Ventura	Murder	American Indian
June 00, 1852	José Cheverino	Jackson	Calveras	Murder	"Spaniard" Mexican
June 00, 1852	John Jackson	Sutter Township	Sutter	Murder	Norwegian
June 00, 1852	Raymond aka Roger	Big Bar on the Cosumnes River	Unknown	Murder	French
June 00, 1852	Unnamed (1 of 2)	Rough and Ready	Nevada	Murder	American Indian
June 00, 1852	Unnamed (2 of 2)	Rough and Ready	Nevada	Murder	American Indian
June 00, 1852	Unnamed (1 of 3)	Bridgeport	Yuba	Murder	American Indian
June 00, 1852	Unnamed (2 of 3)	Bridgeport	Yuba	Murder	American Indian
June 00, 1852	Unnamed (3 of 3)	Bridgeport	Yuba	Murder	American Indian
June 00, 1852 (Hanged by Chinese)	Unnamed	Mud Springs	El Dorado	Murder	American Indian
June 11, 1852	Cruz Flores	Jackson	Calveras	Murder	"Spaniard" Mexican
June 12, 1852	Washington Rideout	Nicholas	Sutter	Murder	African American

Date	Name	Town	County	Alleged Crime	Origin
June 17, 1852	Grovenor I. Layton	Sonora	Tuolumne	Robbery, murder, arson	Anglo/Euro
July 20, 1852	Mariano (Domingo) Hernandez	Santa Cruz	Santa Cruz	Thief	Calif/Mex
July 21, 1852	Capistrano	Santa Cruz	Santa Cruz	Horse thief	Mexican
July 21, 1852	Unnamed	Santa Cruz	Santa Cruz	Horse thief	Mexican
July 31, 1852	Jesús Rivas (1 of 2)	Los Angeles	Los Angeles	Murder	(Sonora) Mexican
July 31, 1852	Doroteo Zavaleta (2 of 2)	Los Angeles	Los Angeles	Murder	Calif/Mex
Oct. 5, 1852	Michael Grant	Weaverville	Trinity	Murder	Anglo/Euro
Nov. 29, 1852	Reyes Feliz	Los Angeles	Los Angeles	Murder, robbery	(Sonora) Mexican
Dec. 5, 1852	Benito López	Los Angeles	Los Angeles	Murder	(Sonora) Mexican
Dec. 5, 1852	Cipriano Sandoval	Los Angeles	Los Angeles	Murder	(Sonora) Mexican
Dec. 25, 1852	Barumas	Los Angeles	Los Angeles	Murder	(Sonora) Mexican
Dec. 25, 1852	William K. Jones	Sacramento	Sacramento	Murder	Unknown
? 1853	Canosky (1 of 2)	Eureka	Humbolt	Murder	Anglo/Euro
? 1853	MacDonald (2 of 2)	Eureka	Humbolt	Murder	Anglo/Euro
Jan. 00, 1853	Big Bill	Yankee (Yaqui) Camp	Calveras	Murder	(Sonora) Mexican
Jan. 00, 1853	Unnamed	Cherokee Flat (Ranch)	Calveras	Murder	Mexican
Jan. 23, 1853	Unnamed	San Andreas	Calaveras	Murder	Mexican

Date	Name	Town	County	Alleged Crime	Origin
Feb. 1, 1853	Unnamed	Angel's Camp	Calveras	Looked suspicious	Mexican
Feb. 8, 1853	Unnamed (1 of 2)	Monterey	Monterey	Horse thief	Mexican
Feb. 8, 1853	Unnamed (2 of 2)	Monterey	Monterey	Horse thief	Mexican
Feb. 11, 1853	Unnamed (1 of 3)	Mud Springs	El Dorado	Larceny	Chinese
Feb. 11, 1853	Unnamed (2 of 3)	Mud Springs	El Dorado	Larceny	Chinese
Feb. 11, 1853	Unnamed (3 of 3)	Mud Springs	El Dorado	Larceny	Chinese
Feb. 15, 1853	Antonio Valencia	Jackson	Now Amador County	Larceny	Mexican
Feb. 20, 1853	Juan Sanchez	San Andreas	Calaveras County	Larceny	Mexican
Feb. 23, 1853	Unnamed	Reading's Ranch	Shasta	Cattle thief	American Indian
March 00, 1853	John Boyd	Colusa	Colusa	Attempted Murder	Anglo/Euro
March 10, 1853	C. Kanasta (1 of 2)	Yreka	Siskiyou	Murder	Anglo/Euro
March 10, 1853	George McDonald (2 of 2)	Yreka	Siskiyou	Murder	Anglo/Euro
April 1, 1853	Noland	Shasta-Whiskey Creek	Shasta Co	Murder	Anglo/Euro
May 23, 1853	Unnamed	American Flat	El Dorado	Murder	Mexican
July 25, 1853	Sánchez	Jackson	Calaveras	Horse thief	Mexican
July 27, 1853	Unnamed	Jackson	Calaveras	Murder	Chilean
Aug. 12, 1853	Charley the Bull Fighter	Gibsonville	Sierra	Murder	"Spaniard"

Date	Name	Town	County	Alleged Crime	Origin
Aug. 17, 1853	John Clare	Santa Cruz	Santa Cruz	Murder	Scottish
Sept. 4, 1853	José María Ochova (Ochoa)	Martinez	Contra Costa	Murder	Mexican
Oct. 00, 1853	Unnamed	Yreka	Siskiyou	Murder	French
Oct. 22, 1853	Higuerro (1 of 3)	San Louis Obispo	San Louis Obispo	Horse thief	Mexican
Oct. 22, 1853	Unnamed (2 of 3)	San Louis Obispo	San Louis Obispo	Horse thief	Mexican
Oct. 22, 1853	Unnamed (3 of 3)	San Louis Obispo	San Louis Obispo	Horse thief	Mexican
Nov. 00, 1853	Unnamed	Alvarado District	Alameda	Murder	"Spaniard" Mexican
Nov. 00, 1853	Unnamed	Columbia	Calaveras	Murder	Italian
? 1854	Mateo Andrade	San Luis Obispo	San Luis Obispo	Larceny	Mexican
? 1854	José Higuera (Guerra)	Monterey	Monterey	Murder	Mexican
Feb. 00, 1854	Unnamed (1 of 4)	Pitt River, Shasta	Shasta	Larceny	American Indian
Feb. 00, 1854	Unnamed (2 of 4)	Pitt River, Shasta	Shasta	Larceny	American Indian
Feb. 00, 1854	Unnamed (3 of 4)	Pitt River, Shasta	Shasta	Larceny	American Indian
Feb. 00, 1854	Unnamed (4 of 4)	Pitt River, Shasta	Shasta	Larceny	American Indian
Feb. 17, 1854	Unnamed	Mariposa	Mariposa	Murder	Mexican
Feb. 17, 1854	Unnamed	Mariposa	Mariposa	Murder	Mexican
March 15, 1854	Schwartz (Swarz)	Jackson	Amador	Horse thief	Swiss
May 30, 1854	Richie	Sonoma	Napa County	Horse stealing	Unknown

Date	Name	Town	County	Alleged Crime	Origin
June 21, 1854	Nemesio Berreyesa	San Vicente Rancho	Santa Clara	Murder	Calif/Mex
Aug. 23, 1854	Pierre Archambault (1 of 2)	San Antonio	Alameda	Cattle thief	Belgian
Aug. 23, 1854	Amedee Canu (2 of 2)	San Antonio	Alameda	Cattle thief	French
Sept. 00, 1854	Unnamed, Weimer Tribe	Grass Valley	Nevada	Murder	American Indian
Dec. 00, 1854	Macy	Volcano	Almador	Murder	Unknown
Dec. 24, 1854	William Johnson aka Long Johnson	Iowa Hill	Placer	Murder	Anglo/Euro
Jan. 00, 1855	David Brown	Los Angeles	Los Angeles	Murder	Anglo/Euro
Jan. 00, 1855	James Moran	Sawyer's Bar	Was Klamath	Murder	New York City
Jan. 3, 1855	George Seldon (Sheldon)	Oakland	Alameda	Horse stealing	Anglo/Euro
Jan. 20, 1855	Edward Crane Griffiths	Sonora	Tuolumne	Murder	English
Jan. 26, 1855	Salvador Valdés (1 of 3)	San Joaquin	Contra Costa	Cattle thief	Chilean
Jan. 26, 1855	Unnamed (2 of 3)	San Joaquin	Contra Costa	Cattle thief	Chilean
Jan. 26, 1855	Unnamed (3 of 3)	San Joaquin	Contra Costa	Cattle thief	Chilean
Jan. 30, 1855	Unnamed	Red Bluffs	Colusa	Mule stealing, escaped convict	Unknown
March 8, 1855	Unnamed (1 of 2)	Tuttletown	Tuolumne	Murder	Chilean
March 8, 1855	Unnamed (2 of 2)	Tuttletown	Tuolumne	Murder	Chilean

Date	Name	Town	County	Alleged Crime	Origin
May 00, 1855	William Watson	Turner Pass		Horse thief	Anglo/Euro
May 5, 1855	William Lomax	Sacramento	Sacramento	Murder	Anglo/Euro
July 1, 1855	John Fenning	San Antonio	Contra Costa	Arson, horse thief	Irish
July 31, 1855	Unnamed	Yreka	Siskiyou	Scott's Bar massacre	American Indian
July 31, 1855	Unnamed	Yreka	Siskiyou	Scott's Bar massacre	American Indian
July 31, 1855	Unnamed (Gave Weapons)	Yreka	Siskiyou	Scott's Bar massacre	African American
Aug. 00, 1855	Manuel Castro	Texas Bar	Amador	(Rancheria) murder	Texan/Mex
Aug. 00, 1855	Unnamed	Campo Seco	Amador	(Rancheria) murder	Mexican or Chilean
Aug. 00, 1855	Unnamed	Gopher Flat	Amador	(Rancheria) murder	Mexican or Chilean
Aug. 00, 1855	Unnamed	Sutter	Amador	(Rancheria) murder	Mexican or Chilean
Aug. 00, 1855	Unnamed (1 of 6)	Unspecified	Unspecified	Various	American Indian
Aug. 00, 1855	Unnamed (2 of 6)	Unspecified	Unspecified	Various	American Indian
Aug. 00, 1855	Unnamed (3 of 6)	Unspecified	Unspecified	Various	American Indian
Aug. 00, 1855	Unnamed (4 of 6)	Unspecified	Unspecified	Various	American Indian
Aug. 00, 1855	Unnamed (5 of 6)	Unspecified	Unspecified	Various	American Indian
Aug. 00, 1855	Unnamed (6 of 6)	Unspecified	Unspecified	Various	American Indian
Aug. 7, 1855	José (1 of 3)	Chili Town (Rancheria)	Amador	Horse thief	Mexican

Date	Name	Town	County	Alleged Crime	Origin
Aug. 7, 1855	Puertovino (2 of 3)	Chili Town (Rancheria)	Amador	Murder	Mexican
Aug. 7, 1855	Tancolino (3 of 3)	Chili Town (Rancheria)	Amador	Murder	Mexican
Aug. 15, 1855	Rafael Escobar	Jackson (Rancheria)	Amador	Murder	Mexican or Chilean
Sept. 00, 1855	Unnamed	Dog Creek	Shasta	Larceny	American Indian
Oct. 10, 1855	John S. Barclay	Columbia	Tuoloumne	Murder	New York
Oct. 20, 1855	Unnamed (1 of 4)	Hills Ferry	Stanislaus	Cattle thief	Mexican
Oct. 20, 1855	Unnamed (2 of 4)	Hills Ferry	Stanislaus	Cattle thief	Mexican
Oct. 20, 1855	Unnamed (3 of 4)	Hills Ferry	Stanislaus	Cattle thief	Mexican
Oct. 20, 1855	Unnamed (4 of 4)	Hills Ferry	Stanislaus	Cattle thief	German
Nov. 00, 1855	Unnamed	San Joaquin River	San Joaquin	Cattle thief	Unknown
Dec. 00, 1855	Harris	Alvarado	Alameda	Horse stealing	Michigan
Dec. 00, 1855	Hill	Alvarado	Alameda	Horse stealing	Illinois
Dec. 00, 1855	Unnamed	Unknown	Merced	Stealing cattle	Mexican
Feb. 00, 1856	Isadoro Soto	San Isidro	Monterey	Stealing cattle	Mexican
March 16, 1856	Unnamed	Coulterville	Maraposa	Murder	Chilean
March 00, 1856	Unnamed (1 of 2)	Bear Valley	Unspecified	Unknown	Chinese
March 00, 1856	Unnamed (2 of 2)	Bear Valley	Unspecified	Unknown	Chinese

Date	Name	Town	County	Alleged Crime	Origin
May 11, 1856	Unnamed (1 of 4)	Monterey	Monterey	Awaiting trial	Mexican
May 11, 1856'	Unnamed (2 of 4)	Monterey	Monterey	Awaiting trial	Mexican
May 11, 1856	Unnamed (3 of 4)	Monterey	Monterey	Awaiting trial	Mexican
May 11, 1856	Salvador (4 of 4)	Monterey	Monterey	Awaiting trial	American Indian
May 22, 1856	James P. Casey	San Francisco	San Francisco	Murder	New York
May 22, 1856	Charles Cora	San Francisco	San Francisco	Murder	(Genoa) Italian
June 27, 1856	A. J. Goff	Surprise Valley	Now Modoc	Murder	Anglo/Euro
July 29, 1856	Philander Brace	San Francisco	San Francisco	Murder	New York
July 29, 1856	Joseph Hetherington	San Francisco	San Francisco	Murder	English
Sept. 00, 1856	C. Colebrook	Angel Camp	Calveras	Murder	English
Oct. 00, 1856	Unnamed (1 of 2)	Happy Camp	Now Del Norte	Murder, Arson	Chinese
Oct. 00, 1856	Unnamed (2 of 2)	Happy Camp	Now Del Norte	Murder, Arson	Chinese
Oct. 00, 1856	Unnamed	Watsonville	Santa Cruz	Horse thief	Mexican
Oct. 00, 1856	Unnamed	Watsonville	Santa Cruz	Larceny	Calif/Mex
Oct. 6, 1856	Tomas J. Bell	Merced River	Sutter	Larceny	Tennessee
Jan. 29, 1857	Pedro López (1 of 4)	San Gabriel	Los Angeles	Barton murder	Mexican
Jan. 29, 1857	Diego Navarro (2 of 4)	San Gabriel	Los Angeles	Barton murder	Mexican
Jan. 29, 1857	José Santos (3 of 4)	San Gabriel	Los Angeles	Barton murder	(Sonora) Mexican
Jan. 29, 1857	Juan Valenzuela (4 of 4)	San Gabriel	Los Angeles	Barton murder	Mexican

Date	Name	Town	County	Alleged Crime	Origin
Jan. 30, 1857	Francisco Ardillero (Guerro Ardillero)	San Gabriel	Los Angeles	Murder	(Sonora) Mexican
Jan. 30, 1857	Juan Catabo (Silvas, Sauripa, El Catabo)	San Gabriel	Los Angeles	Murder	Mexican
Feb. 00, 1857	Encarnación Berreyesa	Near Ventura	Now Ventura	Barton murder	Calif/Mex
Feb. 00, 1857	José Jesús Espinosa	San Buenaventura	Now Ventura	Barton murder	Mexican
Feb. 00, 1857	Unnamed (1 of 2)	Los Nietos	Los Angeles	Unknown	Mexican
Feb. 00, 1857	Unnamed (2 of 2)	Los Nietos	Los Angeles	Unknown	Mexican
Feb. 14, 1857	Juan Flores	Los Angeles	Los Angeles	Barton murder	Calif/Mex
April 2, 1857	Unnamed (1 of 3)	Bangor	Butte	Murder of Chinese man	Unknown
April 2, 1857	Unnamed (2 of 3)	Bangor	Butte	Murder of Chinese man	Unknown
April 2, 1857	Unnamed (3 of 3)	Bangor	Butte	Murder of Chinese man	Unknown
May 1, 1857	Dean	Monterey	Monterey	Attempted murder	Anglo/Euro
Jan. 11, 1858	Lopez	Monterey	Monterey	Murder	American Indian
Feb. 00, 1858	Aaron Bracey	Auburn	Placer	Murder	African American
Feb. 11, 1858	José Anastacio (Anastasia) Garcia	Monterey	Monterey	Murder	"Spaniard" Mexican1
May 00, 1858	Ysidro Silvas	Santa Cruz	Monterey	Larceny	Mexican

Date	Name	Town	County	Alleged Crime	Origin
May 00, 1858	Joaquín Valenzuela	San Luis Obispo	San Luis Obispo	Murder	Mexican
June 00, 1858	Miguel Blanco	San Luis Obispo	San Luis Obispo	Murder	Calif/Mex
June 00, 1858	José Antonio García	San Luis Obispo	San Luis Obispo	Murder	Mexican
June 00, 1858	Desiderio Grijalva	San Luis Obispo	San Luis Obispo	Murder	Mexican
June 00, 1858	El Mesteño	San Luis Obispo	San Luis Obispo	Murder	American Indian
June 27, 1858	Nieves Robles	San Luis Obispo	San Luis Obispo	Murder	Mexican
Oct. 00, 1858	Unnamed	Cooks Bar	Unknown	Larceny and murder	Chinese
Nov. 30, 1858	Pancho Daniel	Los Angeles	Los Angeles	Murder	(Sonora) Mexican
Dec. 00, 1858	Harrison Morgan	Gold Springs near Columbia	Sacramento	Murder	Anglo/Euro
May 00, 1859	Unnamed boy	Unspecified	Tehama	Arson	American Indian
Aug. 23, 1859	Francisco Badillo (1 of 2)	Carpinteria	Santa Barbara	Horse thief	Mexican
Aug. 23, 1859	Francisco Badillo's son (2 of 2)	Carpinteria	Santa Barbara	Horse thief	Calif/Mex
Jan. 31, 1860	Thomas	Los Angeles	Los Angeles	Murder	American Indian
April 00, 1860	John O'Donnell	Downieville	Sierra	Murder	Anglo/Euro
June 8, 1860	Antonio Ruiz	Knight's Ferry	Stanislaus	Murder, rape	Mexican
April 28, 1861	José Claudio Alvitre	El Monte	Los Angeles	Murder	Mexican
Oct. 17, 1861	Francisco Cota	Los Angeles	Los Angeles	Murder	Mexican

Date	Name	Town	County	Alleged Crime	Origin
March 00, 1862	Unnamed (1 of 3)	between Elizabeth Lake and Fort Tejon	Now Kern	Cattle stealing	Unknown
March 00, 1862	Unnamed (2 of 3)	between Elizabeth Lake and Fort Tejon	Now Kern	Cattle stealing	Unknown
March 00, 1862	Unnamed (3 of 3)	between Elizabeth Lake and Fort Tejon	Now Kern	Cattle stealing	Unknown
Nov. 00, 1862	Manuel Cerredel	Los Angeles	Los Angeles	Murder	Mexican
Aug. 24, 1863	Unnamed	Gilroy	Santa Clara	Murder	American Indian
Nov. 21, 1863	Eli Chase (1 of 5)	Los Angeles	Los Angeles	Murder	Anglo/Euro
Nov. 21, 1863	Boston Daimwood (2 of 5)	Los Angeles	Los Angeles	Murder	Anglo/Euro
Nov. 21, 1863	José Olivas (3 of 5)	Los Angeles	Los Angeles	Murder	Mexican
Nov. 21, 1863	Wood (4 of 5)	Los Angeles	Los Angeles	Murder	Anglo/Euro
Nov. 21, 1863	Ybarra (5 of 5)	Los Angeles	Los Angeles	Murder	Mexican
Dec. 00, 1863	Charles Wilkins	Los Angeles	Los Angeles	Murder	English
Jan. 00, 1864	John Daly (1 of 4)	Aurora	Now Mono	Murder	Anglo/Euro
Jan. 00, 1864	Unnamed gang member (2 of 4)	Aurora	Now Mono	Murder	Unknown
Jan. 00, 1864	Unnamed gang member (3 of 4)	Aurora	Now Mono	Murder	Unknown
Jan. 00, 1864	Unnamed gang member (4 of 4)	Aurora	Now Mono	Murder	Unknown
Jan. 00, 1864	Gregorio Orosco	Monterey	Monterey	Deranged	American Indian

Date	Name	Town	County	Alleged Crime	Origin
Jan. 25, 1864	Unnamed	San Juan Capistrano	Los Angeles, now Orange	Murder	Mexican
Feb. 00, 1864	Patricino Lopez	Natividad	Monterey	Murder	Mexican
Feb. 18, 1864	Jesús Arellanes	San Pedro	Los Angeles County	Murder	Calif/Mex
May 00, 1865	Juan Igera	Santa Clara	Santa Clara	Murder	Calif/Mex
June 22, 1865	Charles Barnhart or William Riggs	near Susanville	Now Lassen	Murder	Anglo/Euro
Nov. 19, 1866	Whalebone	Chipps Flat	Sierra	Murder	Chinese
May 16, 1867	Elder Thompson	San Juan Capistrano	Now Orange	Assault	Anglo/Euro
Aug. 21, 1867	Estevan	The Alameda, San Juan Capistrano	Now Orange	Murder	American Indian
Aug. 25, 1868	B. S. Templeton	Visalia	Tulare	Unknown	African American
Aug. 00, 1869	Robbes	Lagrange	Stanislaus	Unknown	Mexican
March 16, 1870	Unnamed	Pajaro	Monterey	Horse thief	Mexican
May 17, 1870	Gregario Gómez (1 of 3)	Pajaro	Monterey	Horse thief	Mexican
May 17, 1870	Jesús Gómez (2 of 3)	Pajaro	Monterey	Horse thief	Mexican
May 17, 1870	Valentine Varaga (3 of 3)	Pajaro	Monterey	Horse thief	Mexican
Aug. 24, 1870	C. Olsen	Oroville	Butte	Murder	Unknown
Sept. 00, 1870	Juan de Dios Sepulveda	Bakersfield	Kern	Unknown	Calif/Mex
Sept. 26, 1870	Sacramento Duarte	Pajaro	Monterey	Horse thief	Mexican
Dec. 17, 1870	Michael Lachenais (Lachensi)	Los Angeles	Los Angeles	Murder	Anglo/Euro

Date	Name	Town	County	Alleged Crime	Origin
Oct. 24, 1871	Ah Cut (1 of 15)	Los Angeles	Los Angeles	Chinese riot	Chinese
Oct. 24, 1871	Ah Long (2 of 15)	Los Angeles	Los Angeles	Chinese riot	Chinese
Oct. 24, 1871	Ah Te (3 of 15)	Los Angeles	Los Angeles	Chinese riot	Chinese
Oct. 24, 1871	Ah Wha (4 of 15)	Los Angeles	Los Angeles	Chinese riot	Chinese
Oct. 24, 1871	Ah Won (5 of 15)	Los Angeles	Los Angeles	Chinese riot	Chinese
Oct. 24, 1871	Chang Linn (Chee Long Tong) (6 of 15)	Los Angeles	Los Angeles	Chinese riot	Chinese
Oct. 24, 1871	Day Kee (7 of 15)	Los Angeles	Los Angeles	Chinese riot	Chinese
Oct. 24, 1871	Fong Won (8 of 15)	Los Angeles	Los Angeles	Chinese riot	Chinese
Oct. 24, 1871	Gene Tong or Chee Lung Tong (9 of 15)	Los Angeles	Los Angeles	Chinese riot	Chinese
Oct. 24, 1871	Ho Hing (10 of 15)	Los Angeles	Los Angeles	Chinese riot	Chinese
Oct. 24, 1871	Leong Quai (11 of 15)	Los Angeles	Los Angeles	Chinese riot	Chinese
Oct. 24, 1871	Lo Hi (12 of 15)	Los Angeles	Los Angeles	Chinese riot	Chinese
Oct. 24, 1871	Unidentified (13 of 15)	Los Angeles	Los Angeles	Chinese riot	Chinese
Oct. 24, 1871	Wau Foo (14 of 15)	Los Angeles	Los Angeles	Chinese riot	Chinese
Oct. 24, 1871	Wong Chin (15 of 15)	Los Angeles	Los Angeles	Chinese riot	Chinese
? 1872	José Castro	Parajo	Monterey	Armed robbery	Mexican
Dec. 24, 1872	James McCrory	Visalia	Tulare	Murder	Anglo/Euro
March 17, 1873	Matt Tarpy	Parajo	Monterey	Murder	Anglo/Euro

Date	Name	Town	County	Alleged Crime	Origin
Aug. 20, 1873	Francke Torres	Santa Ana	now Orange	Murder	Mexicann
June 3, 1874	Jesús Romo aka El Gordo	El Monte	Los Angeles	Armed robbery	Calif/Mex
Dec. 17, 1874	Ernest Reusch	Markleeville	Alpine	Murder	Danish
Dec. 5, 1875	José Alvijo	Campo	San Diego	Horse thief	Mexican
Dec. 5, 1875	Raphael Martínez	Campo	San Diego	Horse thief	Mexican
Dec. 22, 1875	José Antonio Ygarra (Igarra)	Hopland/Ukiah	Mendocino	Murder	Calif/Mex
June 10, 1876	Charles (Thomas) W. Henley	Santa Rosa	Sonoma	Murder	Anglo/Euro
Nov. 24, 1876	Richard Collins aka Fighting Dick	Modesto	Stanislaus	Murder	Anglo/Euro
May 3, 1877	Francisco Arias	Santa Cruz	Santa Cruz	Murder	Calif/ Mestizo/ Mexican
May 3, 1877	José Chamales	Santa Cruz	Santa Cruz	Murder	Mestizo/ Mexican
July 13, 1877	Justin Arayo	San Juan Bautista	San Benito	Murder	"Spaniard" Mexican
Dec. 22, 1877	Fermin Eldeo (1 of 5)	Bakersfield	Kern	Horse thief	Mexican
Dec. 22, 1877	Francisco Ensinas (2 of 5)	Bakersfield	Kern	Horse thief	Mexican
Dec. 22, 1877	Miguel Elias (3 of 5)	Bakersfield	Kern	Horse thief	Mexican
Dec. 22, 1877	Anthony Maron (4 of 5)	Bakersfield	Kern	Horse thief	Mexican
Dec. 22, 1877	Bessena Ruiz (5 of 5)	Bakersfield	Kern	Horse thief	Mexican
Aug. 00, 1877	John McCoy	Unspecified	Modoc	Murder	Anglo/Euro

Date	Name	Town	County	Alleged Crime	Origin
May 2, 1878	Christian Mutchler	Germantown	Colusa	Arson	Anglo/Euro
May 7, 1878	Modoc Charlie	Walker Valley	Mendocino	Assault	American Indian
May 28, 1878	Thomas Yoakum (1 of 2)	Bakersfield	Kern	Murder	Anglo/Euro
May 28, 1878	William Yoakum (2 of 2)	Bakersfield	Kern	Murder	Anglo/Euro
July 6, 1878	Refugio Boca	Riverside	Now Riverside	Murder	Mexican
Sept. 4, 1879	Elijah Frost (1 of 3)	Willits	Mendocino	Larceny	Anglo/Euro
Sept. 4, 1879	Bige Gibson (2 of 3)	Willits	Mendocino	Larceny	Anglo/Euro
Sept. 4, 1879	Tom McCracken (3 of 3)	Willits	Mendocino	Larceny	Anglo/Euro
Jan. 17, 1881	Joseph DeRoche	Bodie	Mono	Murder	French Canadian
April 5, 1881	Francisco Jimemo	Lompoc	Santa Barbara	Rape, murder	American Indian
Aug. 7, 1881	Thomas J. Noakes	Oroville	Butte	Murder	Anglo/Euro
x-June 17, 1883	Encarnación García (Rayfield Morales)	Los Gatos	Santa Clara	Murder	Calif/Mex
x-July 9, 1883	Dennis Hagarty (1 of 2)	Marysville	Yuba	Murder	Anglo/Euro
x-July 9, 1883	Henry Dawling (2 of 2)	Marysville	Yuba	Murder	Anglo/Euro
Dec. 30, 1883	William Richardson	Eel River Island	Humbolt	Assault	Illinois
x-March 20, 1884	Joseph Dean	Modesta	Stanislaus	Murder	Anglo/Euro

Date	Name	Town	County	Alleged Crime	Origin
x-Dec. 00, 1884	William Pitts (William White)	Daggett	San Bernardino	Murder	Anglo/Euro
? 1885	Unnamed	Northern California	Unknown	Murder	Chinese
June 10, 1885	James Delaney	Mohawk/ Quincy	Plumas	Murder	Anglo/Euro
x-Aug. 12, 1885	Henry D. Benner (Henry L. Bemor)	Eureka	Humbolt	Murder	Anglo/Euro
x-Sept. 18, 1885	Dr. A. W. Powers	Bear Valley/ Hollister	San Benito	Incendiarism	Anglo/Euro
x-Jan. 23, 1886	Holden Dick (1 of 2)	Susanville	Lessen	Murder	American Indian
x-Jan. 23, 1886	Vicente Olivas (2 of 2)	Susanville	Lessen	Murder	Mexican
April 1, 1886	Peter Hemmi (1 of 2)	Aroyo Grande	San Luis Obispo	Murder	Anglo/Euro
April 1, 1886	James Hemmi (2 of 2)	Aroyo Grande	San Luis Obispo	Murder	Anglo/Euro
May 5, 1886	George Vuga	Drytown	Amador	Murder	Anglo/Euro
x-July 11, 1887	Hong Di	Colusa	Colusa	Murder	Chinese
x-Nov. 26, 1887	Frank McCutcheon	Oakdale	Stanislaus	Incendiarism	Mexican
x-Jan. 27, 1888	Fritz Auschla	Santa Ana	Now Orange	Murder	Anglo/Euro
x-May 5, 1888	John Wright	St. Helena	Napa	Murder	Anglo/Euro
x-March 18, 1889	B. S. Sprauge (Sprague)	Garvanza	Los Angeles	Murder	Anglo/Euro
April 30, 1890	Tacho	Banning	San Diego	Horse stealing	American Indian
May 12, 1890	E. L. Chriswell	Santa Maria	Santa Barbara	Murder	Anglo/Euro
x-Feb. 22, 1891	Oliver Reilly	Salado	Independence	Murder	Anglo/Euro

Date	Name	Town	County	Alleged Crime	Origin
x-June 15, 1891	Ah Anong Ti (Ah Quong Tis/Tia/Tai)	Bridgeport	Mono	Murder	Chinese
x-Aug. 25, 1891	Lee Oman	Locality undetermined	Unknown	Rape	Chinese
x-July 24, 1892	Charles Ruggles (1 of 2)	Redding	Shasta	Stagecoach robbery	Anglo/Euro
x-July 24, 1892	John D. Ruggles (2 of 2)	Redding	Shasta	Stagecoach robbery	Anglo/Euro
Aug. 21, 1892	Francisco Torres	Santa Ana	Orange	Murder	Mexican
x-Sept. 30, 1892	J. W. Smith	Dunsmuir	Siskiyou	Murder	Anglo/Euro
x-Nov. 11, 1892	Henry Planz	San Jose	Santa Clara	Unknown	African American
x-April 7, 1893	Jesús Fuen (Fulzen/Quien) San Bernardino	San Bernardino	Murder	Murder	Mexican
Dec. 12, 1894	William Dean	Fort Jones	Siskiyou	Murder	American Indian
x-July 26, 1895	Victor Adams	North Fork	Madera	Murder	Anglo/Euro
x-Aug. 26, 1895	Lawrence Johnson (1 of 4)	Yreka	Siskiyou	Murder	Anglo/Euro
x-Aug. 26, 1895	Luis Moreno (2 of 4)	Yreka	Siskiyou	Murder	Mexican National
x-Aug. 26, 1895	William Null (3 of 4)	Yreka	Siskiyou	Murder	Anglo/Euro
x-Aug. 26, 1895	Garland Stemler (4 of 4)	Yreka	Siskiyou	Murder	Anglo/Euro
x-Sept. 23, 1895	William Archor	Bakersfield	Kern	Murder	American Indian
x-Oct. 10, 1895	John Littlefield	Round Valley	Inyo	Murder	Anglo/Euro
x-May 31, 1901	Calvin Hall (1 of 5)	Lookout	Modoc	Petty theft	Anglo/Euro

Date	Name	Town	County	Alleged Crime	Origin
x-May 31, 1901	Frank Hall (2 of 5)	Lookout	Modoc	Petty theft	Unknown
x-May 31, 1901	James Hall (3 of 5)	Lookout	Modoc	Petty theft	Anglo/Euro
x-May 31, 1901	Martin Wilson (4 of 5)	Lookout	Modoc	Petty theft	American Indian
x-May 31, 1901	Daniel Yantis (5 of 5)	Lookout	Modoc	Petty theft	Anglo/Euro
x-July 9, 1901	Ah Sing Yong (Tung Fook)	Mt. Brecken-ridge	Kern	Assault	Chinese
x-March 11, 1904	James Cummings (or no name)	Mojave	Kern	Rape of boy	African American
x-April 15, 1904	B. H. Harrigan or Petrie	Dunamuir	Siskiyou	Rape	Anglo/Euro
x-April 23, 1908	Joseph Simpson	Skidoo	Inyo	Murder	Anglo/Euro
x-Sept. 3, 1918	Marion (Warren) Cezerich	San Pedro	Los Angeles	Murder	Anglo/Euro
x-Dec. 10, 1920	George Boyd (1 of 3)	Santa Rosa	Sonoma	Murder	Anglo/Euro
x-Dec. 10, 1920	Terrance Fitts (2 of 3)	Santa Rosa	Sonoma	Murder	Anglo/Euro
x-Dec. 10, 1920	Charles Valento (3 of 3)	Santa Rosa	Sonoma	Murder	Mexican
x-Nov. 26, 1933	John M. Holmes (1 of 2)	San Jose	Santa Clara	Kidnapping	Anglo/Euro
x-Nov. 26, 1933	Thomas H. Thurmond (2 of 2)	San Jose	Santa Clara	Kidnapping	Anglo/Euro
x-Aug. 3, 1935	Clyde L. Johnson	Yreka	Siskiyou	Murder	Anglo/Euro

Date	Name	Town	County	Alleged Crime	Origin
Excluded from case list:					
Oct. 00, 1849 (widely recorded as Oct. 1850)	Richard Cronin (Crone) aka Irish Dick	Placerville	El Dorado	Murder	Irish

Selected List of Legal and Military Executions

This selected list of legal and military executions was compiled by Kenneth R. Gonzales-Day, March 18, 2005, from an extensive number of sources. Some sources are listed in the individual chapter notes, but a full list of sources could not be included in this publication.

Minor variations in the spelling of names or in the date were common among the multiple sources.

As new sources are uncovered, future scholars may be able to expand and improve the list presented here. Three men committed suicide before they could be executed but are still included in the list. They were Frank Moore in 1857, David Butler in 1858, and Birchbeck in 1862.

The following is a statistical breakdown of legal and military executions:

Total number of cases: 103
Committed suicide prior to execution: 3
Totals by race, ethnicity, and nationality
    Identified as African American: 1
    Identified as American Indian: 10
    Identified as Chinese: 9
    Identified as Mexican or Mexican American: 18
    Anglo-American or European descent: 59

Specifically identified as: Yankee: 1
Australian: 1
English: 2
Irish: 2
Russian: 1
Spanish: 1
Unknown race, ethnicity, or nationality: 6

Year	Name	City	County	Origin
1851	James Hamilton aka Gibson (1 of 2)	Sacramento	Sacramento	Anglo/Euro
1851	John McDermot aka Thompson (2 of 2)	Sacramento	Sacramento	Anglo/Euro
1852	José Antonio	Martinez	Contra Costa	American Indian
1852	John Barrett (Garrat)	Nevada City	Nevada	English
1852	José Corrales	Sonora	Tuolumne	Mexican (Sonora)
1852	José Forner (Forné)	San Francisco	San Francisco	Spanish
1852	Tanner	Unspecified location	Unspecified	(Sydney) Australian
1852	Teodor Vásquez (Basques)	San Jose	Santa Clara	(Sonora) Mexican
1853	Jack Thompson (1 of 3)	Sutter's Fort	Sacramento	Anglo/Euro
1853	Barney Ackerman (2 of 3)	Sutter's Fort	Sacramento	Anglo/Euro
1853	Charles Stewart (Steward) (3 of 3)	Sutter's Fort	Sacramento	Anglo/Euro
1853	Unnamed (1 of 2)	Fort Reading	Shasta	American Indian
1853	Unnamed (2 of 2)	Fort Reading	Shasta	American Indian
1853	Unnamed (1 of 2)	San Diego	San Diego	Unknown
1853	Unnamed (2 of 2)	San Diego	San Diego	Unknown
1854	Robert Bruce	Unspecified location	Unspecified	Anglo/Euro
1854	Ignacio Herrera	Los Angeles	Los Angeles	Mexican
1854	James Logan (1 of 2)	Coloma	El Dorado	Anglo/Euro

Year	Name	City	County	Origin
1854	William Lipsely (2 of 2)	Coloma	El Dorado	Anglo/Euro
1854	Henry H. Monroe	Martinez	Contra Costa	Anglo/Euro
1854	William O'Brian	Mokelumne Hill	Calveras	Anglo/Euro
1854	Jack Roarke	Mariposa	Mariposa	Anglo/Euro
1854	William B. Sheppard	San Francisco	San Francisco	Irish
1854	John Thompson	Mokelumne Hill	Calveras	Anglo/Euro
1855	Felipe (Félix) Alvitre	Los Angeles	Los Angeles	Mestizo/ Mexican
1855	Samuel Garrett	Sacramento	Sacramento	Anglo/Euro
1855	Alex E. Higguns	Shasta	Shasta	Anglo/Euro
1855	José María Escobar (1 of 2)	Unspecified location	Unspecified	Mexican
1855	José Sebada (2 of 2)	Unspecified location	Unspecified	Chilean
1856	Nathan Cottle	Unspecified location	Amador County	Anglo/Euro
1856	Nicholas Graham	San Francisco	San Francisco	Irish
1856	William S. Kelly	Sacramento	Sacramento	Anglo/Euro
1856	Unnamed	Unspecified location	Unspecified	Chinese
1855–57	William S. Davis	Sonora	Tuolumne	Anglo/Euro
1857	James P. Johnson	Los Angeles	Los Angeles	Anglo/Euro
1857	Lyons	Sonora	Tuolumne	Anglo/Euro
1857	McCauley	Sonora	Tuolumne	Anglo/Euro
1857	Frank V. Moore	Nevada City	Nevada	Anglo/Euro
1857	Poer	Sonora	Tuolumne	Anglo/Euro
1858	David Butler aka Major C. Bolin	Nevada City	Nevada	Illinois

Year	Name	City	County	Origin
1858	Indian	Unspecified location	Amador	American Indian
1858	Henry F. W. Mewes aka Charles Dowse	San Francisco	San Francisco	Anglo/Euro
1858	Martín Rodriguez	Unspecified location	Placer	Unknown
1858	Stevenson	Unspecified location	Amador	Unknown
1858	Tomas King (1 of 2)	Los Angeles	Los Angeles	Anglo/Euro
1858	Luciano Tapia aka Leonardo López (2 of 2)	Los Angeles	Los Angeles	(Sonora) Mexican
1858	Fou Sin (1 of 3)	Jackson	Amador	Chinese
1858	Chou Yee (2 of 3)	Jackson	Amador	Chinese
1858	Coon You (3 of 3)	Jackson	Amador	Chinese
1859	William Morris aka Tipperary Bill	San Francisco	San Francisco	Anglo/Euro
1860	Frank Bonney	San Francisco	San Francisco	Anglo/Euro
1860	Albert Lee	San Francisco	San Francisco	Anglo/Euro
1860	Peter Lundberg	Sacramento City	Sacramento	Anglo/Euro
1860	Joseph N. Maes (1 of 2)	Unknown location	Placer	Unknown
1860	Genaro Quintano (2 of 2)	Unknown location	Placer	Unknown
1860	James Whitford	San Francisco	San Francisco	Anglo/Euro
1861	John C. Clarkson	San Francisco	San Francisco	Anglo/Euro
1861	Luis Kahl	Sacramento	Sacramento	Anglo/Euro
1862	Syriaca Arza	Los Angeles	Los Angeles	Mexican
1862	Birchbeck	Nevada City	Nevada	Anglo/Euro
1863	Thomas Burke	Nevada City	Nevada	English

Year	Name	City	County	Origin
1864	Santiago Sánchez	Los Angeles	Los Angeles	Mexican
1864	George N. Symonds	Sacramento	Sacramento	Anglo/Euro
1864	William William	Washington	Yolo	Anglo/Euro
1865	Tom Poole	Unknown location	Unknown	Anglo/Euro
1866	Thomas Byrnes	San Francisco	San Francisco	Anglo/Euro
1866	Robert Dodge	Nevada City	Nevada	Anglo/Euro
1866	Barney Olwell	San Francisco	San Francisco	Anglo/Euro
1866	Antonio Sassovitch	San Francisco	San Francisco	Anglo/Euro
1866	Chung Wong	San Francisco	San Francisco	Chinese
1867	Manuel Jaurez	Martinez	Contra Costa	Mestizo
1871	Ramón Amador	San Leandro	Alameda	Mexican
1872	Francisco García	San Quentin	Marin	Mexican
1873	John Devine aka The Chicken	San Francisco	San Francisco	Anglo/Euro
1873	Kientepoos (Captain Jack)	Unspecified location	Unknown	American Indian (Modoc)
1873	John Schonchin	Unspecified location	Unknown	American Indian (Modoc)
1873	Boston Charley	Unspecified location	Unknown	American Indian (Modoc)
1873	Black Jim	Unspecified location	Unknown	American Indian (Modoc)
1873	Charles Mortimer	Sacramento	Sacramento	Anglo/Euro
1873	Charles A. Russell	San Francisco	San Francisco	Anglo/Euro
1874	Marshall Martin	Martinez	Contra Costa	Anglo/Euro
1874	Unnamed (1 of 2)	Unspecified	Siskiyou or Placer	Chinese
1874	Unnamed (2 of 2)	Unspecified	Siskiyou or Placer	Chinese

Year	Name	City	County	Origin
1875	Filomena Cotta	Sacramento	Sacramento	Mexican
1875	Domingo Estrada	Sacramento	Sacramento	Mexican
1875	Corporal Frank Hudson	Camp Union	Sacramento	Anglo/Euro
1875	Tiburcio Vasquez	San Jose	San Jose	Santa Clara Calif/Mex
1876	Richard Collins aka Fighting Dick	Modesto	Stanislaus	Anglo/Euro
1877	James Hayes	Unspecified location	Unspecified	Anglo/Euro
1877	Chin Mook Sow	San Francisco	San Francisco	Chinese
1878	George Butts	Nevada City	Nevada	Anglo/Euro
1879	Anderson (1 of 2)	Sacramento	Sacramento	Anglo/Euro
1879	Dye (2 of 2)	Sacramento	Sacramento	Anglo/Euro
1880	Ah Luck aka Charlie Lock	Nevada City	Nevada	Chinese
1885	Stephen Jones	San Francisco	San Francisco	African American
1885	James O'Neill	Sierra County		Anglo/Euro
1885	Francisco Martínez (1 of 2)	Los Angeles	Los Angeles	Calif/Mex
1885	Adolfo Rodolfo Silvas (2 of 2)	Los Angeles	Los Angeles	Calif/Mex
1893	José Gabriel aka Indian Joe	San Quentin	Marin	American Indian
1895	Anthony Azoff (1 of 3)	Santa Cruz	Santa Cruz	Russian
1895	Patrick Collins (2 of 3)	Santa Cruz	Santa Cruz	Anglo/Euro
1895	Amelio García (3 of 3)	San Cruz	Santa Cruz	Mexican
1897	Benito López	Folsom	Sacramento	Mexican

Pardons, 1849–59

Term of Office	Governor	Number of Pardons
1849–51	Peter Burnett	1
1851–52	John McDougall	16
1852–56	John Bigler	78
1856–58	J. Neely Johnson	59
1858–59	John Weller	22

Source: *Los Angeles Star*, January 1, 1859.

NOTES

INTRODUCTION

1 *Southern News*, October 23, 1861; Newmark gives an account of the same case. Newmark, *Sixty Years in Southern California*, 309.

2 *Southern News*, October 23, 1861; Newmark, *Sixty Years in Southern California*, 305.

3 *Southern News*, October 23, 1861.

4 Das and Kleinman, *Remaking a World*, 4.

5 In spite of its other shortcomings, California's constitution repeated the precise wording found in the U.S. Constitution. *Constitution of the State of California*, 1849.

6 U.S. Constitution.

7 The *San Francisco Alta California* gives the date as February 8 and identified the posse as being from San Buenaventura. San Buenaventura is the name of the Mission church in Ventura, and Ventura is located between Santa Barbara and Los Angeles. Though the account gives no first name, the case matches in every detail. *San Francisco Alta California* (daily), February 15, 1857; *Los Angeles Star*, February 14, 1857; Boessenecker, *Gold Dust and Gunsmoke*, 128.

8 *Los Angeles Star*, February 14, 1857.

9 Boessenecker, *Lawman*, 104; Boessenecker, *Gold Dust and Gunsmoke*, 68–69.

10 His name was Nemesio Berreyesa. Bancroft refers to him as "Derassio Berreyessa" but cites the same exact date. Bancroft, *Popular Tribunals*, 1:476.

11 Nemesio is identified as "Derrasio Berreyesa" in the *San Francisco Alta California* and the lynching is dated as having occurred on July 21, 1854. The *Alta California* report confuses two of the brothers, as the posse may have, and based on reputation, another one of the brothers by the name of Demaso may have been an even more likely match. He lived until 1861, when he was killed escaping San Quentin prison. The initial "Derrasio" account matches every detail as the

"Nemesio" and "Nemasio" versions found elsewhere. *San Francisco Alta California* (weekly), July 29, 1854, 5; *San Francisco Alta California* (daily), July 30, 1854, 2; Pitt, *The Decline of the Californios*, 172; Boessenecker, *Lawman*, 104.

12 *San Francisco Alta California* (daily), June 30, 1854, 2.

13 Boessenecker claims that Ezekiel Rubottom headed the band of vigilantes from Los Angeles and that upon seeing the rope scar on Encarnación's neck the men hanged him. Pitt, *The Decline of the Californios*, 172; Boessenecker, *Lawman*, 104.

14 Readings on California's earliest vigilance committees, such as those found in San Francisco in 1851 and 1856–57, suggest that every attempt was made to emulate a legal trial; often representatives were assigned to the prosecution and the defense. With regard to their nationality, the Berreyesa brothers were all born in California before it became a state. *San Francisco Alta California* (weekly), July 29, 1854, 5; for more on vigilance committees, see Bancroft, *Popular Tribunals*, Vols. 1 and 2.

15 Boessenecker, *Gold Dust and Gunsmoke*, 68–69; Pitt, *The Decline of the Californios*, 30, 119, 172, 173; Boessenecker, *Lawman*, 104.

16 Vanderwood and Samponaro give a remarkable history of the picture postcard and have noted that the words *post card* only became legal in the United States in 1901 when changes in postal law allowed for the mailing of these now familiar objects. Vanderwood and Samponaro, *Border Fury*, 1.

17 For a detailed description of changes in postal law in the 1890s, and the increased availability of photographic technology made possible by George Eastman and others, see ibid., 1–7.

18 Gold was discovered at John Sutter's sawmill by James Marshall on January 24, 1848. Office of Historic Preservation, *California Historical Landmarks*, 45.

19 One contributing factor may have been the passage of 1854 legislation that required that all capital offenses be tried in the county seats.

20 My own case list confirms 352 lynchings and summary executions for the state of California between 1850 and 1935; Carrigan and Webb record a total of 597 persons of Mexican origin and descent being lynched nationally from 1848 to 1928. Carrigan and Webb, "The Lynching of Persons of Mexican Origin or Descent in the United States, 1848–1928."

21 Initial information on the case was established through a series of e-mails with Professor Michael Pfeifer at Evergreen State College. Pfeifer has been unable to definitively confirm the lynching in his own research on the case and he directed me to an article entitled "The Last Lynching in California." The article states that in 1995, Sgt. Giley of the Siskiyou County Sheriff's Department concluded that the alleged lynching was nothing more than "an effigy of the local town drunk, hanging from a utility pole, and that no lynching took place." Professor Pfeifer learned of the case from a man named Begley, who claimed to have seen a body hanged from a utility pole in 1947. Keith Arnold, "The Last Lynching in California," *Siskiyou Daily News*, May 12, 2003.

22 Letts, *California Illustrated*, 109; Varley, *The Legend of Joaquín Murrieta, California's Gold Rush Bandit*, 14; Hittell, *History of California*, 277–78.

23 Letts reported that the event occurred prior to his arrival. He left the gold fields by Fall 1849. Likewise, his account is the earliest to appear in print. Letts, *California Illustrated*, 109.

24 Alvitre has been identified as mestizo. Pitt, *The Decline of the Californios*, 160.

25 *San Francisco Alta California*, January 23, 1855.

26 Pitt, *The Decline of the Californios*, 161; Mayo, *Los Angeles*, 48.

27 Wilson, *Reproduction of Thomson and West, History of Los Angeles County with Illustrations and Biographical Sketches of its Prominent Men and Pioneers*, 78–79; Bancroft, *Popular Tribunals*, 1:494–95.

28 Mayo, *Los Angeles*, 38.

29 Pitt, *The Decline of the Californios*, 161.

30 Ibid.

31 Referred to as David or "DG" Brown in Windeler, *The California Gold Rush Diary of a German Sailor*, 127; and as William Brown in Shirley, *The Shirley Letters from California Mines*, 95.

32 The case also appears in Hittell's *History of California* as "William Brown" and matches details found in other accounts. Hittell, *History of California*, 3:305; Hittell cites *Pioneer Magazine* (vol. 2, 214, 219; vol. 3, 20), which published *The Shirley Letters from California Mines* in 1854–55.

33 Shirley, *The Shirley Letters from California Mines*, 95–96.

34 Windeler, *The California Gold Rush Diary of a German Sailor*, 127.

35 Ibid.

36 Ibid., 140–41; Shirley, *The Shirley Letters from California Mines*, 169.

37 Shirley, *The Shirley Letters from California Mines*, 169.

38 From letter nineteen, written to her sister in Massachusetts from Indian Bar on August 4, 1852. Ibid., 166–73.

39 The Tuskegee Institute Archives, the NAACP, and Walter White each record two cases involving the lynching of African Americans in the State of California. Their specific records will be addressed at length in the following chapter. Tuskegee Institute Archives, *Lynchings by State and Race, 1882–1968*, 37, 38, 40; NAACP, *Thirty Years of Lynching in the United States*, 52; White, *Rope and Faggot*, 235–36.

40 Tuskegee records a total of thirty cases for California, the NAACP records twenty-five, and White records fifty. Tuskegee Institute Archives, *Lynchings by State and Race, 1882–1968*, 37, 38, 40; NAACP, *Thirty Years of Lynching in the United States*, 52; White, *Rope and Faggot*, 235–36.

41 The statistics of my own case list can be found in appendix 1.

42 See appendix 1 for a complete summary of the case history.

43 White, *Rope and Faggot*, 235–36.

44 Ibid., 234–36.

45 Windeler discussing making coffee from acorns, eating raw meat, etc. The historian Susan Lee Johnson writes about the role of Mexican miners who traveled to the gold fields with their families during the Gold Rush, but it must also be acknowledged that not all Mexican miners brought their families with them. However, in invoking families, Johnson is able to provide an innovative analy-

sis of domestic and personal service work in both the northern and southern mining camps, and she effectively explores the relationship between homosocial behavior and Western racial formation: Johnson, *Roaring Camp*, 100, 101, 125. See Windeler, *The California Gold Rush Diary of a German Sailor*.

46 San Francisco's vigilance committees of 1851, 1856, and 1857 have been extensively studied. See Bancroft, *Popular Tribunals*, Vols. 1 and 2.

47 Tuskegee Institute, "When Is Murder Lynching?" *Montgomery Advertiser*, June 7, 1959; reproduced in Ginzburg, *One Hundred Years of Lynchings*, 245.

48 *San Francisco Alta California* (daily), February 1, 1851, 2; Davis, *California Criminal Justice Time Line*," 1; McKanna, "Crime and Punishment," 2.

49 *San Francisco Alta California* (daily), September 5, 1879; *Ukiah Weekly Dispatch*, September 6, 1879; *Mendocino Weekly Democrat*, September 6, 1879; Webb, *A History of Lynching in California since 1875*, 28.

50 See the same sources in the previous note.

51 Tuskegee records nearly thirteen hundred, and White records over fourteen hundred cases for the same period. Tuskegee Institute Archives, "Lynchings: By Year and Race," May 2002, unpaginated; White, *Rope and Faggot*, table 2, 233.

52 The category of black or African American has been recognized as being as problematic as Anglo or Mexican because, according to scholars like Neil Folley, it reasserts blacks as a separate racial group rather than acknowledging that blacks can be as ethnically diverse as Anglos or Mexicans. Folley, *The White Scourge*, 13.

53 For an in-depth analysis of these three approaches, see Omi and Winant, *Racial Formation in the United States from the 1960s to the 1990s*, 11.

54 In 1948, Andrea Perez, a Mexican American woman, and Sylvester Davis, an African American man, were denied a marriage license from the Los Angeles County Clerk's Office because Perez was racially classified as white and Davis as Negro. The case eventually made it to the California Supreme Court, and the couple was able to overturn California's miscegenation laws. *Perez vs. Sharp*, October 1, 1948.

55 These names were gleaned from maps of the northern and southern mine regions. Bancroft, *California*, 368–69.

56 To further explore how contemporary anthropologists have used the critical interpretation of photographic images to rethink, for example, British anthropology from 1860–1920, I would recommend Elizabeth Edwards's anthology, *Anthropology and Photography, 1860–1920*, in which she assembles a variety of responses to modern recording and interpretive problems. While this project does not make use of anthropological images per se, it does wrestle with many of the same questions relating to the interpretation of images.

57 Located in El Dorado County, Placerville was one of the first mining camps to spring up around Coloma where James Marshall discovered gold. Initially known as Dry Diggings or the Diggins, it would later be renamed Placerville as it is still officially known. It received the nickname Hangtown after a series of men were hanged to a giant oak that stood at the center of town. As recently as 2005, Placerville's street signs had the emblem of a hangman's noose incorpo-

rated into their design. Persons of various nationalities and ethnicities died on Placerville's hang tree.

58 According to one of the foremost scholars on California history, Hubert Howe Bancroft (1832–1918), three men had actually met their deaths on Placerville's hang tree in January 1849; two Frenchman by the name of Garcia and Bissi (or a Canadian by the name Montreuil) and a Chilean by the name of Manuel (or Pepe). Office of Historic Preservation, *California Historical Landmarks*, 43; Bancroft, *Popular Tribunals*, 1:144–145; Bancroft cites the *San Francisco Alta California*, January 18, 1849.

59 In the Chinese Massacre of 1872, several of those who died were hanged from the cross beam of a corral gate, and one was reported to have been hanged from a covered wagon. Frank, *Scrapbook of a Western Pioneer*, 241–42.

60 A small selection of photographs from my series "Searching for California's Hang Trees" are included in the pages of this book.

61 For a detailed history of the antilynching movement, see Zangrando, *The NAACP Crusade Against Lynching, 1909–1950*, and Grant, *The Anti-Lynching Movement, 1883–1932*.

62 San Francisco's 1856 committee of vigilance not only invoked the 1851 committee, but its first meeting reunited many of its members. Bancroft, *Popular Tribunals*, 2:84–88.

63 For a general discussion of the archive, see Sekula, "The Body and the Archive," 343–78; S. Smith, *American Archives*; Firstenberg, "Autonomy and the Archive in America," 313–34.

64 Montejano, *Anglos and Mexicans in the Making of Texas, 1836–1986*, 4.

65 Horsman, *Race and Manifest Destiny*, 62–77.

ONE Counting the Dead

1 In "On Torture," Asad suggests that Darius Rejali misread Foucault in his book *Torture and Modernity*. Asad insists that Foucault's thesis about disciplinary power "is not subverted by evidence of *surreptitious* torture in the modern state." Asad, "On Torture," 288.

2 Heizer and Almquist, *The Other Californians*, 151.

3 Ibid.

4 Boessenecker, *Gold Dust and Gunsmoke*, 51; Pitt, *The Decline of the Californios*, 61–64.

5 *Sacramento Placer Times*, April 26, 1850.

6 Hundley, *The Great Thirst*, 66.

7 Ibid. Hundley cites Sherburn F. Cook, *The Population of the California Indians, 1769–1970* (Berkeley: University of California Press, 1976), 44; Cook, "Historical Demography," in *Handbook of North American Indians*, Vol. 8: *California*, ed. by Robert F. Heizer (Washington, D.C.: Smithsonian Institution, 1978), 91, 93; U.S. Department of Commerce, Bureau of the Census, *Historical Statistics of the United States* (Washington, D.C.: Government Printing Office, 1975), Vol. 1, 25.

8 Mountaineer, "Letter to the Editor," *San Francisco Alta California* (daily), June 24, 1853, 1.

9 "Monthly Record of Current Events," *Harper's New Monthly Magazine*, Vol. 3, no. 13 (June 1851): 130.

10 See appendix 3.

11 This information is derived from appendix 1 of this publication. By the end of 1849, California's population has been estimated to have included some 80,000 Yankees, 8,000 Mexicans, and 5,000 South Americans. Combined with American Indians (depending on which statistics one used), Chinese, and African Americans, the percentage of Latinos in the state's overall population would hover somewhere around 10 percent. Heizer and Almquist, *The Other Californians*, 144.

12 Tuskegee Institute Archives, "Lynchings in California, 1883–1935."

13 *Los Angeles Star*, October 26, 1871, 3.

14 See appendix 3.

15 U.S. Census Bureau, *Race for the United States, Regions, Divisions, and States: 1850*, table A-20.

16 *San Francisco Alta California*, April 7, 1854, 2.

17 "Monthly Record of Current Events," *Harper's New Monthly Magazine*. Vol. 5, no. 28 (September 1852): 403.

18 U.S. Census Bureau, *Race for the United States, Regions, Divisions, and States: 1860*, table A-19.

19 Shirley, *The Shirley Letters from California Mines*, 158–59.

20 For a detailed description of the origins of the "Anglo-Saxon" race and its specific uses in the 1840s to distinguish Americans of northern European descent from American Indians, Asians, blacks, Mexicans, and Spaniards on this continent, see Horsman, *Race and Manifest Destiny*, 4, 5, 210, 211.

21 Ibid., 4, 5, 63, 210.

22 Ibid.

23 Ibid., 5.

24 The "white" races in this passage referred to the presence of persons of Spanish descent. Farnham, *Life, Adventures, Travels in California*, 413; Horsman, *Race and Manifest Destiny*, 210; Heizer and Almquist, *The Other Californians*, 140.

25 Wells, *New Physiognomy*, 407–11.

26 Ibid., 407–8.

27 Ethnology was popular in the 1840s not only because of questions over slavery or how to address the nation's Indian populations, but because it was also tied to whether or not Genesis accurately described the origins of all human beings. In this period, the theory of polygenesis was seen as a direct challenge to Genesis, even as arguments for innate physical and mental differences between the races came to be widely accepted. Proslavery advocates used these arguments to justify slavery, just as expansionists used them to argue for westward expansion, and even to justify the war with Mexico. For more on the nature and dissemination of "scientific racialism" and its relationship to the concept of Manifest Destiny, see Horsman, *Race and Manifest Destiny*, 139–57.

28 Spencer, *First Principles*, 278.

29 Spencer, "Progress: Its Law and Causes," *The Westminster Review*, 464–65.

30 Spencer, *First Principles*, 342–43.

31 Ibid.

32 Pitt, *The Decline of the Californios*, 27.

33 According to Irving Lewis Allen, "greaser" was used as a derogatory term for Italians, Puerto Ricans, and Mexicans as early as 1836. Allen, *Unkind Words*, 55–56.

34 Thompson, *American Character*, 187.

35 Lighton, "The Greaser," 750.

36 Ibid.

37 Ibid., 753.

38 In appendix 1, the term "Mexican" is used if it appeared in the historical record. In some cases the same individual might be referred to with more than one term, sometimes by the same author. In these cases, the additional terms appear alongside of the term "Mexican."

39 Omi and Winant, *Racial Formation*, 55.

40 Farnham, *Life, Adventures, and Travels in California*, 413; Heizer and Almquist, *The Other Californians*, 140.

41 Rosales, "Viaje a California," 68.

42 In the case list, "Anglo/Euro" is intended as an abbreviation for persons of Anglo-American or European descent.

43 *San Francisco Alta California*, February 3, 1855, 2.

44 *Los Angeles Star*, August 20, 1853.

45 Cooper, *The Lesson of the Scaffold*, 101; Maestro, *Cesare Beccaria and the Origins of Penal Reform*, 137.

46 *San Francisco Alta California* (daily), August 11, 1855, 2.

47 Ibid.; and August 10, 1855, 2.

48 Ibid., August 13, 1855, 2.

49 Ibid.

50 Ibid., August 11, 1855, 2.

51 I have only included eight of the sixteen cases in appendix 1 because they are confirmed in multiple sources. Ibid., August 10, 11, 1855, 2; Puertovino, Tancolino, and José are also identified in Bancroft, *Popular Tribunals*, 1:546; Manuel Castro and one unnamed Mexican are identified in Boessenecker, *Gold Dust and Gunsmoke*, 55; Rafael Escobar is mentioned as hanged in Jackson Tree. Boessenecker, *Gold Dust and Gunsmoke*, 57–58; Escobar is also mentioned in Burns, *The Robin Hood of El Dorado*, 205, 208. Another account reported that the men were Chileans and Mexicans and that "six of the gang were taken, tried, and hung." "Monthly Record of Current Events," *Harper's New Monthly Magazine*, Vol. 11, no. 65 (October 1855): 689. Still another account stated that no less than seven were hanged and countless others were shot, including one suspect hanged on Main Street, another in Sutter, and a third at Campo Seco; *San Francisco Alta California* (daily), August 11, 1855, 2.

52 Boesseneker, *Gold Dust and Gunsmoke*, 54.

53 *San Francisco Alta California* (daily), August 14, 1855, 2.

54 Ibid.

55 Boesseneker, *Gold Dust and Gunsmoke*, 55.

56 Hittell, *History of California*, 300.

57 Ibid.

58 Ibid; *History of Touloumne County*, 81, 187–98.

59 De la Guerra, *Speech of Hon. Pablo de la Guerra*, 7.

60 Citing Theodore Roosevelt's use of the phrase "waste spaces" to refer to the un-industrialized spaces of the world, the historian Matthew Frye Jacobson has convincingly argued that Roosevelt's juxtaposition of "Barbarism" and "Virtue" can be seen as the controlling metaphor for the period from 1876 to 1917, which Jacobson characterizes as the period in which industrialization and republicanism meet. Roosevelt takes already established themes from American expansionism and applies them on a global scale. Begun thirty years earlier with the war against Mexico, the removal of American Indians and Roman Catholic Mexicans was not seen as a challenge to American virtue, but proof of it. Jacobson, *Barbarian Virtues*, 3–5; he cites Theodore Roosevelt, *The Winning of the West* (Lincoln: University of Nebraska Press, 1995), Vol. 1, 1.

61 Royce, *California*, 254–55; *San Francisco Alta California* (steamer edition), April 5, 1852.

62 *California Journals of the Senate and Assembly*, 3rd session, 1852, 75; *California Political Code*, section 1669, 1872, which provided for the education of black and Indian children; Homestead Act, *California Statutes*, 1860, 87; *Constitution of the State of California*, 1849, article 2, section 1.

63 Lapp, "Negro Rights Activities in Gold Rush California," 3–20.

64 Newmark, *Sixty Years in Southern California*, 141.

65 Hittell, *History of California*, 283–84.

66 *Sonora Herald*, July 12, 1851, quoted in Lang, *Early Justice in Sonora*, 36–37.

67 See appendix 2.

68 Hittell, *History of California*, 283–84.

69 Royster, introduction, 9.

70 Tuskegee Institute, "When Is Murder Lynching?" as published in the *Montgomery Advertiser*, June 7, 1959; reproduced in Ginzburg's *100 Years of Lynchings*, 245. The Tuskegee definition is accepted by Ginzburg, the NAACP, the Tuskegee Institute Archives, and in employing this definition, California's history of lynching may finally be seen as a part of the history of lynching nationwide.

71 Royser, introduction, 8.

72 Percy, *Origin of the Lynch Law*, 65.

73 Ibid.

74 Ibid., 34.

75 Dray, *At the Hands of Persons Unknown*, 21.

76 Percy, *Origin of the Lynch Law*, 30.

77 The sentence was usually, "forty lashes save one" and was probably derived from

Second Corinthians in the King James Bible, which references thirty-nine lashes, also called stripes, as a frequent punishment for a wide range of crimes and misdeeds. Percy, *Origin of the Lynch Law*, 67.

78 Under Jim Crow, blacks were barred from voting, holding public office, and serving on juries. For more on lynching and the history of Jim Crow, see Zangrando, *The NAACP Crusade Against Lynching*.

79 Grant, *The Anti-Lynching Movement*, 20.

80 Douglas addressed lynching in his initial call for the National Convention, but the fact that lynching was a topic of interest to black delegates from many of states reveals that lynching was already a national issue. Ibid.

81 Ibid., 21.

82 Ibid., 167.

83 The Archives at the Tuskegee Institute date the last three lynchings in the United States to 1964 and record only fifteen cases between 1948 and 1963. Tuskegee Institute Archives, "Lynchings: By Year and Race," August 14, 2002, unpaginated.

84 Grant, *The Anti-Lynching Movement*, 167; letter from the NAACP dated February 10, 1938, private collection (photographs of the letter in the collection of the author).

85 White, *Rope and Faggot*, 237.

86 Ibid., 227–28.

87 Based on a phone conversation with Cynthia Wilson, Coordinator of Archives, Tuskegee Institute Archives, Tuskegee, Ala., January 6, 2004; White, *Rope and Faggot*, 229.

88 The NAACP number includes those cases recorded between 1882 and 1927; White, *Rope and Faggot*, 237–38; NAACP, *Thirty Years of Lynching in the United States*, 41; additional statistics provided by Archives of the Tuskegee Institute. Tuskegee Institute Archives, *Lynchings by State and Race, 1882–1968*.

89 Ida Wells-Barnett began writing on lynching in 1892 after three prosperous businessmen were lynched in Memphis. Wells-Barnett had known the three men and the neighborhood in which their businesses were located. According to her, they managed a grocery business that competed with a white-owned store, and this competition led to the lynching. Collins, introduction, 11–14.

90 Chadbourn, *Lynching and the Law*, 3.

91 White, *Rope and Faggot*, vi.

92 NAACP, *Thirty Years of Lynching in the United States*, 29.

93 White, *Rope and Faggot*, 236.

94 Ibid., 267.

95 Tuskegee Institute Archives, *Lynchings by State and Race, 1882–1968*; Philip Dray, in his book *At the Hands of Persons Unknown*, recognized that the full data on lynching may never be known and cites numerous statistics not included in either the NAACP or Tuskegee Institute lists. Among these studies, he includes Richard Maxwell Brown's study, which estimated that there were over four hundred lynchings by the Ku Klux Klan in the South between 1868 and 1871; Ida Wells-Barnett, who estimated the number of African Americans killed by whites to be approxi-

mately ten thousand between 1865 and the 1890s; and Dorothy Sterling, who claimed that nearly twenty thousand black Americans were killed by the Klan between 1868 and 1871. Dray, *At the Hands of Persons Unknown*, 49.

96 White, *Rope and Faggot*, 254.

97 Ibid., 234–55.

98 See appendix 1.

99 In this incident, an inquest was held, and according to Circuit Judge Harold Cohen, Golden's death resulted from suicide; others argued that Golden was lynched, noting that his clothes were not even soiled, even though he was alleged to have climbed the treé on a rainy night. Rumors that Golden had been dating a white police officer's daughter only further fueled the debate, and there were still some questions as to whether his hands had been tied behind his back. Sales, "Somebody Hung My Baby," 328–35.

100 White, *Rope and Faggot*, 232. The Tuskegee Institute Archives records forty-one cases for California between 1883 and 1968. Tuskegee Institute Archives, *Lynchings in California, 1883–1935*.

101 NAACP, *Thirty Years of Lynching in the United States*, 31, 52.

102 In examining the case records, it is unclear whether the "Mexican" was a Mexican native or a Mexican American. The case is identified as that of "Jesus Fulzen" and appears in appendix 1 of this publication; NAACP *Thirty Years of Lynching in the United States*, 52.

103 See appendix 1. Luis Moreno was a Mexican national and was lynched in 1895; Martin Wilson and James Hall were half-brothers and their mother was American Indian. They were lynched in 1901.

104 Boessenecker, *Lawman*, 158.

105 Labeled "A Ready Reckoner for Hangman," the chart consulted provided the approximate distances necessary to effectively hang a man based on his weight in stones. A stone is a British measurement of mass that equals approximately fourteen pounds. See Charles Duff, *A Handbook on Hanging*, 197.

106 Bancroft, *California*, 741, 743; Bancroft, *Popular Tribunals*, 1:226–37.

107 Bancroft also makes note of the fact that San Francisco's first Committee of Vigilance was organized along a "police system" and did not have the military organization of the 1856 committee. Bancroft, *California*, 743; Bancroft, *Popular Tribunals*, 1:294–98.

108 Lavater is addressed in chapter 5; Bancroft, *Popular Tribunals*, 1:267.

109 Bancroft, *Popular Tribunals*, 1:353, 360.

110 Ibid., 1:360–61; Bancroft, *California*, 743.

111 Bancroft, *Popular Tribunals*, 1:406.

112 Boessenecker, *Gold Dust*, 36.

113 Bancroft, *California*, 744.

114 Bancroft, *Popular Tribunals*, 1:97, 176–243.

115 Ibid., 2:487–500; Bancroft, *California*, 752–53; Sherman, "Gold Hunters of California," 297.

116 Bancroft, *California*, 754.

117 California Department of Corrections, "History of Capital Punishment in California," 1.

118 Cooper, *The Lesson of the Scaffold*, 177.

119 Ibid.

120 See appendix 2.

121 California Department of Corrections, "History of Capital Punishment in California," 1.

122 *San Francisco Alta California* (daily), July 25, 1854, 2.

123 Ibid.

124 *Los Angeles Star*, December 25, 1858, 2.

125 The credit on the photograph names only the Brisly Drug Company and states that the card was printed by the Albertype Company in Brooklyn.

126 *Sacramento Daily Record-Union*, August 25, 1895.

127 Ibid.; *Sacramento Evening Bee*, August 26, 1895; *San Francisco Examiner*, August 27, 1895.

128 Bill 10691 requested the funds to pay out of "humane consideration" an indemnity to the family of Luis Moreno who was lynched in 1895 at Yreka, California. Webb, *A History of Lynching in California since 1875*, 65–66. This case was included in the NAACP's *Thirty Years of Lynching in the United States*, which made no mention of Moreno's national or racial origin.

129 Around the border of the image someone had written, along with the time and date of the lynching, that three hundred people had participated in the lynching which took place in front of the County Courthouse in Yreka; *San Francisco Examiner*, August 27, 1895.

130 *Sacramento Daily Record-Union*, August 25, 1895; *Sacramento Bee* (evening), August 26, 1895; *San Francisco Examiner*, August 27, 1895.

131 *Sacramento Daily Record-Union*, August 25, 1895; *Sacramento Bee* (evening), August 26, 1895; *San Francisco Examiner*, August 27, 1895.

132 *Sacramento Daily Record-Union*, August 25, 1895; *Sacramento Bee* (evening), August 26, 1895; *San Francisco Examiner*, August 27, 1895.

133 Available since the 1880s, flash powder could be dangerous to work with and required some degree of technical expertise. Flashbulbs would dramatically broaden not only the number of images that could be captured on film, but also the number of people that had access to the technology. The Mazda Photoflash Lamp, first advertised in 1932, was one of the first battery operated flashes to become commercially available. Mazda Photoflash Lamp, *American Annual of Photography*, 1932, adv. 25.

134 See Villon, "Éclairage à l'Aluminium," *Photo-Gazette*, 204–6.

135 Prosch Manufacturing Co., advertisement for Proschlite Flash Lamps, *American Annual of Photography and Photographic Times 1904*, xxxiii.

136 Scoville and Adams, advertisement for Solograph Flash Pistol, *American Annual of Photography and Photographic Times*, 1900, cxv.

137 Barthes recognized the signifying force of the photographer's camera when he described the photographer's subject, the "person or thing photographed" as a target. Barthes, *Camera Lucida*, 9.

138 The Mazda Photoflash Lamp, advertisement, *American Annual of Photography 1932*, adv. 25.

139 Barthes, *Camera Lucida*, 119.

140 Ibid.

141 Ibid.

142 Ibid., 9.

143 Kristeva, *Powers of Horror*, 4.

144 Ibid.

TWO The Greatest Good

1 For more on the origins of criminology, see Gault, *Criminology*, 24–25.

2 Adam Smith's *Inquiry into the Nature and Causes of the Wealth of Nations* was published in 1776, but Beccaria's writing had no direct influence on Smith. Catherine II began her rule with plans to establish a radical new code of law and had invited Beccaria to Russia to help write her new code. He did not accept her invitation and instead used the offer to negotiate a teaching position in Milan. Greatly influenced by Beccaria's text, Catherine's own document was to serve as a guide for a new and enlightened code of law. She even went so far as to organize a legislative commission with representatives of various classes (excluding the serfs), but the group was disbanded before any code was completed. Maestro, *Cesare Beccaria and the Origins of Penal Reform*, 7–18, 70–71, 87–88.

3 Beccaria, *Of Crimes and Punishment*, 48.

4 David Young argued that Beccaria may have been influenced by Jean Jacques Rousseau, who also argued against capital punishment in all but the most extreme circumstances. Ibid.

5 Ibid., 49–50.

6 With regard to the U.S. Constitution, Beccaria's influence can be seen in the right to trial by jury, along with several provisions within the amendments, specifically the right to confront the witnesses, the right to counsel, and the right to witnesses of one's own: Maestro, *Cesare Beccaria and the Origins of Penal Reform*, 142–43.

7 Wells, *History of Nevada County with Illustrations and Biographical Sketches of Its Prominent Men and Pioneers*, 106. Hereafter referred to as *History of Nevada County*.

8 Ibid.

9 The article notes that the California legislature had passed a bill making grand larceny a capital offense. The bill would come to be known as the Criminal Practices Act of 1851. "Monthly Calendar of Events," *Harper's New Monthly Magazine*, Vol. 3, no. 13 (June 1851):130.

10 Wright, *Reproduction of Thompson and West's The History of Sacramento County, Cali-*

fornia: With Illustrations Descriptive of its Scenery, Residences, Public Buildings, Fine Blocks, and Manufactories from Original Sketches by Artists of the Highest Ability (Berkeley, Calif.: Howell-North, 1960), 125–26.

11 Ibid.

12 The four members of the vigilance committee were Milne, Rightmire, Duncombe, and Hutchinson. Ibid.

13 Ibid.

14 Ibid.

15 Ibid.

16 Ibid.

17 Ibid.

18 According to the report, the woman who let out the room believed him to be a hard worker, but he was apparently also suspected of horse stealing and attempted arson. The event occurred in a small town known then as San Antonio, not far from present-day Martinez in Contra Costa County. *San Francisco Alta California* (daily), July 4, 1855, 2.

19 *Sacramento Transcript* (steamer edition), May 1, 1851.

20 Ibid.

21 Royster, introduction, 27–33.

22 *Los Angeles Star*, September 17, 1853, 1.

23 *The Literary Digest*, November 27, 1909, 938–39.

24 Ibid., 938.

25 California had many immigrants and miners from Sonora, Mexico, and so it was not uncommon for them to be identified as "Sonorans" (but properly spelled Sonoranians). However, in the southern mines, so many Mexicans had settled in one area that it became Sonora, California. *New York Times*, January 17, 1852, 3; Hittell, *History of California*, 3: 294.

26 Because of the extreme lag time for communications to travel between the coasts, news of Corrales's sentencing did not appear in the *Times* until eleven days after the execution was scheduled to occur. *New York Times*, January 17, 1852, 3.

27 Wells, *History of Nevada County*, 108.

28 *Washington National Intelligencer*, August 12, 1851, 3; Royce, *California*, 266; *San Francisco Herald*, June 26, 1851.

29 [Munro-Fraser], *History of Contra Costa County, California*, 341.

30 Ibid.

31 Baudelaire, *Baudelaire*, 230.

32 Ibid.

33 Pitt, *The Decline of the Californios*, 160.

34 Dated to February 13, 1854, by Judge Benjamin Hayes. He goes on to explain that he had "some doubts as to whether I ought not to have fixed the execution of Ignacio Herrera for to-day, instead of yesterday. Today (14th) would have been the last of the term allowed by law (60 days), but in the view that this was my birth-day, (and for no other reason), I designated yesterday at 3 P.M. for this exe-

cution. And the poor fellow suffered the penalty with evident repentance, and the prayers of all the Catholic population went up to Heaven for him." The date is given as February 20, 1854, in the San Francisco newspaper, which adds that the original date of the thirteenth was postponed until the twentieth. Hayes, *Pioneer Notes from the Diaries of Judge Benjamin Hayes, 1849–1875*, 104; *San Francisco Alta California* (daily), February 22, 1854, 2.

35 *San Francisco Alta California* (daily), February 22, 1854, 2.

36 Hayes, *Pioneer Notes from the Diaries of Judge Benjamin Hayes, 1849–1875*, 104.

37 *San Francisco Alta California* (daily), May 13, 1854, 2.

38 Murray uses "Native Californian" to refer to those communities presently known as Latino or Hispanic, and "American" to refer to Anglos or persons of European descent. [Angel], *History of San Luis Obispo County with Illustrations and Biographical Sketches of Its Prominent Men and Pioneers*, 295; *San Francisco Alta California* (daily), May 13, 1854, 2.

39 López, *White by Law*, 42, cites *Act of March 26, 1790*, U.S. Congress, ch. 3, 1 stat. 103.

40 López, *White by Law*, 204; Martinez, "Mexican-Americans and Whiteness," 211.

41 Martinez, "Mexican-Americans and Whiteness," 211.

42 As most contemporary readers will be aware, Mexican nationality is no guarantee of racial origin, and Mexican nationals can be of any racial background. Ibid.

43 Amador was executed for killing a man near Pleasanton. Pitt, *The Decline of the Californios*, 261.

44 The *Oakland Daily News*, September 23, 1871, ran a slightly different version which included the statement, "That is a hell of a law you have here for a poor man. Them God damned judges don't care for a poor man." For more on the case, see Pitt, *The Decline of the Californios*, 261, which cites *San Francisco Call*, September 23, 1871, and Boessenecker, *Lawman*, 171, which cites *Oakland Daily News*.

45 Pitt, *The Decline of the Californios*, 260; Boessenecker, *Lawman*, 173.

46 Pitt, *The Decline of the Californios*, 261.

47 Ibid.

48 Wells, *History of Nevada County*, 107.

49 California Department of Corrections, "History of Capital Punishment in California."

50 Ibid.

51 California Department of Corrections, "Number of Executions, 1893 to Present."

52 California Department of Corrections, "History of Capital Punishment in California."

53 California Department of Corrections, "Death Row Tracking System," 1.

54 Hitchens, introduction to *A Handbook on Hanging*, xxiii.

55 American Civil Liberties Union, "DNA Testing and the Death Penalty"; California Department of Corrections, "Number of Executions, 1893 to Present"; Welsh-Huggins, "Death Row Inmates Yet to Seek DNA Testing," *Columbus Dispatch*, February 27, 2001.

56 American Civil Liberties Union, "Statement of Diann Rust-Tierney, Director ACLU Capital Punishment Project."

57 Amnesty International, "Death Penalty Facts"; Death Penalty Focus, "The High Cost of the Death Penalty to Taxpayers," New York, press release, July 23, 2003.

58 Death Penalty Focus, "The High Cost of the Death Penalty to Taxpayers."

59 See appendix 1, which, along with the names of those summarily executed, provides city and county information.

60 In March 1855, a bill to establish a U.S Circuit Court for the District of California became law. By the 1860s the court met four times a year, twice in San Francisco and twice in Los Angeles. Gordon, *Authorized by No Law*, 4–5.

61 *Sacramento Transcript* (steamer edition), March 14, 1851, 3.

62 Ibid., January 14, 1851, 3.

63 Los Angeles had its first police force, and its badges read "City Police—Organized by the Council of Los Angeles." Guinn, *Historical and Biographical Record of Los Angeles and Vicinity*, 134; *Los Angeles Star*, August 6, 1853, 2; February 11, 1854, 2.

64 Boessenecker, *Lawman*, 48.

65 Hittell, *History of California*, 3:292.

66 The 1879 state constitution gave the superior court the duties of the grand jury. See Searcy, "For the Record"; *Sacramento Transcript* (steamer edition), October 31, 1850.

67 *Sacramento Transcript* (steamer edition), October 31, 1850.

68 Congress created California's federal court system on September 29, 1850. Several individuals were already nominated and confirmed but turned down the positions due to the low salaries being offered. See Fritz, *Federal Justice in California*, 18.

69 Marryatt, "Admission Day Celebration."

70 Ibid.

71 Fritz, *Federal Justice in California*, 9.

72 Ibid., 21–22.

73 Ibid., 21.

74 After 1855, Hoffman increasingly ruled on land grant cases, which, not surprisingly, is an equally contested legacy of the old West, particularly for many early Latino families whose claims were contested, overturned, or flatly rejected depending upon their ability to provide legal documentation of ownership. After executions, land grant claims were probably the most contested and widely covered cases in the newspapers of the day. See ibid., 32.

75 The first case referenced in the article appears to be the lynching of a man named Brown. The case is listed in appendix 1. *Washington National Intelligencer*, August 12, 1851, 3.

76 The incident took place in Columbia. Columbia is now preserved as a state park. *Sacramento Union* (steamer), August 14, 1852, 2.

77 Ibid.

78 Mayo, *Los Angeles*, 36; Blew, "Vigilantism in Los Angeles, 1835–1874," 13; Pitt and Pitt, *Los Angeles A to Z*, 528; Bancroft, *California*, 3:417; Guinn, *Historical and Biographical Record of Los Angeles and Vicinity*, 137.

79 Numbers vary slightly in the sources, but newspapers from the time are quite

specific and state that no less than fifteen persons were hanged and three were shot in the Chinese Massacre. *New York Times*, October 26, 1871, 8; Mayo, *Los Angeles*, 36; Blew, "Vigilantism in Los Angeles," 13.

80 For more information of the San Francisco committees of vigilance, see Bancroft, *Popular Tribunals*, Volumes 1 and 2.

81 In two phone conversations in May 2002 with a representative from the Los Angeles coroner's office, I was told that these records have been indefinitely "misplaced."

82 Frank, *Scrapbook of a Western Pioneer*, 241.

83 Frank claimed that $40,000 to $50,000 was stolen by the mob. Ibid.

84 Rasmussen records a total number of fifteen hanged and four additional men shot. Newmark records eighteen Chinese hanged and four additional men shot. The *Los Angeles Star* reported that fifteen had been hanged, or shot and hanged, and that three had been shot only. Other accounts report as many as twenty-two, but I am including in the case list in appendix 1 only the fifteen whose names are identified in the *Los Angeles Star*, since it was based on the bodies that had actually been laid out in a double row before the jail house after the massacre. Rasmussen, "A Forgotten Hero," *Los Angeles Times*, May 16, 1993, 3; Newmark, *Sixty Years in Southern California*, 434; *Los Angeles Star*, October 26, 1871, 3.

85 Rasmussen, "A Forgotten Hero," *Los Angeles Times*, May 16, 1993, 3.

86 *Sacramento Union* (steamer edition), June 15, 1852, 2.

87 Ibid.

88 Ibid.

89 Ibid.; "Monthly Record of Current Events," *Harper's New Monthly Magazine*, Vol. 5, no. 28 (September 1852), 545; Burns, *The Robin Hood of El Dorado*, 205; Varley, *The Legend of Joaquin Murrieta*, 14; Royce, *California*, 270.

90 Varley, *The Legend of Joaquin Murrieta*, 14.

91 *Los Angeles Star*, April 21, 1860, 1.

92 *San Francisco Call*, June 11, 1876; Webb, *A History of Lynching in California since 1875*, 14.

93 *San Francisco Alta California*, June 11, 1876, 2; *San Francisco Call* (morning), June 11, 1876; Webb, *A History of Lynching in California since 1875*, 14.

94 Same sources as in previous note.

95 *San Francisco Call* (morning), June 11, 1876; Webb, *A History of Lynching in California since 1875*, 14.

96 *Sacramento Record-Union* (daily), May 29, 1879; *San Francisco Chronicle*, May 29, 1879; *Kern County Gazette*, May 31, 1879; Webb, *A History of Lynching in California since 1875*, 24.

97 Webb, *A History of Lynching in California since 1875*, 25.

98 Ibid.

99 *Sacramento Record-Union* (daily), May 29, 1879; *San Francisco Chronicle*, May 29, 1879; *Kern County Gazette* (Bakersfield), May 31, 1879; Webb, *A History of Lynching in California since 1875*, 24.

100 *Sacramento Record-Union* (daily), May 29, 1879; Webb, *A History of Lynching in California since 1875*, 26–27.

101 *Kern County Courier* (Bakersfield), June 15, 1879; Webb, *A History of Lynching in California since 1875*, 26–27.

102 *San Francisco Daily Evening Bulletin*, December 28, 1875; Webb, *A History of Lynching in California since 1875*, 12.

103 Bancroft spelled his name "Igarra" and identifies the hang tree as an oak. *San Francisco Bulletin* (evening), December 28, 1875; Webb, *A History of Lynching in California since 1875*, 12; Bancroft, *Popular Tribunals*, 1:573.

104 For more on the Vasquez band, see chapter 4.

105 *San Francisco Bulletin* (evening), December 28, 1875; Webb, *A History of Lynching in California since 1875*, 12.

106 *San Francisco Bulletin* (evening), December 28, 1875; Webb, *A History of Lynching in California since 1875*, 12.

107 *San Francisco Bulletin* (evening), December 27, 28, 1875; Webb, *A History of Lynching in California since 1875*, 12.

108 *Los Angeles Star*, January 24, 1857.

109 Pitt, *The Decline of the Californios*, 259, cites *Monterey Gazette*, January 8, 1864.

110 *Bodie Free Press*, January 18, 1881.

111 McGrath, *Gunfighters, Highwaymen and Vigilantes*, 256.

112 Ibid.

113 Ibid.

114 *Los Angeles Star*, March 28, 1857.

THREE In the Shadow of Photography

1 *San Francisco Call* (morning), May 5, 1877; Bryam, *Edward Byram Scrapbooks*, January 2, 1877–May 26, 1878; Bancroft, *Popular Tribunals*, 1:573–74.

2 *Santa Cruz Sentinel*, May 3, 1877; *San Jose Herald*, May 3, 1877; *San Francisco Call* (morning), May 5, 1877; Bryam, *Edward Bryam Scrapbooks*, January 2, 1877–May 26, 1878; Webb, *A History of Lynching in California since 1875*, 16.

3 In some accounts the mob was estimated to have numbered up to three hundred. *San Francisco Call* (morning), May 5, 1877; Bryam, *Edward Bryam Scrapbooks*, January 2, 1877–May 26, 1878; Bancroft, *Popular Tribunals*, 1:573–74; *San Francisco Chronicle*, May 4, 1877; *San Jose Herald*, May 3, 1877; *Santa Cruz Sentinel*, May 3, 5, 1877; Webb, *A History of Lynching in California since 1875*, 17.

4 Accounts vary slightly, but most agree that the mob got the two suspects to admit to murdering De Forest to get money to go to the circus. Others accounts suggest they admitted to the crimes while in custody. See Bancroft, *Popular Tribunals*, 1:573–74; *San Francisco Chronicle*, May 4, 1877; *San Jose Herald*, May 3, 1877; *Santa Cruz Sentinel*, May 3, 5, 1877; *San Francisco Call* (morning), May 5, 1877; Bryam, *Edward Bryam Scrapbooks*, January 2, 1877–May 26, 1878; Webb, *A History of Lynching in California since 1875*, 17.

5 *San Francisco Chronicle*, May 4, 1877; *San Jose Herald*, May 3, 1877; *Santa Cruz Sentinel*, May 3, 5, 1877; *San Francisco Call* (morning), May 5, 1877; Bryam, *Edward Bryam Scrapbooks*, January 2, 1877–May 26, 1878; Webb, *A History of Lynching in California since 1875*, 17.

6 Bancroft, *Popular Tribunals*, 1:573.

7 Bancroft, *Popular Tribunals*, 1:573; *San Francisco Call* (morning), May 5, 1877; Bryam, *Edward Bryam Scrapbooks*, January 2, 1877–May 26, 1878.

8 *San Francisco Call* (morning), May 5, 1877; Bryam, *Edward Bryam Scrapbooks*, January 2, 1877–May 26, 1878.

9 *San Francisco Call* (morning), May 5, 1877; Bryam, *Edward Bryam Scrapbooks*, January 2, 1877–May 26, 1878.

10 *San Francisco Bulletin* (evening), May 4, 1877; Webb, *A History of Lynching in California since 1875*, 18.

11 Prior to the photographic postcard, printed pamphlets were sometimes produced for local and national sales. For a discussion of early pamphlets, see Johnson, *Roaring Camp*, 317–33.

12 For more on the relationship between photography and the archive, see Sekula, "The Traffic in Photographs," 111–27; Sekula, "The Body and the Archive," 343–78.

13 *New York Tribune* (weekly), January 1, 1890, 9.

14 The lynching of J. L. Compton and Joseph Wilson took place on April 30, 1870. The tree upon which they were hanged was said to have been used to take the lives of over twenty men. Compton and Wilson were also accused of shooting and robbing an elderly gentleman by the name of George Lenhart. Allen et al., *Without Sanctuary*, 177.

15 The two men have been misidentified as American Indians in some accounts.

16 Terrence Wright has written that the photographic blur can function as both symbol and index, insisting that by rejecting the retinal image as the basis for visual perception one is also able to rethink photographic realism and conventionalism. Wright, "Theories of Realism and Convention," 26–27.

17 *Santa Cruz Local Item*, May 4, 1877; Webb, *A History of Lynching in California since 1875*, 18.

18 *San Francisco Bulletin* (evening), May 4, 1877; Webb, *A History of Lynching in California since 1875*, 18.

19 *Santa Cruz Local Item*, May 4, 1877; *San Francisco Post* (evening), May 4, 1877; *San Francisco Bulletin* (evening), May 4, 1877.

20 Bancroft, *Popular Tribunals*, 1:575; Webb, *A History of Lynching in California since 1875*, 18–20.

21 Spelled "Arajo" in Bancroft, *Popular Tribunals*, 1:575. See also Webb, *A History of Lynching in California since 1875*, 18–20.

22 *San Francisco Daily Evening Post*, July 16, 1877, cited in Webb, *A History of Lynching in California since 1875*, 20.

23 *Santa Cruz Sentinel*, July 21, 1877, cited in Webb, *A History of Lynching in California since 1875*, 20.

24 *Eugene Morning Register*, December 10, 1920, 1.

25 Ibid.

26 Webb, *A History of Lynching in California since 1875*, 77, notes that the rumors of police involvement were never proven.

27 Vanderwood and Samponaro explore the evolution of the picture postcard from its early development in Europe to its explosive popularity during Mexico's revolution. They also provide a concise history of the changes in postal law and photographic technology which allowed for the production and distribution of these now familiar objects. Vanderwood and Samponaro, *Border Fury*, 1–7.

28 Valento had served five years in San Quentin for robbery and assault and was discharged in 1912. *Eugene Morning Register*, December 10, 1920, 1; Webb, *A History of Lynching in California since 1875*, 76.

29 See chapter 2. After being executed Ramón Amador's heart didn't stop beating for five minutes. Boessenecker, *Lawman*, 173.

30 One article claims that all three men had been involved in a series of attacks upon a number of young women, but it is unclear whether these attacks would have resulted in death penalties for all three men. See *Eugene Morning Register*, December 10, 1920, 1.

31 Webb, *A History of Lynching in California since 1875*, 76.

32 Ibid.; *Santa Rosa Republican*, December 10, 1920; *San Francisco Chronicle*, December 11, 1920; *San Francisco Examiner*, December 11, 1920.

33 According to the archivist at the *San Francisco Chronicle* there were no photographers by the name of "Borne Miller" working for the *Chronicle* at the time, which greatly diminishes the possibility that he was a newspaper photographer, since newspaper photographers often worked freelance in this period.

34 Biographical information on Dobbin from California State Library records.

35 Webb, *A History of Lynching in California since 1875*, 76.

36 The photographic images are in the Allen/Littlefield Collection and are titled, "The burning and mutilated corpse of William Brown, male and female onlookers, September 28, 1919, Omaha, Nebraska," and "The lynching of Thomas Shipp and Abram Smith, a large gathering of lynchers. August 7, 1930, Marion, Indiana." The images are reproduced in Allen et al., *Without Sanctuary*, plates 31 and 97.

37 *Oakland Tribune*, November 27, 1933, 1, fourth extra.

38 Ibid.; Webb, *A History of Lynching in California since 1875*, 79; Farrell, *Swift Justice*, 4.

39 On November 22, 1933, a federal grand jury indicted the two men for using the U.S. postal system to extort and conspiracy to extort money from the family; at nearly the same time, the State of California issued warrants charging the two men with kidnapping. *Oakland Tribune*, November 27, 1933, 1, fourth extra; Webb, *A History of Lynching in California since 1875*, 76–79; Farrell, *Swift Justice*, 4.

40 Webb, *A History of Lynching in California since 1875*, 80; Farrell, *Swift Justice*, 195.

41 *Oakland Tribune*, November 27, 1933, 3, fourth extra.

42 Farrell, *Swift Justice*, 201.

43 KQW's newscaster Sam Hayes encouraged everyone to "Come on down," and

hundreds of cars filled the area surrounding the jail. In the end, newspapers reported the crowd to be between five and fifteen thousand, while the FBI officially reported some three thousand. Farrell, *Swift Justice*, 214.

44 *Oakland Tribune*, November 27, 1933, 1, fourth extra.

45 Farrell, *Swift Justice*, 216.

46 *Oakland Tribune*, November 27, 1933, 1, fourth extra.

47 Ibid.

48 Farrell, *Swift Justice*, 242.

49 *Oakland Tribune*, November 27, 1933, 2–3, fourth extra.

50 Farrell, *Swift Justice*, 214–16.

51 Webb, *A History of Lynching in California since 1875*, 80.

52 *Oakland Tribune*, November 27, 1933, 2–3, fourth extra.

53 Farrell, *Swift Justice*, 216.

54 Ibid.

55 The *San Jose News* referred to the lynching as the result of a vigilance committee, stating that "San Jose is made up of the finest citizens of any city in the entire United States—peace loving, quiet, cultured people." Cited in Farrell, *Swift Justice*, 251.

56 In her combined-media piece, "Accused/Blowtorch/Padlock," 1986, the artist Pat Ward Williams writes a series of questions around an appropriated and rephotographed image of a lynching that originally appeared in *Life Magazine*. Among the questions are "How long has he been locked to that tree? Can you be black and look at this without fear? Who took this picture?" The piece is in the collection of the Whitney Museum of Art in New York City.

57 Royster, introduction, 7–8.

58 Bancroft, *Popular Tribunals*, 1:472.

59 *Sacramento Transcript*, February 1, 1851, 5; February 14, 1851, 2–3, 8; May 1, 1851, 7, 8; *Sacramento Transcript* (steamer edition), May 1, 1851, 9.

60 *Sacramento Transcript* (steamer edition), February 14, 1851, 3.

61 Ibid., April 1, 1851, 8.

62 Ibid.

63 *Sacramento Transcript*, February 14, 1851.

64 Ibid.

65 Ibid.

66 *Sacramento Transcript* (steamer edition), April 1, 1851, 8.

67 *San Francisco Alta California* (daily), May 10, 1853; *Los Angeles Star*, November 12, 1853, 1.

68 "The 'souvenir' is the form of the commodity in the arcades." Benjamin, "First Sketches," *The Arcades Project*, 864.

69 Extending his analysis to "Spleen," a poem from Baudelaire's *Fleurs du Mal*, Benjamin argued that the psychic alienation described in the poem could be traced to a series of "psychic" souvenirs identified in the poem. The historian Susan Buck-Morss echoes Benjamin's own claims that within the souvenir, one uncovers the increasing self-alienation of those who inventory their past through

such "dead possessions." Buck-Morss, *The Dialectics of Seeing*, 189, cites Walter Benjamin, "Zentralpark" (1939–40), *Gesammelte Schriften* (Frankfurt on Main: Suhrkamp Verlag, 1972), 1:669–89.

70 The 1920 Santa Rosa triple lynching was one such example, and I found no less than three generations of the image, each one shot from another. This was also true in the double lynching of Holmes and Thurmond, where one lynching postcard was created by rephotographing the two trees that were used and printing them together as if the two men had been hanged to the same tree.

71 Benjamin characterizes Atget's photographic images of Paris streets as objects that function as "standard evidence for historical occurrences," but which also contain a "hidden political significance." See "The Work of Art in the Age of Mechanical Reproduction" in *Illuminations*, 226.

72 With regard to photography, Benjamin argues that "to ask for the 'authentic' print makes no sense" and concludes that once the authenticity of the object is put into question, the discourse of art shifts from one based on *ritual* to one of *politics*. Benjamin, *Illuminations*, 224.

73 In 1861, Mathew Brady made a deal with Anthony and Company, the largest photographic supply house in the country, to mass produce his photographs in Anthony's card factory, a deal which made the Brady negatives the legitimate property of Anthony and Company, in return for which he received approximately $4,000 a month. Cobb, *Mathew B. Brady's Photographic Gallery in Washington*, 22, cites *Humphrey's Journal of the Daguerreotype and Photographic Art* 12 (1861): 9; 14 (1862–63): 26.

74 *Oakland Tribune*, November 27, 1933, 2, fourth extra.

75 I must extend thanks to Michael Hutter for our many conversations on art, economics, and value as well as for directing me to Thompson's *Rubbish Theory*.

76 Thompson, *Rubbish Theory*, 7–9.

77 Ibid., 8.

78 An increasing number of archives now supply digital files instead of copy prints to researchers or for use in publications such as this one.

79 "World's First Photograph snaps £1/4m," *Times* (London), March 22, 2002, 18.

80 Ibid.

81 Smith, *American Archives*, 3.

82 Carey McWilliams employed the term "fantasy heritage" in 1949 when she described the Anglo-American "propensity to romanticize and mythify the white European, Spanish presence in the American Southwest." Griswold del Castillo, "The del Valle Family and the Fantasy Heritage," 2.

83 This image has been mistakenly dated 1875 in Griswold del Castillo, "The del Valle Family and the Fantasy Heritage," 2–15.

84 Two additional photographs document the famous Fourth of July Celebrations at Camulos in 1888 or possibly before; in one, Josepha holds a U.S. flag in her hand.

85 Their ranch was part of a Mexican land grant, measuring some eleven square leagues (roughly 48,000 acres); it was given to Antonio del Valle, their grandfather, in 1839. He called it Rancho San Francisco. After Antonio's death in 1841

the Mexican government divided the ranch among his heirs. Ygnacio senior, born in Mexico in 1818, received 1,800 acres and called it Rancho Camulos. He was commissioner in the secularization of Santa Cruz and Dolores Missions, was the alcalde of Los Angeles in 1850, and under American rule was elected recorder of the county. Wilson, *Reproduction of Thomson and West, History of Santa Barbara and Ventura County*, 350.

86 Rancho Camulos Museum, *Where the History, Myth and Romance of Old California Still Linger.*

87 Reginaldo F. del Valle was born in Los Angeles on December 15, 1854, went to public schools in Los Angeles, and continued his education at the University of Santa Clara, where he graduated in 1873. Newmark, "Historical Profiles," 74.

88 Ibid.

89 Griswold del Castillo, "The del Valle Family and the Fantasy Heritage," 9; Smith, *This Land Was Ours*, 177.

90 Griswold del Castillo, "The del Valle Family and the Fantasy Heritage," 10, cites *La Fe en la Democracia*, November 23, 1884.

91 Major Horace Bell credits all the horses to del Valle. Leonard Pitt credits the horses to both del Valle and Pio Pico, as does the *Star*. Bell, *Reminiscences of a Ranger*, 110–11; Pitt, *The Decline of the Californios*, 158; *Los Angeles Star*, August 6, 1853.

92 The Rangers were to be supported by both county funds and private subscription. It was hoped that they could eventually hire twenty-five men, but that they were funded at all marks a significant point in the evolution of a police force. The county hoped to be reimbursed by the state legislature. *Los Angeles Star*, August 6, 1853, 2; February 11, 1854, 2.

93 As an interesting side note, the del Valle family once owned parts of El Tejon Ranch, which lies just north of Los Angeles County. An extremely reliable source told me that at least one lynching had occurred on the ranch in the twentieth century (under different owners), but since the source would not go on record, the case could not be included in the final count.

94 Griswold del Castillo, "The del Valle Family and the Fantasy Heritage," 9.

95 First published in 1884, *Ramona* eventually went through 135 editions and was the subject of three feature films, the most notable of which may have been the 1927 version that starred Dolores del Río. Monroy, "Ramona, I Love You," 134–36.

96 After 1890 there were a number rival claims to the Ramona myth from Rancho Guajome, but it has been argued that this claim was derived more as part of a scheme to aid land developers than based in actual fact. Griswold del Castillo, "The del Valle Family and the Fantasy Heritage," 3, 137; Monroy, "Ramona, I Love You," 137.

97 The house is now preserved as a historical landmark; its orientation and unusual porch as well as the overall configuration of the ranch all appear to match Hunt's narrative description.

98 In the 1850s many of the wealthiest families, including the del Valles, had kept

"city" homes on the plaza square, but as the area began to decline the del Valles sold their home and took up permanent residence at Camulos.

99 "State of California against Adolfo Silvas," *Pardon Papers for Adolfo Silvas*, 201.

100 Ibid., 1–2.

101 He was sentenced to fifty years in prison. *Los Angeles Daily Times*, Friday, March 20, 1885, 4.

102 Rodolfo Silvas and Francisco Martínez were executed on March 20, 1885. *Los Angeles Daily Herald*, March 20, 1885; Thompson, *American Character*, 53.

103 A detailed example of this practice is addressed in the following chapter.

104 "State of California against Adolfo Silvas," *Pardon Papers for Adolfo Silvas*, 29–30.

105 Ibid., 28.

106 Ibid., 78.

107 Ibid., 80.

108 Ibid., 82.

109 Ibid., 178–79.

110 Ibid., 179–81.

111 Ibid., 183.

112 It seems unlikely that Juana hid the knife, and she was never charged with any crime. Ibid., 199.

113 Ibid., 187.

114 Ibid.

115 Ibid., 186–202.

116 Ibid.

117 Griffin, "Letter to Governor, March 10, 1885," ibid.

118 Ibid.

119 Ibid.

120 Howard, "Letter to the Governor, March 17, 1885," in *Pardon Papers for Adolfo Silvas*.

121 White, "Letter to the Governor on March 13, 1885," in *Pardon Papers for Adolfo Silvas*.

122 *Los Angeles Daily Times*, March 21, 1885, 4.

123 Ibid.

124 In the *sistema de castas* of colonial Mexico there was a wide variety of terms which covered just about every racial combination one could think of. For example, the first generation from a European and an Indian was mestiza (half-Indian), and subsequent generations were *cuarterona* (one-quarter Indian), *ochavona* (one-eighth Indian), and the *punchuela* (white). For a detailed discussion of the *sistema de castas*, see Katzan, *Casta Paintings*, 44–49.

FOUR Signifying Bodies

1 See chapter 1.

2 Graham, *Lavater's Essays on Physiognomy*, 77.

3 Ibid.

4   *San Francisco Alta California*, March 18, 1853, 2.

5   Rivers, *Face Value*, 20, cites Aristotle, *Complete Works*, 1:1240.

6   Ibid.

7   Darwin specifically references Lavater's *Essays on Physiognomy*. Darwin, *Expressions of the Emotions in Man and Animals*, 3.

8   Ibid., 122.

9   Ibid., 310.

10 Ibid. Darwin cites volume 3 of an earlier edition. In a 1907 edition, the passage reads: "It is only in white men that the instantaneous penetration of the dermoidal system by the blood can produce that slight change of the colour of the skin which adds so powerful an expression to the emotions of the soul. 'How can those be trusted who know not how to blush?' says the European, in his dislike of the Negro and the Indian." Alexander Von Humboldt, *Personal Narrative of Travels to the Equinoctial Regions of America During The Years 1799–1804*, Vol. 1, Chapter 1.9 (London: George Bell and Sons, 1907), unpaginated.

11 Darwin, *Expressions of the Emotions in Man and Animals*, 320.

12 Degeneration is "a condition analogous to illness in which the human organism is said to exist in a state of silent and for the most part invisible decay." Lombroso and Ferrero, glossary, *Criminal Woman, the Prostitute, and the Normal Woman*, 287.

13 Paredes, *"With His Pistol in His Hand,"* 16.

14 Graham, *Lavater's Essays on Physiognomy*, 35.

15 Ibid.

16 *Sacramento Union*, October 31, 1851.

17 Ibid., 2.

18 *New York Times*, March 13, 1889, 7, cites *Cleveland Leader*.

19 *New York Times*, October 6, 1889, 4.

20 For a discussion of the relationship between the antilynching movement and frontier justice, see chapter 1.

21 Special thanks to Julie Carson for her discussion and e-mails on Barthes (December 19–20, 2004).

22 "All images are polysemous; they imply, underlying their signifiers, a 'floating chain' of signifieds, the reader is able to choose some and ignore others." Barthes, "Rhetoric of the Image," 274.

23 Ibid.

24 Ibid., 275.

25 This handwritten comment is found on the back of a lynching postcard in the author's collection.

26 Barthes, *Camera Lucida*, 5.

27 *San Francisco Call*, May 15, 1874; *San Francisco Call*, March 20, 1875, in Bryam, *Edward Byram Scrapbooks*, February 19, 1873–August 30, 1876. See also May, "Tiburcio Vasquez," 123–35. The photography session is mentioned in *San Francisco Call*, May 28, 1874, in Bryam, *Edward Byram Scrapbooks*, February 19, 1873–August 30, 1876.

28 See appendix 2.

29 *San Francisco Call*, March 19, 1875, in Bryam, *Edward Byram Scrapbooks*, February 19, 1873–August 30, 1876; *San Francisco Call*, May 28, 1874, in Bryam, *Edward Byram Scrapbooks*, February 19, 1873–August 30, 1876.

30 *Los Angeles Star*, July 25, 1857.

31 *Los Angeles Star*, August 15, 1857; Vasquez arrived at San Quentin on August 26, 1857, and escaped on June 25, 1859. He was returned to San Quentin in August 1859 and completed his term and was released on August 13, 1863. He was caught attempting to steal a herd of cattle and was again sent to San Quentin in January 1867. He was released on June 4, 1870. *San Francisco Call*, May 16, 1874, in Bryam, *Edward Byram Scrapbooks*, February 19, 1873–August 30, 1876.

32 Rasmussen, "A Forgotten Hero," 3; Truman, *Life, Adventures and Capture of Tiburcio Vasquez*, 14–15.

33 Boessenecker, *Gold Dust and Gunsmoke*, 133; see also Boessenecker, "California Bandidos," 419–34.

34 Vasquez Rocks is a regional park located just northeast of Los Angeles County; the medical center is in Union City, California.

35 See Boessenecker, "California Bandidos," 419–34.

36 Truman, *Life Adventures and Capture of Tiburcio Vasquez*, 14–15.

37 One newspaper reported that Tiburcio was born in 1838; he claimed to have been born in 1837. His actual birthday was August 11, 1835. Secrest, *California Desperados*, 141; *San Francisco Call*, May 15, 1874, and March 20, 1875, in Bryam, *Edward Byram Scrapbooks*, February 19, 1873–August 30, 1876; May, "Tiburcio Vasquez," 122.

38 The reference to speech making is borrowed from the Arayo case in the previous chapter. Vasquez was said to have received scores of visitors. Truman, *Life Adventures and Capture of Tiburcio Vasquez*, 14–15. *San Francisco Call*, March 19, 1875, in Bryam, *Edward Byram Scrapbooks*, February 19, 1873–August 30, 1876.

39 It specifically states: "A Judgment of death must be executed within the walls or yard of a jail, or some convenient private place in the county." It also specifies that the sheriff must be present as well as a physician, the district attorney, twelve reputable citizens, ministers (two optional), relatives or friends of the condemned (five optional), and as many officers as necessary. California Department of Corrections, "History of Capital Punishment in California."

40 *San Francisco Call*, May 15, 1874–1875, in Bryam, *Edward Byram Scrapbooks*, February 19, 1873–August 30, 1876.

41 The pathognomical method was not favored by pseudo-Aristotle and is distinguished from physiognomy in Lavater's *Essays on Physiognomy*. See Lavater, *Essays on Physiognomy*, Vol. 1; Rivers, *Face Value*, 19–20; Graham, *Lavater's Essays on Physiognomy*, 35.

42 Hastings, *The Emigrant's Guide to Oregon and California*, 113.

43 Ibid.

44 *San Francisco Call*, May 28, 1874–1875, in Bryam, *Edward Byram Scrapbooks*, February 19, 1873–August 30, 1876.

45 For more on Herbert Spencer, see chapter 1.

46 Secrest, *California Desperados*, 139.

47 Lombroso's born criminal is, "A pure or natural offender, someone with four or more degenerative characteristics and who can thus be defined as belonging to the full criminal type." Lombroso and Ferrero, glossary, *Criminal Woman, the Prostitute, and the Normal Woman*, 285.

48 For a detailed analysis of the influence of physiognomy on artists and criminologists alike, see Cowlings, *The Artist as Anthropologist*. Cowlings specifically traces the many ways in which the concept of the type was applied and misapplied to the criminal body in England, noting that such characterizations were regularly identified as both class and race. The phrase "anthropological monster" is taken from Charles Goring, whose book *The English Convict* rejected the existence of a distinct criminal type. Cowling, *The Artist as Anthropologist*, 304–14, cites Goring, *The English Convict*, 370.

49 Like "desperado," "bandito" is another English language word that has its roots in Spanish but is not a Spanish word (*bandido*). With regard to "greaser," a second use of the term emerged in the middle of the twentieth century, when it was applied to rebellious young Anglo men who slicked their hair back, but even with such new uses, it continued to be directed at persons of Mexican and Latin American heritage as a racial slur in much of the American West.

50 *San Francisco Call*, March 20, 1875, in Bryam, *Edward Byram Scrapbooks*, February 19, 1873–August 30, 1876.

51 For a detailed description of the life of Gregorio Cortez, see Paredes, *"With His Pistol in His Hand."* A lynch mob of 300 to 350 men from Karnes County was disbanded by the sheriff, a man by the name of F. M. Fly. Ibid., 91.

52 *San Antonio Express*, June 25, 1901, cited in Paredes, *"With His Pistol in His Hand,"* 89.

53 *Los Angeles Star*, June 8, 1861, 4.

54 The original article was written in an intentionally heavy twang with phonetic spelling, which would have also added humor to the piece. Below is my translation, which may be easier for the contemporary reader to follow:

> His mouth, his paw and his feet are the principal features, and the striking point is the way them there legs of his get into his body. They go into each edge, sort of like the prongs go into a pitchfork. Of all the darned scary looking old cases for a president, ever I seen, he is decidedly the darndest. He looks like a ladder with half the rungs knocked out. I knocked an old bullfrog once, and drove a nail through his lips, into a post, tied two rocks to his hind legs, and stuck a darning needle into his body to let out the moisture, and left him there to dry. I saw him two weeks afterwards, and when I seen old Abe I thought it was an offal retribution come unto me, and that it was the same frog, only stretched a little longer, and had taken to wearing cloths to keep me from knowing him, a catching him and nailing him up again; a natural born fool am I, I swear I seen the same watery scary look in the eyes, and the same sorter knots on the backbone. I'm afraid George, something is

to come of my nailing up that frog, I swear I am ever since I seen old Abe; same shape, same color, same feel (cold as ice), and I'm damned if it isn't the same smell. Sut Lovegood (*Los Angeles Star*, June 8, 1861, 4).

55 George Washington Harris created and published a variety of adventures for Sut Lovingood in the *Spirit of the Times* during the 1850s. See *Spirit of the Times: A Chronicle of Field Sports, the Turf, Literature, and the Stage* (1831–1902).

56 There are also some interesting overlaps between anthropology, ethnography, and nineteenth-century erotic photography that could be addressed here, but that is outside the scope of this text. For a discussion of nineteenth-century erotic photography I would recommend Alloula, *The Colonial Harem*. For a general discussion of the type in anthropology, see Roslyn Poignant, "Surveying the Field of View: The Making of the RAI Collection," in *Anthropology and Photography*, 55.

57 Benjamin, *The Arcades Project*, 429.

58 "This individual, presented as always the same in his multiplicity, testifies to the anguish of the city dweller who is unable to break the magic circle of the type even though he cultivates the most eccentric peculiarities." Ibid., 430.

59 For a discussion of the influence of physiognomical thought in French literature, see Rivers, *Face Value*, in which he discusses the work of Balzac, Gautier, Marivaux, Zola, and others. For a discussion on physiognomical thought in Stendal, Poe, and others, see Graham, *Lavater's Essays on Physiognomy*.

60 Benjamin, *The Arcades Project*, 22.

61 It has been widely suggested that Samuel Langhorne Clemens (1835–1910), also known as Mark Twain, was so intrigued by the Sut Lovingood character that he modeled the youthful protagonist in *Huckleberry Finn* after him.

62 Avery, *The Harp of a Thousand Strings*, 19.

63 Lincoln was inaugurated on March 4, 1861. Meredith, *Mr. Lincoln's Contemporaries*, 128.

64 Perret, *Lincoln's War*, 30.

65 Pitt, *The Decline of the Californios*, 57–60, 183, 205.

66 Meredith, *Mr. Lincoln's Cameraman*, 66–76.

67 At least one collodian glass-plate negative (NPG.81.M8) from the series is in the Frederick Hill Meserve Collection in the National Portrait Gallery of the Smithsonian Institution in Washington. It measures 3 1/2 by 2 5/16 inches and is dated 1861.

68 Cobb, *Mathew B. Brady's Photographic Gallery in Washington*, 22.

69 Kunhardt and Kunhardt, *Mathew Brady and His World*, 85.

70 See Meredith, *Mr. Lincoln's Cameraman*.

71 The negatives may be at the Smithsonian National Portrait Gallery that now holds the Meserve collection; at the time of publication, only one of the series of portraits had been definitively identified. According to Frank Goodyear, the curator of the Smithsonian National Portrait Gallery, many of the negatives have not yet been examined, catalogued, or printed.

72 The chair and table also appear in an 1863 portrait of Lincoln taken in the Mathew

Brady Studio and credited to Tomas Le Mere. In fact, the pose, arrangement, and even the expression appear to be identical. This later image is part of the Frederick Hill Meserve Collection at the National Portrait Gallery in Washington, D.C.

73 George H. Story, a friend and associate of Brady's, was at the sitting and recalled the incident. His job was to assist in positioning the model. Meredith, *Mr. Lincoln's Cameraman*, 72.

74 Meredith, *Mr. Lincoln's Contemporaries*, 88.

75 The *Southern News* was only published in 1861 and 1862. *Southern News* (semiweekly; Los Angeles), July 24, 1861, 1.

76 In the 1850s and 1860s, lynching in California included whipping, flogging, and even blanket tossing. For additional information on these practices, see chapter 3. These practices are not included in the final appended case list because it only includes those cases that conform to the Tuskegee Institute Archives definition of lynching.

77 "Abraham Lincoln," *Phrenological Journal*, 98.

78 Ibid.

79 Ibid., 97.

80 Lavater, *Essays on Physiognomy*, 1:128.

81 Ibid., 3: 418.

82 Ibid., 2:97.

83 See Rivers, *Face Value*.

84 Lavater, *Essays on Physiognomy*, 4:188.

85 Ibid.

86 Ibid., 3:303.

87 Ibid., 3:423.

88 Ibid., 2:98.

89 Wells, *New Physiognomy*, 622.

90 Lavater, *Essays on Physiognomy*, 3:303.

91 Ibid.

92 Ibid.

93 Lavater, *Essays on Physiognomy* (abridged), 44.

94 Baudelaire, "The Painter of Modern Life."

95 Lavater, *Essays on Physiognomy*, 2:241.

96 "I am a miner, who wandered 'from away down east,' and came to sojourn in a strange land and 'see the elephant.' " *Miner's Ten Commandments*; "I may without vanity affirm, that I have 'seen the elephant.' " Shirley, *The Shirley Letters from California Mines*, 173.

97 Lavater, *Essays on Physiognomy*, 3:177–78.

98 Smith, *American Archives*, 69.

99 Lavater's great unfinished work, according to him, would have been to complete and publish a project he referred to as "Physiognomical Lines." Lavater, *Essays on Physiognomy*, 2:178, 236.

100 Ibid., 2:236.

101 Date given as December 10, 1852, in "Execution of Jose Forner on Russian Hill, S.F. for the murder of Jose Rodrigues," State Library, Prints Collection, Sacramento, California. His name also appears as "Forne" in a number of sources, including the *San Francisco Alta California* (daily), November 21, 1855, 2. It was not uncommon to see names spelled phonetically in the newspapers of the day; many examples were discovered while compiling the case list. His name is spelled "Forin" in Bancroft, *Popular Tribunals*, 1:746–47.

102 *San Francisco Alta California* (daily), November 21, 1855, 2.

103 Ibid. A daguerreotype is a unique photographic image that would have been produced by traveling photographers such as Robert H. Vance and William Shew, who traversed the state in this period. For more information on early daguerreotypes in California, see Johnson and Eymann, eds., *Silver and Gold*.

104 *San Francisco Alta California* (daily), November 21, 1855, 2.

105 See Wells, *New Physiognomy*, 41–42.

106 Ibid., 413.

107 Ibid.

108 Ibid., 412.

109 Ibid.

110 Ibid.

111 Ibid.

112 *San Francisco Examiner*, July 12, 1887.

113 *Weekly Colusa Sun*, July 16, 1887; *Sacramento Daily Record-Union*, July 11, 1887; Hong Di is identified as "Hong, Du, Chinaman," in Tuskegee Institute Archives, *Lynchings in California, 1883–1935*, 37.

114 *San Francisco Examiner*, July 12, 1887.

115 *Weekly Colusa Sun*, July 16, 1887; *Sacramento Daily Record-Union*, July 11, 1887; *Yolo Weekly Mail*, July 1887; *San Francisco Examiner*, July 11, 1887; Webb, *A History of Lynching in California since 1875*, 42.

116 Webb, *A History of Lynching in California since 1875*, 43.

117 *Yolo Weekly Mail*, July 16, 1887.

118 *Colusa Sun*, July 16, 1887, cites *New York Tribune*.

119 Gilman, *Difference and Pathology*, 21.

120 Johann Kaspar Lavater, *Essays on Physiognomy: Designed to Promote the Knowledge and the Love of Mankind*, trans. Thomas Holcroft, 9th ed. (London: William Tegg, 1855), 10–11, cited in Sobieszek, *Ghost in the Shell*, 93.

121 The statement was drafted by the coroner's jury at the inquest into Hong Di's cause of death and published in *Sacramento Record-Union*, July 12, 1887.

122 Zangrando, *The NAACP Crusade Against Lynching, 1909–1950*, table 3, 8.

123 On May 9, 1894, an unnamed black man was lynched for writing a letter to a white woman in West Texas. On May 23 of that same year, a man by the name of William Brooks was lynched for asking a white woman to marry him. Wells, *Southern Horrors*, 151–52.

124 Boessenecker, *Gold Dust and Gunsmoke*, 135; Varley, *The Legend of Joaquín Murrieta, California's Gold Rush Bandit*, 153, cites *Sacramento Union*, May 28, 1858.

FIVE The Wonder Gaze

1 A man named Joaquín Gurrieta is mentioned as early as 1852; "Gurrieta" is believed to be "Murrieta." Varley, *The Legend of Joaquín Murrieta, California's Gold
Rush Bandit*, 17; "Confession of Teodor Basquez [Vasquez]," *Benicia Gazette*, February 21, 1852, ibid., 174–79.

2 Ridge, *The Life and Adventures of Joaquín Murieta*, 158.

3 Ibid.

4 Ridge's grandfather, Major Ridge, had agreed to move the Cherokee people to
Indian territory and to give up their lands after the federal government prom-
ised that they would not be molested. At age twelve, Ridge's father, grandfather
(Major Ridge), and cousin were brutally murdered by Cherokees who disap-
proved of the move and blamed Ridge. Jackson, introduction to *The Life and
Adventures of Joaquín Murieta*, xiii.

5 He is referred to as "Carillo" in March 1853. *San Francisco Alta California*, March 4,
1853, 1. Neruda, *Splendor and Death of Joaquín Murrieta*; Latta, *Joaquín Murrieta and
His Horse Gangs*; Varley, *The Legend of Joaquín Murrieta, California's Gold Rush Bandit*; Rodriguez, *Days of Obligation*; Boessenecker, *Gold Dust and Gunsmoke*; Johnson, *Roaring Camp*.

6 Tom Bell, the "Gentleman Highwayman," was also said to wear a suit of armor
under his clothes. Captured on the Merced River, he was summarily executed
in 1856. Thompson and West, *History of Sutter County California with illustrations
descriptive of its scenery, residences, public buildings, fine blocks and manufactories . . .* , 80.

7 James Knowlton, also known as Yankee Jim, was lynched in Bridgeport, Nevada
County. One text claimed that all the lynchers died, from both natural and in-
flicted deaths. This idea is also found in the Murrieta myth. See Hittell, *History
of California*, 280; Ridge, *The Life and Adventures of Joaquín Murieta*, 13.

8 *San Francisco Alta California*, January 29, 1853, 2.

9 Ibid., November 16, 1853, 2.

10 Love's absence was also noted in an article in the *Los Angeles Star*, August 6, 1853, 2.

11 The term "banditti" is used in the *Union* and the *Star*. It is also used to describe
the 1857 actions of the Daniel-Flores gang in 1859. It is used by Bancroft and Bell
and noted in Varley and others. *Sacramento Union*, November 29, 1851, 3; *Los Angeles Star*, July 11, 1857, 2; August 27, 1859, 2; Bancroft, *Popular Tribunals*, 1:498. Bell,
Reminiscences of a Ranger, 43; Varley, *The Legend of Joaquín Murrieta, California's Gold
Rush Bandit*, 53.

12 Speaking of the greaser, Lighton wrote, "Anomalous as he is, he is one of the
few distinct types in our national life whose origin is fully known to us." The
full quotation can be found in chapter 1. Lighton, "The Greaser," 750.

13 For a discussion of physiognomical thought in the work of Balzac, Gautier, Marivaux, Zola and others, see Rivers, *Face Value*. For a discussion on physiognomical
thought in Stendal, Poe, and others, see Graham, *Lavater's Essays on Physiognomy*.

14 Graham, *Lavater's Essays on Physiognomy*, 188.

15　Ibid.

16　Ibid.,118.

17　Honoré de Balzac, *Le Cousin Pons*, 130; passage cited in Benjamin, *The Arcades Project*, 437.

18　*Sacramento Union*, December 12, cited in Varley, *The Legend of Joaquín Murrieta, California's Gold Rush Bandit*, 124.

19　The display was advertised in the *Herald* and noted in the *Star*; the admission fee was $1. *San Francisco Herald*, August 18, 1853; *Los Angeles Star*, September 3, 1853.

20　Pennoyer, *This Was California*, 43.

21　Well-respected locals like Andrés Pico and J. J. Warner also claimed to have recognized the head as that of Joaquín.

22　Burns, *The Robin Hood of El Dorado*, 280; Varley, *The Legend of Joaquín Murrieta, California's Gold Rush Bandit*, 126.

23　Varley, *The Legend of Joaquín Murrieta, California's Gold Rush Bandit*, 134.

24　They were sold for $36. *Los Angeles Star*, October 13, 1855, 2.

25　This time they were sold for $100. *Los Angeles Star*, October 13, 1855, 2.

26　They fetched a mere $11 in this sale. Varley, *The Legend of Joaquín Murrieta, California's Gold Rush Bandit*, 170–71.

27　Corcoran, "Robber Joaquin," 4.

28　Burns claims they vanished in the 1890. Burns, *The Robin Hood of El Dorado*, 281; Varley, *The Legend of Joaquín Murrieta, California's Gold Rush Bandit*, 170–71.

29　Rodriguez, *Days of Obligation*, 148.

30　Ibid.

31　Stevens, *Charles Christian Nahl*, 10.

32　There is some debate as to whether it may have been for political asylum, but Stevens convincingly argues that the Nahls did not leave France until a year after the 1848 revolution and thus considered any direct involvement to be unlikely. Stevens, *Charles Christian Nahl*, 10, 27.

33　See appendix 1; Stevens, *Charles Christian Nahl*, 37.

34　Stevens, *Charles Christian Nahl*, 54.

35　See Jackson, introduction to *The Life and Adventures of Joaquín Murieta*, xxviii.

36　If you are still unconvinced that Murrieta's expression has been manipulated to give him a deeply disturbing expression, I would like to suggest that you stand in front of a mirror and try to get the whites above your own irises to show. Several of my students have tried—to the great amusement of their classmates.

37　Varley, *The Legend of Joaquín Murrieta, California's Gold Rush Bandit*, 110.

38　*Los Angeles Star*, September 3, 1853, 2.

39　Graham, *Lavater's Essays on Physiognomy*, 36.

40　*San Francisco Alta California*, February 19, 1853.

41　For Lacan, this is "The split in which the drive is manifested at the level of the scopic field." Lacan, *The Seminar of Jacques Lacan, Book XI*, 73.

42　Using the ideas of the imaginary, the symbolic, and the real, Lacan revised orthodox Freudian ideas about a stable psychic reality. Central to this work was the mirror stage (l'étage du miroir) which argued that the subject at the mirror stage finds subjectivity through language, culture, and the reflected image of a unified self. Ibid., 257, 279.

43 Ibid., 73.

44 Ibid., 73.

45 Allen, *Mexican Treacheries and Cruelties, Incidents and Suffering in the Mexican War*, unpaginated.

46 *Los Angeles Star*, September 3, 1853.

47 Bancroft referred to her as "Juanita" but the contemporary historian William B. Secrest has demonstrated that her name was "Josefa." Secrest cites the *Pacific Star* (steamer edition), July 15, 1851, along with Franklin Buck's eyewitness account of the lynching which refers to her as "Josefa." Alejandro Murguía also insists that her name was "Josefa" and not "Juanita." Bancroft, *Popular Tribunals*, 1:581; Secrest, *Juanita*, 29; Buck, *A Yankee Trader in the Gold Rush*, 29; Murguía, *The Medicine of Memory*, 41.

48 Secrest includes other "eyewitness" accounts that placed the crowd in the thousands. Numerous accounts confirm that "Josefa" was tried on the same platform Senator Weller made his speech the previous day. Bancroft defends Cannon's actions and describes it as a "glorious night" of drunken reverie and insisted that the broken down door was an accident. Secrest, *Juanita*, 22–24; Hurtado, *Intimate Frontiers*, 134–35; Bancroft, *Popular Tribunals*, 1:582–87.

49 Most accounts suggest that Josefa lived with a Mexican man, and some accounts suggest that Cannon had threatened him as well. Murguía, *The Medicine of Memory*, 51; Pitt, *The Decline of the Californios*, 73.

50 Excerpt from *San Francisco Alta California*, "A Woman Hung in Downieville—We are informed by Deputy Sheriff Gray; that on Saturday afternoon a Spanish woman was hung for stabbing to the heart a man by the name of Cannon, killing him instantly. Mr. Gray informs us that the deceased, in company with some others, had the night previously entered the house of the woman and created a riot and disturbance, which so outraged her, that when he presented himself the next morning to apologize for his behavior, he was met at the door by the female, who had in her hand a large Bowie knife, which she instantly drove into his heart." Passage quoted in Secrest, *Juanita*, 15.

51 Secrest, *Juanita*, 11.

52 A Dr. Aiken testified that she was pregnant but his statements were contested by the crowd and believed be a ploy to save the woman's life. Ibid., 23.

53 Murguía, *The Medicine of Memory*, 55.

54 Secrest, *Juanita*, 15.

55 Ibid.

56 Ibid., 29, cites *San Jose Pioneer*, November 12, 1881.

57 Bancroft, *Popular Tribunals*, 1:587.

58 *Los Angeles Star*, October 22, 1853, 2.

59 The note and the name appear on the back of the photograph in the Regional History Collection at the University of Southern California. According to the 1850 (completed in 1851) California census there does not appear to be a "Martina" listed in any of the Sepulveda households. There was a fourteen-year-old Indian girl in the Juan Sepulveda household but her name was María Dolores. In the 1880 census, a Mexican woman by the name of Martina Espinoza is listed as a housekeeper in San Juan Capistrano, and her age is given as thirty-nine, so she would have been sixteen in 1857. U.S. Census Bureau, 1880 Federal Census, Capistrano, Los Angeles, Calif., 236.

60 The image can also be found at the Henry E. Huntington Library and Art Gallery, which records her name as Martina Espinoza. Martina is also identified in Boessenecker, *Gold Dust and Gunsmoke*, 117; Rasmussen, "When Justice was a Mob and a Rope," *Los Angeles Times*, October 4, 1998, 3.

61 "Martina" is identified as Flores's sweetheart, but her role is considered by some scholars to be unverifiable. Rasch, "The Story of the Hangman's Tree," 60.

62 In 1901, Pierce bought the George Wharton James Southwestern Native American Portraits Collection, which contained 2,000 to 3,000 negatives of Indians, along with images of the southwestern frontier. The C. C. Pierce Collection was eventually sold and became part of the Title Insurance and Trust Company Collection. The Title Insurance Collection eventually became a part of the California Historical Society Collection. This collection can be broken down into two main collections: the Los Angeles Chamber of Commerce Collection (1890–1960) and the Title Insurance Collection (1860–1960). In 1990, the Historical Society Collection was placed on "long-term deposit" in the Regional History Collection, formerly housed in the Regional History Center at the University of Southern California. In fall 2001, the photographs were in the process of being moved again, though only from one building to another.

63 *Los Angeles Star*, March 3, 1860, 2.

64 Ibid.

65 Ibid., November 27, 1858, 2.

66 Ibid.

67 Bell, *Reminiscences of a Ranger*, 382.

68 Ibid.

69 Pitt, *The Decline of the Californios*, 167.

70 Identified as Charles Fluggart in the *Los Angeles Star*, January 31, 1857, 2; Identified as Pflugardt in Rasch, "The Story of the Hangman's Tree," 60.

71 Pitt notes the war of reform may have motivated some men to join Flores, but this idea has not gained much support from other scholars. Pitt, *The Decline of the Californios*, 168.

72 Pitt claims Barton had six men. Horace Bell says Barton had twelve men. The *Star* identified six men and a French guide. Bell, *Reminiscences of a Ranger*, 385; Pitt, *The Decline of the Californios*, 168; *Los Angeles Star*, January 31, 1857, 2.

73 Bell claims the "insurgents" lost no men. The *Star* claims that the bandits lost

three. Bell, *Reminiscences of a Ranger*, 386–87; *Los Angeles Star*, January 31, 1857, 2; Newmark, *Sixty Years in Southern California*, 204–10.

74 *Los Angeles Star*, August 27, 1859, 2.

75 The *Star* claimed there were 119 men including the Indians. *Star*, February 7, 1857, 2.

76 Traveling through Texas during the Mexican-American war, Lt. Rankin Dilworth notes the general attitude of Mexicans toward the Texas Rangers. He writes, "The Mexicans dread the Texans more than they do the devil, and they have good reason for it if all the reports that we hear are true." Dilworth, *The March to Monterrey*, 24.

77 The Berreyesa case is addressed in the introduction.

78 *Los Angeles Star*, February 14, 1857.

79 Santos is identified as having been shot at the mission, presumably when the noose broke. *Los Angeles Star*, February 7, 14, 1857, 2.

80 Soto was shot through the heart. He was then decapitated, and his head was brought to town to be identified by a W. H. Peterson. Peterson had met Soto previously when he had been interrogated in connection with charges of robbery and attempted murder. *Los Angeles Star*, January 31, 1857, 2.

81 There are differing accounts of the event, some suggesting three and others four hangings. However, in comparing the names and cases that were cited, along with published firsthand testimony, four is the number that will be used in this text. *San Francisco Alta California*, February 15, 1857.

82 Ibid.; *Los Angeles Star*, February 14, 1857; Newmark, *Sixty Years in Southern California*, 208; Boessenecker, *Gold Dust and Gunsmoke*, 126; Pitt, *The Decline of the Californios*, 169.

83 Bell, *Reminiscences of a Ranger*, 388–89.

84 *San Francisco Alta California*, February 15, 1857, 2.

85 Ibid., February 14, 15, 1857; Newmark gives the 16th as the date and San Buenaventura as the site, but the case is reported in the *Star* on the 14th and gives the 8th as date and reports that it was the posse on the way to San Buenaventura. Newmark, *Sixty Years in Southern California*, 209; *San Francisco Alta California*, February 15, 1857; Boessenecker, *Gold Dust* and Gunsmoke, 127.

86 Bancroft, *California*, 502; *Los Angeles Star*, February 7, 1857, 2; *San Francisco Alta California*, February 15, 1857, 2.

87 *Los Angeles Star*, February 14, 1857, 2.

88 Pitt, *The Decline of the Californios*, 171; *Los Angeles Star*, February 21, 1857, 2; Newmark, *Sixty Years in Southern California*, 209.

89 *El Clamour Público*, February 21, 1857, cited in Pitt, *The Decline of the Californios*, 171.

90 Newmark, *Sixty Years in Southern California*, 209; [Angel], *History of San Luis Obispo County with Illustrations and Biographical Sketches of Its Prominent Men and Pioneers*, 298; Pitt, *The Decline of the Californios*, 171.

91 Pitt, *The Decline of the Californios*, 172.

92 *Los Angeles Star*, February 20, 1858, 2.

93 Boessenecker, *Gold Dust and Gunsmoke*, 194; *Santa Cruz Sentinel*, February 28, 1857, cited in Secrest, *California Desperados*, 156.

94 The *San Jose Daily Patriot* spelled his name "Jose Guerra" [Higuera]; cited in Seacrest, *California Desperados*, 130, 148.

95 *Los Angeles Star*, October 18, 1856.

96 *Los Angeles Star*, January 3, 1857.

97 Boessenecker, *Gold Dust and Gunsmoke*, 37.

98 *Monterey Gazette*, January 11, 1858, cited in *New York Times*, January 22, 1858, 4; *Los Angeles Star*, February 27, 1858, 2.

99 For a detailed account of the Bracey case, see Boessenecker, *Gold Dust and Gunsmoke*, 37–38.

100 Ibid., 136; *Los Angeles Star*, December 18, 1858; Boessenecker, *Badge and Buckshot*, 25.

101 Walter Murray wrote to Anne Murray Evans, "That night we visited the jail and endeavored to disclose his accomplices. He was silent as the grave. We left him hanging from the roof of his cell." Letter cited in Boessenecker, *Gold Dust and Gunsmoke*, 111.

102 Varley, *The Legend of Joaquín Murrieta, California's Gold Rush Bandit*, 153; Boessenecker, *Gold Dust and Gunsmoke*, 113.

103 *Los Angeles Star*, June 19, 1858; [Angel], *History of San Luis Obispo County with Illustrations and Biographical Sketches of Its Prominent Men and Pioneers*, 298, 301; Boessenecker, *Gold Dust and Gunsmoke*, 113–16; Pitt, *The Decline of the Californios*, 174–77.

104 *Los Angeles Star*, September 9, 10, 1859; Boessenecker, *Gold Dust and Gunsmoke*, 70–71; Pitt, *The Decline of the Californios*, 178–79.

105 Wilson, *Reproduction of Thomson and West, History of Los Angeles County with Illustrations and Biographical Sketches of its Prominent Men and Pioneers*, 82; *Los Angeles Star*, November 27, 1858, 2.

106 *Los Angeles Star*, November 27, 1858, 2.

107 Ibid.

108 Ibid.; Wilson, *History of Los Angeles County*, 82; Newmark, *Sixty Years in Southern California*, 223; Boessenecker, *Gold Dust and Gunsmoke*, 131; *Los Angeles Star*, December 4, 1858.

109 *Los Angeles Star*, December 4, 1858, 2.

110 Ibid.

111 Ibid.

112 Ibid.

113 Pitt, *The Decline of the Californios*, xv.

114 Ibid., 291.

115 Bell, *Reminiscences of a Ranger*, 148.

116 Ibid.

117 Ibid., 149–50.

118 Ibid.

119 Ibid.

120 Ibid.

121 Smelser, Wilson, and Mitchell, *America Becoming*, 3.

CONCLUSION

1 Ken Gonzales-Day, "Twisted." Read at Angles Gallery in Santa Monica, Californian. The reading was organized by Susan Silton to commemorate her image series entitled "Tornado in a Box," which included the text. Susan Silton, "Tornado in a Box," 2004.

2 Ralph Ellison's *Invisible Man* used the idea of "invisible" as a metaphor for the African American experience in the United States. In the book's darkest moments, Ellison's character sought to suggest that blacks did not even register in the social consciousness of Anglo-American society. In the prologue to the book the narrator states, "I am invisible, understand, simply because people refuse to see me. Like the bodiless heads you see sometimes in circus sideshows, it is as though I have been surrounded by mirrors of hard, distorting glass. When they approach me they see only my surroundings, themselves, or figments of their imagination—indeed, everything and anything except me." *Lynching in the West* has sought to demonstrate that many of these cases were noted in their own day and that it was only later that racial, ethnic, and regional subtexts came to obscure this history, less as a willful act of denial than a systemic misrecognition. Ellison, *Invisible Man*, 3.

BIBLIOGRAPHY

NEWSPAPERS

Bodie Free Press
Columbus [Ohio] *Dispatch*
Colusa Sun
El Clamor Público (Los Angeles)
Eugene [Oregon] *Morning Register*
Kern County Courier (Bakersfield)
Kern County Gazette (Bakersfield)
Los Angeles Daily Herald
Los Angeles Daily Times
Los Angeles Star
Los Angeles Times
Mendocino Democrat
Monterey Gazette
Montgomery [Ala.] *Advertiser*
New York Times
New York Weekly Tribune
Oakland Daily News
Oakland Tribune
Sacramento Bee
Sacramento Placer Times
Sacramento Record-Union

Sacramento Transcript
Sacramento Union
San Antonio Express
San Francisco Alta California
San Francisco Bulletin
San Francisco Call
San Francisco Chronicle
San Francisco Examiner
San Francisco Herald
San Francisco Post
San Jose Herald
Santa Cruz Local Item
Santa Cruz Sentinel
Santa Rosa Republican
Siskiyou Daily News
Sonora Herald
Southern News (Los Angeles)
Times (London)
Washington [D.C.] *National Intelligencer*
Yolo Weekly Mail
Yreka Herald

"Abraham Lincoln." *Phrenological Journal* 40, October 1864, 97–98.

Allen, G. N. *Mexican Treacheries and Cruelties, Incidents and Suffering in the Mexican War.* Boston: Lieut. G. N. Allen, 1847.

Allen, Irving Lewis. *Unkind Words: Ethnic Labeling from Redskin to WASP.* New York: Bergin and Garvey, 1990.

Allen, James, Hilton Als, John Lewis, and Leon F. Litwack. *Without Sanctuary: Lynching Photography in America.* Foreword by John Lewis. Santa Fe: Twin Palms Publishers, 2000.

Alloula, Malek. *The Colonial Harem.* Translated by Myrna Godzich and Wlad Godzich. Minneapolis: University of Minnesota Press, 1986.

[Angel, Myron]. *History of Placer County with Illustrations and Biographical Sketches of Its Prominent Men and Pioneers.* Oakland: Thompson and West, 1882.

————. *History of San Luis Obispo County with Illustrations and Biographical Sketches of Its Prominent Men and Pioneers.* Oakland: Thompson and West, 1883.

Aristotle. *Complete Works.* Edited by Jonathan Barns. Princeton: Princeton University Press, 1984.

Asad, Talal. "On Torture." In *Social Suffering.* Edited by Arthur Kleinman, Veena Das, and Margaret Lock. Berkeley: University of California Press, 1997.

Athearn, Robert G. *The Mythic West in Twentieth-Century America.* Lawrence: University Press of Kansas, 1986.

Avery, Samuel Putnam. *The Harp of a Thousand Strings; or, Laughter for a Lifetime. Konceived, Comp., and Komically Konkokted, by Spavery [pseud.] . . . Aided, Added, and Abetted by Over 200 Kurious Kutz, from Original Designs . . . The whole engraved by S. P. Avery.* New York: Dick and Fitzgerald, ca. 1858.

Balzac, Honoré de. *Le Cousin Pons.* Translated by Herbert J. Hunt. London: Penguin, 1968.

Bancroft, Hubert Howe. *California.* 7 volumes. San Francisco: History Company, 1884–1900.

————. *Popular Tribunals,* Volumes 1–2. San Francisco: History Company, 1887.

Barthes, Roland. *Camera Lucida: Reflections on Photography.* Translated by Richard Howard. New York: Hill and Wang, 1981.

————. "Rhetoric of the Image." In *Classic Essays on Photography.* Edited by Alan Trachtenberg. New Haven, Conn.: Leete's Island Books, 1980.

Baudelaire, Charles. *Baudelaire: His Prose and Poetry.* Edited by T. R. Smith. New York: Modern Library, 1919.

————. *Les Fleurs du Mal* (1857). Paris: Musée d'Orsay, 1861.

————. *Mirror in Art: Critical Studies.* Translated by Jonathan Mayne. New York: Doubleday/Anchor Books, 1955.

————. *Baudelaire: Selected Poems.* Translated by Joanna Richardson. New York: Penguin, 1975.

————. "The Painter of Modern Life." In *The Painter of Modern Life and Other Essays.* Translated by J. Mayne (1964). Reprinted in *Modern Art and Modernism: A Critical*

Anthology. Edited by Francis Frascina and Charles Harrison. New York: Harper and Row, 1982, 12–15. Originally published in *Figaro*, November 1863, 23–27.

Beccaria, Cesare Bonesana. *Of Crimes and Punishment.* 1764. Translated by David Young. Indianapolis: Hackett Publishing, 1986.

Bell, Horace. *Being further Reminiscences of a Ranger, Major Horace Bell.* Edited by Lanier Bartlett. New York: William Morrow, 1930.

————. *Reminiscences of a Ranger; or, Early Times in Southern California.* Los Angeles: Yarnell, Caystile and Mathes, Printers, 1881.

Benjamin, Walter. *Illuminations.* Translated by Harry Zohn. Edited with an introduction by Hannah Arendt. New York: Schocken Books, 1968.

————. *Gesammelte Schriften*, Volume 1. Frankfurt on Main: Suhrkamp Verlag, 1982.

————. *The Arcades Project.* Translated by Howard Eiland and Kevin McLaughlin. Cambridge, Mass.: Belknap Press of Harvard University Press, 1999.

————. *Walter Benjamin: Selected Writing.* Volume 2: *1927–1934.* Edited by Michael W. Jennings, Howard Eiland, and Gary Smith. Translated by Rodney Livingston et al. Cambridge, Mass.: Belknap Press of Harvard University Press, 1999.

Blew, Robert. "Vigilantism in Los Angeles, 1835–1874." *Southern California Quarterly* 54, no. 1 (spring 1972): 11–30.

Boessenecker, John. "California Bandidos: Social Bandits or Sociopaths?" *Southern California Quarterly* 80, no. 4 (fall 1998): 419–34.

————. *Badge and Buckshot: Lawlessness in Old California.* Norman: University of Oklahoma Press, 1988.

————. *Gold Dust and Gunsmoke: Tales of Gold Rush Outlaws, Gunfighters, Lawmen, and Vigilantes.* New York: Wiley, 1999.

————. *Lawman: The Life and Times of Harry Morse, 1835–1912.* Norman: University of Oklahoma Press, 1998.

Buck, Franklin. *A Yankee Trader in the Gold Rush.* Boston: Houghton Mifflin, 1930.

Buck-Morss, Susan. *The Dialectics of Seeing.* Cambridge, Mass.: MIT Press, 1989.

Burns, Walter Noble. *The Robin Hood of El Dorado: The Saga of Joaquin Murrieta, Famous Outlaw of California's Age of Gold.* 1854. Foreword by Richard Griswold del Castillo. Albuquerque: University of New Mexico Press, 1999.

Byram, Edward. *Edward Byram Scrapbooks.* San Francisco: California Historical Society, 1874–75.

California Department of Corrections. "Number of Executions, 1893 to Present." Sacramento: California Department of Corrections, Communications Office, March 2003. Available online. Printout in possession of author.

————. "Death Row Tracking System: Condemned Inmate Summary List." Sacramento, January 7, 2005. Available online. Printout in possession of author.

————. "History of Capital Punishment in California." Sacramento, 2004. Available online. Printout in possession of author.

Carrigan, William D., and Clive Webb. "The Lynching of Persons of Mexican Origin or Descent in the United States, 1848–1928." *Journal of Social History* 37, no. 2 (winter 2003): 411–38.

Chadbourn, James Harmon. *Lynching and the Law*. Chapel Hill: University of North Carolina Press, 1933.

[Chamberlain, William Henry and Henry Laurenz Wells]. *History of Sutter County, California: with Illustrations Descriptive of its Scenery, Residences, Public Buildings, Fine Blocks and Manufactories*. Oakland, Calif.: Thompson and West, 1879.

"Civil Cases, 1850–1851." *Alcalde's Docket*. Volume 1: 1851. Sacramento: Sacramento Archives Museum and Collection Center.

Cobb, Josephine. *Mathew B. Brady's Photographic Gallery in Washington*. Reprinted from the Columbia Historical Society Records, Volumes 53–56. Washington, D.C., 1955.

Collins, Patricia Hill. Introduction to Ida B. Wells-Barnett, *On Lynchings*. Amherst, N.Y.: Humanity Books, 2002, 9–24.

Conquergood, Dwight. "Lethal Theatre: Performance, Punishment, and the Death Penalty." *Theatre Journal* 54 (2002): 339–67.

Constitution of the State of California. Sacramento: California State Archives, 1849.

Cook, "Historical Demography," in *Handbook of North American Indians*, Volume 8: *California*, ed. by Robert F. Heizer. Washington, D.C.: Smithsonian Institution, 1978.

Cooper, David D. *The Lesson of the Scaffold: The Public Execution Controversy in Victorian England*. Athens: Ohio University Press, 1974.

Corcoran, May S. "Robber Joaquin." *Grizzly Bear*, June 1921.

Coronel, Antonio. *Tales of Mexican California*. Edited by Boyce B. Nunis Jr. Translated by Diane de Avalle-Arce. Los Angeles: Bellerophon Books, 1994. Original transcription dictated to Tomas Savage for H. H. Bancroft (1877) in the Bancroft Library.

Cowlings, Mary. *The Artist as Anthropologist: The Representation of Type and Character in Victorian Art*. Cambridge: Cambridge University Press, 1989.

Darwin, Charles. *The Expression of the Emotions in Man and Animals*. New York: D. Appleton and Company, 1873.

Das, Venna, and Arthur Kleinman. "Introduction." In *Remaking a World: Violence, Social Suffering and Recovery*, edited by Veena Das, Arthur Kleinman, Margaret Lock, Mamphela Ramphele, and Pamela Reynolds. Berkeley: University of California Press, 2001.

Davis, Tad. *California Criminal Justice Time Line*. Edited by Tad Davis. Research by Adel Spears. Sacramento: California Department of Justice, Division of Criminal Justice Information Services, Bureau of Criminal Information and Analysis, Criminal Justice Statistics Center, 2002.

De la Guerra, Pablo. *Speech of Hon. Pablo de la Geurra, of Santa Barbara, In the Senate of California, on the 17th of April, 1855*. Sacramento: State Tribune Office, 1855.

Dilworth, Rankin. *The March to Monterrey: The Diary of Lieutenant Rankin Dilworth, U.S. Army*. Edited by Lawrence R. Clayton and Joseph E. Chance. El Paso: University of Texas at El Paso, 1996.

[Dobbin, Hamilton Henry]. *Album of San Francisco: A Collection of Miscellaneous Photographs of Places, Events and Persons of San Francisco, 1836–1927*. 2 volumes, compiled and signed by Hamilton Henry Dobbin (1836–1927). Sacramento: California State Library, History Room.

Dray, Philip. *At the Hands of Persons Unknown: The Lynching of Black America.* New York: Random House, 2002.

Duff, Charles. *A Handbook on Hanging.* Revised and enlarged edition, 1961. Reprint. New York: New York Review of Books, 2001.

Edwards, Elizabeth, ed. *Anthropology and Photography, 1860–1920.* New Haven: Yale University Press in association with The Royal Anthropological Institute, London, 1992.

Ellison, Ralph. *Invisible Man.* 1952. New York: Vintage International, 1980.

Farnham, T. J. *Life, Adventures, and Travels in California.* 1844. New York: Nafis and Cornish, 1855.

Farrell, Harry. *Swift Justice: Murder and Vengeance in a California Town.* New York: St. Martin's Press, 1992.

Firstenberg, Lauri. "Autonomy and the Archive in America: Reexamining the Intersection of Photography and Stereotype." In *Only Skin Deep.* Edited by Coco Fusco and Brian Wallis. New York: Abrams, 2003.

Folley, Neil. *The White Scourge: Mexicans, Blacks, and Poor Whites in Texas Cotton Culture.* Berkeley: University of California Press, 1997.

Foucault, Michel. *Discipline and Punish: The Birth of the Prison.* Berkeley: University of California Press, 1966.

———. *The Order of Things: An Archaeology of the Human Sciences.* New York: Pantheon Books, 1971.

Frank, Herman W. *Scrapbook of Western Pioneer.* Los Angeles: Times-Mirror Press, 1934.

Fritz, Christine. *Federal Justice in California: The Court of Ogden Hoffman, 1851–1891.* Lincoln: University of Nebraska Press, 1991.

Galton, Francis. *Hereditary Genius: An Inquiry into Its Laws and Consequences.* 1892. New York: Horizon Press, 1952.

Gault, Robert. *Criminology.* Boston: D. C. Heath and Company, 1932.

General Electric. Advertisement. *American Annual of Photography* 46 (1932): Adv. 25.

Gilman, Sander L. *Difference and Pathology: Stereotypes of Sexuality, Race, and Madness.* Ithaca: Cornell University Press, 1985.

Ginzburg, Ralph. *One Hundred Years of Lynchings.* Baltimore: Black Classic Press, 1962.

Gordon, John D., III. *Authorized by No Law: The San Francisco Committee of Vigilance of 1856 and the U.S. Circuit Court for the Districts of California.* Pasadena: Ninth Judicial Circuit Historical Society; San Francisco: U.S. District Court for the Northern District of California Historical Society, 1987.

Goring, Charles. *The English Convict: A Statistical Study.* London: H. M. Stationery Office, 1913.

Graham, John. *Lavater's Essays on Physiognomy: A Study in the History of Ideas.* Bern: Peter Lang, 1979.

Grant, Donald L. *The Anti-lynching Movement, 1883–1932.* San Francisco: R and E Research Associates, 1975.

Griffin, John S. "Letter to the Governor, March 10, 1885." Pardon Papers: Adolfo Silvas. California State Archive, Sacramento.

Griswold del Castillo, Richard. "The del Valle Family and the Fantasy Heritage." *California History* 59, no. 1 (spring 1980): 2–15.

Guinn, J. M. *A History of California*. Los Angeles: Historic Record Company, 1907.

———. *Historical and Biographical Record of Los Angeles and Vicinity*. Chicago: Chapman Publishing Company, 1901.

Harris, George Washington. *Sut Lovingood. Yarns Spun by a "Nat'ral Born Durn'd Fool." Warped and Wove for Public Wear*. New York: Dick and Fitzgerald, 1867.

Harris, Robert. [Coroner's Inquest] "In the Matter of the Inquisition upon the Body of Calvin Hall, Held at Lookout, Modoc County. . . ." June 1901. Inquisition folder, documents relating to lynching. Bancroft Library, University of California, Berkeley.

Hastings, Lansford W. *The Emigrant's Guide to Oregon and California*. 1845. Reprint. New York: Da Capo Press, 1969.

Hayes, Benjamin. *Pioneer Notes from the Diaries of Judge Benjamin Hayes, 1849–1875*. Edited by Marjorie Tisdale. Los Angeles: Marjorie Tisdale, 1929.

Heizer, Robert F., and Alan J. Almquist. *The Other Californians: Prejudice and Discrimination under Spain, Mexico, and the United States to 1920*. Berkeley: University of California Press, 1977.

History of Toulumne County, California: Compiled from the Most Authentic Records. San Francisco: B. F. Alley Publishers, 1882.

Hitchens, Christopher. "Introduction." *A Handbook on Hanging* by Charles Duff. Revised and enlarged edition, 1961. Reprint. New York: New York Review of Books, 2001. xv–xxiv.

Hittell, Theodore Henry. *History of California*. Volume 3. San Francisco: N. J. Stone and Company, 1897.

Horsman, Reginald. *Race and Manifest Destiny: The Origins of American Racial Anglo-Saxonism*. Cambridge, Mass.: Harvard University Press, 1981.

Howard, Rene. "Letter to the Governor, March 17, 1885." Pardon papers: Adolfo Silvas. California State Archive, Sacramento.

Hundley, Norris. *The Great Thirst*. Revised edition. Berkeley: University of California Press, 2001.

Huntley, Henry Veel. *California: Its Gold and Its Inhabitants*. London: Thomas Cautley Newby, Publisher, 1856.

Hurtado, Albert L. *Intimate Frontiers: Sex, Gender, and Culture in Old California*. Albuquerque: University of New Mexico Press, 1999.

Hutchings, James. M. *Miner's Ten Commandments*. Placerville Calif.: James M. Hutchings, 1853.

Jackson, Helen Hunt. *Ramona*. Boston: Little Brown, 1884.

Jackson, Joseph Henry. "Introduction." *The Life and Adventures of Joaquín Murieta: The Celebrated California Bandit*. 1854. Norman: University of Oklahoma, 1955, xi–1.

Jacobson, Matthew Frye. *Barbarian Virtues: The United States Encounters Foreign Peoples at Home and Abroad, 1876–1917*. New York: Hill and Wang, 2000.

Johnson, Drew Heath, and Marcia Eymann. *Silver and Gold: Cased Images of the California Gold Rush*. Iowa City: University of Iowa Press, 1998.

Johnson, Susan Lee. *Roaring Camp*. New York: Norton, 2000.

Katzew, Ilona. *Casta Painting: Images of Race in Eighteenth-Century Mexico*. New Haven and London: Yale University Press, 2004.

Kristeva, Julia. *Powers of Horror: An Essay on Abjection*. Translated by Leon S. Roudiez. New York: Columbia University Press, 1982.

Kunhardt, Dorothy Meserve, and Philip B. Kunhardt Jr. *Mathew Brady and His World: Produced by Time-Life Books from the Pictures in the Meserve Collection*. New York: Time Life Books, [1977].

Lacan, Jacques. *The Seminar of Jacques Lacan, Book XI: The Four Fundamentals Concepts of Psychoanalysis*. 1973. Edited by Jacques-Alan Miller. Translated by Alan Sheridan. New York: Norton, 1977.

Lang, Margaret Hanna. *Early Justice in Sonora*. Sonora, Calif.: Mother Lode Press, 1963.

Langford, Nathaniel P. *Vigilante Days and Ways*. Helena: American and World Geographic Publishing, 1996.

Lapp, Rudolph M. "Negro Rights Activities in Gold Rush California." *California Historical Society Quarterly* 45 (March 1966): 3–20.

Latta, Frank F. *Joaquín Murrieta and His Horse Gangs*. Santa Cruz, Calif.: Bear State Books, 1980.

Lavater, Johann Caspar. *Essays on Physiognomy: Designed to Promote Knowledge and the Love of Mankind, Illustrated by More than Eight Hundred Engravings Accurately Copied; and Some Duplicates Added from Originals. Executed by, or under the Inspection of, Thomas Holloway*. Translated by Henry Hunter. London: J. Murray, 1789–98.

———. *Essays on Physiognomy: For the Promotion of the Knowledge and the Love of Mankind. Abridged from Mr. Holcroft's Translation*. Boston: William Spotswood and David West, 1794.

———. *Essays on Physiognomy: Designed to Promote the Knowledge and the Love of Mankind*. Translated by Thomas Holcroft. 9th ed. London: William Tegg, 1855.

Letts, John M. *California Illustrated: Including a Description of the Panama and Nicaragua Routes by a Returned Californian*. New York: William Holdredge, Publisher, 1852.

Lighton, William R. "The Greaser." *Atlantic Monthly* 83, no. 500 (June 1899): 750–56.

Lombroso, Cesare, and Guglielmo Ferrero. *Criminal Woman, the Prostitute, and the Normal Woman*. Translated with a new introduction by Nicole Hahn Rafter and Mary Gibson. Durham, N.C., and London: Duke University Press, 2004.

López, Ian F. Haney. *White by Law: The Legal Construction of Race*. New York: New York University Press, 1996.

"Lynchings: Los Angeles." Folder at the History and Genealogy Department, Los Angeles Public Library.

McGrath, Roger D. "A Violent Birth: Disorder, Crime, and Law Enforcement, 1849–1890." *California History* 81, no. 3/4 (2003): 27–73.

———. *Gunfighters, Highwaymen and Vigilantes: Violence on the Frontier*. Berkeley: University of California Press, 1984.

McKanna, Clare V., Jr. "Crime and Punishment: The Hispanic Experience in San Quentin, 1851–1880." *Southern California Quarterly* 72, no. 1 (spring 1990): 1–17.

Maestro, Marcello T. *Cesare Beccaria and the Origins of Penal Reform*. Translated by David Young. Philadelphia: Temple University Press, 1973.

Marryatt, Francis. "Admission Day Celebration." Catalogue entry notes. 1850. Washington, D.C.: Library of Congress.

Martinez, George A. "Mexican-Americans and Whiteness." In *Critical White Studies: Looking Behind the Mirror*. Edited by Richard Delgado and Jean Stefancic. Philadelphia: Temple University Press, 1997.

May, Ernest R. "Tiburcio Vasquez." *The Quarterly: Historical Society of Southern California* 29, no. 3/4 (September–December 1947): 123–35.

Mayo, Marrow. *Los Angeles*. New York: Alfred A. Knopf, 1933.

Mazda photoflash Lamp. Advertisement. *American Annual of Photography*. 1932. Adv. 25.

Meredith, Roy. *Mr. Lincoln's Cameraman: Mathew B. Brady*. New York: Charles Scribner's Sons, 1946.

———. *Mr. Lincoln's Contemporaries: An Album of Portraits by Mathew B. Brady*. New York: Charles Scribner's Sons, 1951.

Monroy, Douglas. "Ramona, I Love You." *California History* 81, no. 2 (2002): 134–53.

———. *Thrown Among Strangers: The Making of Mexican Culture of Frontier California*. Berkeley: University of California Press, 1990.

Montejano, David. *Anglos and Mexicans in the Making of Texas, 1836–1986*. Austin: University of Texas Press, 1987.

"Monthly Record of Current Events," *Harper's New Monthly Magazine*, Volume 3, no. 13 (June 1851): 123–38.

"Monthly Record of Current Events," *Harper's New Monthly Magazine*, Volume 5, no. 28 (September 1852): 402–6.

"Monthly Record of Current Events," *Harper's New Monthly Magazine*, Volume 2, no. 65 (October 1855): 688–92.

[Munro-Fraser, J. P.]. *History of Contra Costa County, California, Including Its Geography, Geology, Topography, Climatography and Description* . . . San Francisco: W. A. Slocum and Company, 1882.

Murguía, Alejandro. *The Medicine of Memory: A Mexican Clan in California*. Austin: University of Texas Press, 2002.

National Association for the Advancement of Colored People (NAACP). *Thirty Years of Lynching in the United States: 1889–1918*. 1919. New York: National Association for the Advancement of Colored People, 1969.

Neruda, Pablo. *Splendor and Death of Joaquín Murrieta*. Translated by Ben Belith. New York: Farrar, Straus and Giroux, 1972.

Newmark, Harris. *Sixty Years in Southern California: 1853–1913*. 1916. Los Angeles: Zeitlin and Ver Brugge, 1970.

Newmark, Marco, R. "Historical Profiles: IX, Reginaldo F. Del. Valle." *Historical Society of Southern California Quarterly* 37, no. 1 (March 1955): 74–75.

Office of Historic Preservation. *California Historical Landmarks*. Sacramento: California State Parks, 1996.

Olson, Steve. *Mapping Human History: Genes, Race, and Our Common Origins*. Boston: Mariner Books, 2002.

Omi, Michael, and Howard Winant. *Racial Formation in the United States from the 1960s to the 1990s*. New York: Routledge, 1994.

Paredes, Américo. *"With His Pistol in His Hand": A Border Ballad and Its Hero*. Austin: University of Texas Press, 1958.

Pennoyer, A. Sheldon. *This Was California: A Collection of Woodcuts and Engravings Reminiscent of Historical Events*. . . . New York: G. P. Putnam's Sons, 1938.

Percy, Alfred. B. *Origin of the Lynch Law, 1780: A Study in Patriotism*. Madison Heights, Va.: Percy Press, 1959.

Perret, Geoffrey. *Lincoln's War: The Untold Story of America's Greatest President as Commander in Chief*. New York: Random House, 2004.

Pitt, Leonard. *The Decline of the Californios: A Social History of the Spanish-Speaking Californians, 1846–1890*. 1966. Foreword by Ramón A. Gutiérrez. Berkeley: University of California Press, 1998.

Pitt, Leonard, and Dale Pitt. *Los Angeles A to Z: An Encyclopedia of the City and County*. Berkeley: University of California Press, 1997.

Pomeroy, Earl S., ed. "The Trial of the Hounds, 1849: A Witness's Account." *California Historical Society Quarterly* 29, no. 1 (March 1950): 161–65.

Proschlite Flash Lamps. Advertisement. *American Annual of Photography*. 1904. xxxiii.

Rancho Camulos Museum. *Where the History, Myth and Romance of Old California Still Linger*. Brochure. Piru, Calif.: Rancho Camulos Museum, n.d.

Rasch, Philip J. "The Story of the Hangman's Tree." *Historical Society of Southern California Quarterly* 39, no. 1 (March 1957): 59–64.

Reader, Phil. *Anthony Azoff and the Murder of Detective Len Harris*. Santa Cruz: Santa Cruz Public Libraries, 1991.

Reid, Bernard J. "Life in the California Goldfields in 1850: The Letters of Bernard J. Reid." Edited by Mary McDougall Gordon. *Southern California Quarterly* 67, no. 1 (spring 1985): 51–69.

Reproduction of Thompson and West's History of Santa Barbara and Ventura County with Illustrations and Biographical Sketches of Its Prominent Men and Pioneers. Introduction by Allan R. Ottley. Berkeley, Calif.: Howell-North, 1961.

Ridge, John Rollin (Yellow Bird). *The Life and Adventures of Joaquín Murieta: The Celebrated California Bandit*. 1854. Norman: University of Oklahoma, 1955.

Rivers, Christopher. *Face Value*. Madison: University of Wisconsin Press, 1994.

Rodriguez, Richard. *Days of Obligation: An Argument with My Mexican Father*. New York: Viking, 1992.

———. *Brown*. New York: Viking, 2002.

Rosales, Vincente Pérez. "Viaje a California: Recuerdoes de 1848, 49, 50." In *We Were 49ers! Chilean Accounts of the Gold Rush*. Edited by Edwin A. Beilharz and Carlos U. Lopez. Pasadena: Ward Ritchie Press, 1976.

Royce, Josiah. *California: From the Conquest in 1846 to the Second Vigilance Committee in San Francisco: A Study of American Character*. New York: Alfred A. Knopf, 1886.

Royster, Jacqueline Jones. Introduction to Ida B. Wells, *Southern Horrors and Other Writings: The Anti-Lynching Campaign of Ida B. Wells, 1892–1900*. Boston: Bedford Books, 1997.

Sales, Nancy Jo. "Somebody Hung My Baby." *Vanity Fair* 520 (December 2003): 328–35.

Saussure, Ferdinand de. *Course in General Linguistics.* 1916. Translated and annotated by Roy Harris. Chicago: Open Court Publishing Company, 1986.

Searcy, Susan E. "For the Record." In *Catalogue of the Public Records, City of Sacramento, 1848–1982.* Sacramento: City of Sacramento, Museum and History Division of the Department of Community Services, in cooperation with Sacramento County, 1982.

Secrest, William B. *California Desperados: Stories of Early California Outlaws in Their Own Words.* Clovis, Calif.: Quill Driver Books/Word Dancer Press, Inc., 2000.

———. *Juanita.* Fresno, Calif.: Saga-West Publishing Co., n.d. (ca. 1967).

Sekula, Allan. "The Body and the Archive." In *The Contest of Meaning: Critical Histories of Photography.* Edited by Richard Bolton. Cambridge, Mass.: MIT Press, 1989.

———. "The Traffic in Photographs." In *Only Skin Deep.* Edited by Coco Fusco and Brian Wallis. New York: Abrams, 2003.

Sherman, W. T. "Gold Hunters of California: Sherman and the San Francisco Vigilantes." *Century* 43, no. 2 (December 1891): 296–309.

Shirley, Dame [Louise Amelia Knapp Smith Clappe]. *The Shirley Letters from California Mines: 1851–1852.* New York: Alfred A. Knopf, 1949.

Smelser, Neil J., William Julius Wilson, Faith Mitchell, eds. *America Becoming: Racial Trends and Their Consequences.* Volume 1. Washington, D.C.: National Academy Press, 2001.

Smith, Shawn Michele. *American Archives: Gender, Race, and Class in Visual Culture.* Princeton: Princeton University Press, 1999.

Smith, Wallace E. *This Land Was Ours: The Del Valles and Camulos.* Edited by Grant W. Heil. Ventura, California: Ventura County Historical Society, 1977.

Sobieszek, Robert. *Ghost in the Shell: Photography and the Human Soul, 1850–2000.* Los Angeles: Los Angeles County Museum of Art and Cambridge, Mass.: MIT Press, 2000.

Solograph Flash Pistol. Scovill and Adams Company. Advertisement. *American Annual of Photography and Photographic Times.* 1900. cxv.

Spencer, Herbert. "Progress: Its Law and Causes." The Westminster Review 67 (April 1857): 445–47, 451, 454–56, 464–65.

———. *First Principles: A System of Synthetic Philosophy* (1862). 4th ed. London: Williams and Norgate, 1884.

"State of California against Adolfo Silvas." Pardon Papers. Californian State Archive, Sacramento, California.

Stevens, Moreland L. *Charles Christian Nahl: Artist of the Gold Rush, 1818–1878.* Sacramento: E. B. Crocker Art Gallery, 1976.

Thompson, Mark. *American Character: The Curious Life of Charles Fletcher Lummis and the Rediscovery of the Southwest.* New York: Arcade Publishing, 2001.

Thompson, Michael. *Rubbish Theory: The Creation and Destruction of Value.* Oxford: Oxford University Press, 1979.

Truman, Benjamin C. *Life, Adventures and Capture of Tiburcio Vasquez.* Los Angeles: Los Angeles Star, 1874.

Tuskegee Institute Archives. *Lynchings by State and Race, 1882–1968*. Tuskegee, Ala.: Tuskegee Institute Archives, [August 2002]. Unpaginated.

———. *Lynchings: By Year and Race*. Tuskegee, Ala.: Tuskegee Institute Archives, [August 2002]. Unpaginated.

———. *Lynchings in California, 1883–1935*. Tuskegee, Ala.: Tuskegee Institute Archives, [August 2002]. Unpaginated.

United States Census Bureau. *1880 Federal Census*. Capistrano, Los Angeles, California. 236.

———. *Race for the United States, Regions, Divisions, and States: 1850*. Table A-20. Internet release date: September 13, 2002.

———. *Race for the United States, Regions, Divisions, and States: 1860*. Table A-19. Internet release date: September 13, 2002.

University of Virginia Geospatial and Statistical Data Center. *United States Historical Census Data Browser*. 1998. http://fisher.lib.virginia.edu/census/.

Vanderwood, Paul J., and Frank N. Samponaro. *Border Fury: A Picture Postcard Record of Mexico's Revolution and U.S. War Preparedness, 1910–1917*. Albuquerque: University of New Mexico Press, 1988.

Varley, James F. *The Legend of Joaquín Murrieta, California's Gold Rush Bandit*. Twin Falls, Idaho: Big Lost River Press, 1995.

Villon, A.-M. "Éclairage à l'Aluminium." *Photo-Gazette*, September 25, 1892. 204–6.

Von Humboldt, Alexander. *Personal Narrative of Travels to the Equinoctial Regions of America During The Years 1799–1804*, Volume 1. London: George Bell and Sons, 1907.

Webb, Warren Franklin. *A History of Lynching in California since 1875*. M.A. thesis. Berkeley: University of California, 1935.

Wells, Harry Laurenz. *History of Nevada County with Illustrations and Biographical Sketches of Its Prominent Men and Pioneers*. Oakland: Thompson and West, 1880.

Wells, Ida B. *Southern Horrors and Other Writings: The Anti-Lynching Campaign of Ida B. Wells, 1892–1900*. Ed. Jacqueline Jones Royster. Boston: Bedford Books, 1997.

Wells, Samuel R. *New Physiognomy; or, Signs of Character, as Manifested Through Temperament and External Forms, and Especially in "The Human Face Devine."* Revised edition, 1866. New York: Fowler and Wells, 1896.

Wells-Barnett, Ida B. *On Lynchings*. Introduction by Patricia Hill Collins. Amherst, N.Y.: Humanity Books, 2002.

White, Walter. *Rope and Faggot: A Biography of Judge Lynch*. 1929. New York: Arno Press and the *New York Times*, 1969.

Widney, R. M. "Chinese Riot and Massacre in Los Angeles." *Grizzly Bear*, January 1921, 3–4, 22. "Lynchings: Los Angeles" folder, History and Genealogy Department, Los Angeles Public Library, Los Angeles.

[Wilson, John Albert]. *Reproduction of Thomson and West, History of Los Angeles County with Illustrations and Biographical Sketches of its Prominent Men and Pioneers*. Introduction by W. W. Robinson. Berkeley: Howell-North, 1959.

Windeler, Adolphus. *The California Gold Rush Diary of a German Sailor: Illustrated with Pencil Sketches by His Inseparable Partner Carl (Charley) Friderich Christendorff*. Edited by W. Turrentine Jackson. Berkeley: Howell-North Books, 1969.

Wright, Terrence. "Theories of Realism and Convention." In *Anthropology and Photography*. Edited by Elizabeth Edwards. New Haven: Yale University Press, in association with the Royal Anthropological Institute, London, 1992.

Zangrando, Robert L. *The NAACP Crusade Against Lynching, 1909–1950*. Philadelphia: Temple University Press, 1980.

INDEX

Page numbers in italics refer to figures.

75; expedience of, idealized, 68; extralegal executions, 24, 69, 83, 84, 181–82; financial costs of, 75, 88; as metaphor for moral transformation, 70; for preservation of society, 69; racialization of, 72; religious aspects of, 64, 69, 70, 71, 251n34; victim's assent to, 69

Carrigan, William D., 240n20

Carte de visite images, 155–56, plate 10

Casey, James P., 52

Catabo, Juan (alias Juan Silvas), 192, 218

Catabo, El, Juan (alias of Juan Catabo), 192

Chamales, José, 93–95, 223

Charley the Bull Fighter, 34, 212

Chileans, 10, 13, 26, 27, 33, 37, 144

Chinese: criminality of, 169; economic opportunities for, 146; execution of, by committee, 194; murder of, 218; population statistics of, in California, 27, 244n11; racial bias against, 10, 33, 169. *See also* Chinese Massacre

Chinese Massacre (1871), 80, 81–82, 253n79, 254n84

Chola Martina, La (alias of Martina Espinoza), 187–89, 190, 271n59, plate 12

Citizenship, 25, 26, 71–72

Civil Practice Act, section 394, 395

Civil Rights Act of 1875, 44

Clamor Público, El, 193

Clappe, Louise Amelia Knapp Smith (Dame Shirley), 8, 9, 162, 266n96

Clarke, Frederick, 73

Commodity culture, 113, 258n69

Comparative physiognomy, 189–90

Compton, J. L., 256n14

Confederacy, 154, 156

Constitution, U.S., 64, 250n9

Contra Costa County, 68

Copy prints, 117–19, 183, 188, 202–3

Cora, Charles, 52

Corrales, José, legal execution of, 67–68

Cortez, Gregorio, 148

Cota, Francisco, 2, 9, 219

Cowlings, Mary, 264n48

Creaner, Charles M., Judge, 76

Criminal physiognomy, 147, 264n48

Criminal Practices Act of 1851, 66, 250n9

Cronin (Crone), Richard, lynching of, 7, 38, 228

Daguerreotype, 166, 267n103

Dame Shirley (Louise Amelia Knapp Smith Clappe), 8, 9, 162, 266n96

Daniel, Pancho, 189, 190–91, 195–97, 219, 271n73

Daniel-Flores band, 190–91, 193–97, 271n73

Darwin, Charles: on blushing, 136–37, 262n10; Herbert Spencer and, 29–30, 146; racial anxiety in theory of evolution and, 167; social Darwinism and, 13, 18, 19, 29, 134, 146

Das, Venna, 3

Death row, 72–73, 75

de Balzac, Honoré, 177

Decapitations, 73, 174, 175, 177–78, *179*, 181, 191, 272n80

DeForest, Henry, 25n4, 93–94

Degeneration, 137, 262n12

de la Guerra, Pablo, Hon., 37

de la Torre, Joaquín, 194

del Valle, Josepha, *121*, *122*, plate 7

del Valle, Reginald, 123

del Valle, Ygnacio, 123, 259n85

del Valle family, *121*, 122–24, 259n84, 259n85, 260nn93, 95

Desparadoes, 99, 119, 148, 175, 189, 194, 203, 264n49

Disappearance (Spencer), 29–30

Dissolution, concept of, 29, 31

DNA testing, 75

Dobbin, Hamilton Henry, 104–5, *106*

26; imagined in performance piece, 202, 203; Mexicans identified as, 31, 32, 144; physiognomic analysis of, 147, 148; racial mixing and, 148, 167, 168, 176; as racial slur, 8, 30–31, 36, 71, 264n49; Spanish-speaking persons as, 137

Grijalva, Desiderio, 195, 219

Gubernatorial pardons, 237

Guerro Ardillero (alias of Francisco Ardillero), 191–92, 218

Hale, Justice, 196

Hanging trees, 6, 7, 8, 14–15, 43, 68, *106*

Hangman's Tree Bar, 14–15

Hangtown, 14–15, 243n58

Harp of a Thousand Strings, The (Avery), 150–51

Harris, George Washington, 150–51, 152

Hart, Brooke, kidnapping of, 105, 108

Hastings, Lansford, 146

Hayes, Benjamin, Judge, 251n34

"Head preserved in spirits," 19

Head shaving, 112

Henley, Charles W., 84, 223

Herrera, Ygnacio, legal execution of, 70, 72, 251n34

Hetherington, Joseph, 52–53

Hickey, Tomas, 125

Higuera, José, 194, 213

Higuera, Manuel, 125

Hittel, Theodore Henry, 41–42

Hoffman, Ogden, Jr., 77, 79, 253n74

Holmes, John M., and Hart kidnapping, 105, 107–8, *109*, *110*, 111, 115, 227, 257n39

Holmes and Thurmond, double lynching of, 105, 107–8, *109*, *110*, 111, 257nn39, 70

Hong, Di, murder trial of, 168, 225

Horsman, Reginald, 28

Howard Street Gang, 103–4

Howell, Edgar Wade, 56, 57

Invisible Man (Ellison), 274n2

Jackson, Helen Hunt, 124, 260n95

Jackson, Miles, 104, *106*

Jacobson, Matthew Frye, 246n60

Jails. *See* Prisons

Jenkins, John (Sydney Ducks), 50

Jim Crow laws, 44, 247n78

Johnson, J. E., 189

Johnson, Lawrence, 56–57

Johnson, Susan Lee, 241n45

Johnson, William, 85

Josefa (Juanita), lynching of, 185–87, 270n48

Judge Lynch, 36, 39, 40, *41*, 98–99

Judicial system: due process in, 3, 4, 7, 25, 65, 68, 83, 84, 87; judges in, 84, 112–13, 189, 251n34; juries in, 8, 71, 76–77, 84, 85, 194, 195, 199–200; legislation for, 76, 253n60; unequal treatment of Latino community by, 70–71

Kidnapping, 105–8, *109*, *110*, 111, 115, 227, 257n39

King, Thomas, 193

Kleinman, Arthur, 3

Kristeva, Julia, 60

Ku Klux Klan, 111, 247n95

Lacan, Jacques, 183–84, 269n41

Land claims, 10, 13–14, 37, 253n74

Latinos: Californios, 10, 33, 144; contestation of legal executions of, 67–68, 70–71; del Valle family, *121*, 122–24, 259n84, 259n85, 260nn93, 95; differences of body of, 199–200; disenfranchisement of, 7, 10, 71–72, 117; erased from historical record, 39; fantasy heritage of the ranchero and, 122, 123–24, 259n82; on lynching postcards, 101; performance piece on lynching and, 201–2; in *Ramona*,

Latinos (*continued*)
124, 260n95; schizoid heritage of, 197, 198; scholarship on experience of, 197–98; Sheriff Barton's murder and, 193; Sonoranians, 41, 67–68, 124, 135, 144, 170, 191, 194, 251n25; Treaty of Guadalupe Hidalgo and, 25, 136. *See also* Mexicans

Lavater, Johann Caspar: on comparative physiognomy, 160; on criminal physiognomy, 50, 146; de Balzac influenced by, 177; on diversity, 159; influence of, 134–35, 160–61; on monsters, 158, *159*; on positivism, 158; on silhouette drawing, 162

Law enforcement officers: deaths of, 190–91, 193, 194; ineffectiveness of, 66, 86–87, 94, 99, 100, 104, 107, 204; mobs and, 87; vigilance committees and, 76, 89–90

Layton, Charles, 194

Legal executions: audiences at, 18; due process and, 68; legislation for, 18; newspaper accounts of, 67–68, 70; popular opinion of, 68; scheduling of, 251n34; sheriff supervision of, 68; unequal treatment of Latino community and, 71

Letts, John, 241n23

Life and Times of Joaquín Murieta, The (Ridge), 174

Lighton, William R., 31

Linares, Pío, 194

Lincoln, Abraham: election of, 154; photograph of, 154, 155, plate 10; phrenological analysis of, 157; physiognomic analysis of, 149–50, 152, 155–56, 264n54; racial formation of, 149–50, 152, 264n54

Lombroso, Cesare, 147

López, Pedro, 191, *192*

Los Angeles: coroner records in, 80, 254n81; deparadoes in, 189; 1871 Chinese massacre in, 80, 81–82, 123, 253n79; El monte Rangers in, 191–92; gallows in, 193; incidence of extralegal execution in, 80; legal executions in, 70; lynchings in, 7–8; police force in, 76; pro-Confederate *Southern News* in, 156; Rudolpho Silvas as last execution in, 124; Sonoratown in, 124; vigilance committee of, 80, 190, *192*, 193

Los Angeles Rangers, 123

Los Angeles Star: Ardillero-Catabo case in, 192; Barton posse coverage in, 190–91, 271n73; Daniel-Flores band coverage in, 190–91, 271n73; description of Murrieta's head in, 181; ears as trophies of lynchings in, 192; Latinos in, 189; on lynchings of Mexicans, 193; "The Photograph of Lincoln" and, 149–50, 151, 155–57, plate 10; on violence in Los Angeles, 189

Love, Harry, Capt., 173, 174

Lovegood (Lovingood), Sut, 149–50, 152, 154, 264n54, 265n61

Lummis, Charles F., 31

Lynch, Charles, Jr., Colonel, 43

Lynchings: of Anglos, 14, 26, 84; antilynching movement and, 16, 44–46, *46*, 67, 170, 247nn89, 95; brutality of, 7–8, 67, 73, 85, 156; confessions before, 65, 83, 94, 187, 255n4; crowds at, 164, *166*; decapitations after, 73, 174, 175, 191, 272n80; definition of, 11, 18, 42–43; demographic change of, in California, 198; disappearance in dissolution theory and, 29–30; ears as trophies of, 192–93; erasures from history of, 26, 31, 39, 47, 103, 119; etymology of, 43–44; executioners and, 8, 193; expediency of, 68, 100; as expression of public frustration with legal system, 85, 88; floggings described as, 112; illumination of, 100, 101–2; indemnity for families of victims of, 56,

249n128; landmarks of, 14–16, 87, 100, 242–43n57, 243n58; legal hangings vs., 66–68; methods of, 11, 15, 18, 48–49, 148, 243n59, 248n105; night as time for, 65; physicians at, 65, 148; postcard images of, 16, 56, 95, 100, 108, 115, 240n16, 257n27; in private spaces, 54, 56, 143–44, 194–95, 263n39, 273n101; racial bias in, 12–13, 96–97, 101, 169, 197–98, 242n52; radio announcements about, 107, 257n43; as rebuke of criminal justice system, 73, 252n44; related capital punishments and, 75, 80, 266n76; romanticization of, 39, 53; ropes used at, 8, 48–50, 73, 74, 76, 191, 193, 194; by San Francisco vigilance committee, 50, 52; shootings and, 49, 191; souvenirs of, 67, 108, 115; statistical data on, 26–27, 45–47, 247nn89, 95; symbolic lynching of Abraham Lincoln, 149–50, 154, 156, 264n54, 265n61; Tory Conspiracy of 1780 and, 43–44; tradition's impact on, 65; unidentified cases of, 34; women and, 19, 107, 108, 110, 185–86. *See also* Law enforcement officers; Photographic images; Prisons; Tuskegee Institute

Lynch's law, 41, 43–44, 79

Manifest Destiny, 13, 28, 29, 171, 202
Martínez, Francisco, 125
Marxism, 146
Mazda photoflash (General Electric), 58
McCracken, Tom, 12, 224
McIntyre, James, 125
McKenzie, Robert, 50, 209
McWilliams, Carey, 259n82
Mewes, Henry F. W. (alias Charles Dowse), 54, 56
Mexican-American War, 28, 71, 184, 246n60, 272n76
Mexican folk heroes. *See* Cortez, Gregorio; Vasquez, Tiburcio

Mexicans: caricatures of, 184, *185*; cholos as slur on, 188; criminal character of, 119, 147; criminality associated with, 99; decomposition of bodies of, 182, 183; denial of land grants to, 37; as desparadoes, 99; female Mexican body, 184–85; forced migrations of, 36; gangs of, 149; greasers identified as, 30, 31, 32, 143, 144; legal prosecution of, 68; Leonard Pitt on, 197; Mexican Americans vs., 56; Mexican women, 180, 184–85, 187; mining and, 25, 26, 241n45; misidentification of, 34, 72, 94, 190, 270n50; monster imagery of, 180–81, *182*, 187; murder of Americans near Cerralvo and, 184; population statistics of, in California, 27, 244n11; racial formation of, 27, 135, 144, 145–46, 167, 168, 176; regional types of, 152, *153*; social class status and, 28; as unwashed, 195; use of term, 14, 32, 135, 245n38; white designation of, 72, 252n42

Migrations, 10, 13–14, 25, 26, 55, 64, 67–68, 251n25

Miners, mining: food provisions for, 10, 241n45; Foreign Miner's Tax (1851) and, 25, 26; intercultural exchange and, 10; land claims of, 10, 13–14; lynch law and, 79; mob violence and, 88; out-migration of Latin American miners, 26; vigilance committees of, 69

Miner's Ten Commandments, 162, *163*, 266n96

Mirror stage, 183

Miscegenation, 2, 30, 31, 167–68, 170

Mob justice described and criticized, 196–97

Mob law: death of Sheriff Phoenix and, 37; murder of Mexicans and, 37; Rancheria tragedy and, 36, 37

Mobs: abduction of prisoners by, 12, 50, 52, 94, 96, 99, 100, 107–8, *109*, 181–

Mobs (*continued*)

82, 196; African Americans hanged by, 67, 96; identification of members of, 84–86, 89, 95, 99–101, 105, 169, 258n55; illusion of spontaneity of, 87; lynching methods of, 49, 102–3; in mining towns, 88; newspaper accounts of, 56, 85, 86, 95; in photographic images, 102, 104, 105; police officers in, 104, 105; size of, 84–85, 86, 87, 255n3; storming of jails by, 8, 169, 194; violent passions of, 64, 65. *See also* Vigilance committees

Monster imagery, 81, 156, 157, 158, *159*, 169, *182*, 187, 198

Montejano, David, 18

Monterey County, lynchings in, 99–100

Moreno, Luis, 56, 249n128

Morse, Sheriff, 72–73

Murphy, Sheriff, 195

Murray, Walter, "Honorable," 71–72, 195, 252n38, 273n101

Murrieta, Joaquín, *182*, plate 11; confirmation of stories about, 175; decapitated head of, 174, 177–78, *179*, 181; identification of, 195; Nahl's painting of, 178, 180, plate 11; physiognomy's impact on characterization of, 177, 180; in *Sacramento Union*, 177

NAACP, 27, 44–46, *46*, 88

Nahl, Charles Christian, 176, 178, 180–81, plate 11

Native Americans. *See* American Indians

Navarro, Diego, 191, *192*, 217

Necktie parties, 12, 100

Newmark, Harris, 40, 41

New Physiognomy (Wells), 167

Newspaper accounts: on Arias-Chamales case, 95; on bias against Chinese, 169; of the Chinese Massacre (1871), 253n79, 254n84; of crowds at lynchings, 107, 257n43; on failures

of the judicial system, 71; of government sanctioning of lynchings, 108, 109; of Holmes and Thurmond lynchings, 109, 111, 258n55; of Josefa's (Juanita's) lynching, 270n50; justification of lynching in, 98–99; on Justin Arayo case, 99–100; of legal executions, 18, 67–68, 70; of lynch mobs, 56, 85, 86, 95; of Pancho Daniel, 195–96; on physiognomic analysis by, 134–35, 143–45; of posses, 4, 190–91, 239n7, 271n73; of prison escapes in, 11; of private executions, 54; race hatred in, 99–100; of the Rancheria tragedy, 36–37; on Reginald del Valle, 123; of San Jose kidnapping, 107, 257n43; of Santa Rosa lynching, 104; of the spectacle of hanging bodies, 113, 182; of vigilante committees, 5, 79, 89

Niépce, Joseph Nicéphore, 118

Norton, Myron, Judge, 189–90

Null, William, 56, 57

Oak trees, 15–16, 87, 100

O'Donnell, John, 84, 219

Of Crimes and Punishments (Beccaria), 63

Olivier, Alfred, 126

Omi, Michael, 32–33

Outdoor photography, 119–20, 122–23, plate 7

Pathognomy, *145*

Pérez Rosales, Vincente, 33

Peterson, W. H., 272n80

Pfeifer, Michael, 240n21

Pflugardt, George W. (alias Charles Fluggart), 190, 195, 271n70

Phoenix, Sheriff, 36–37

Photographic images, 56, 57–59; in Arias-Chamales case, 93–95, 96, 97, 98; authenticity of, 259n72; Barthes on, 59, 140; cameras and, 97–98,

155; of La Chola Martina (alias of
Martina Espinoza), 188–89, 271n59,
plate 12; copy prints of, 117–19, 183,
188, 202–3; cult of remembrance
and, 114; emotional reactions to, 5,
102, 103; flash equipment in, 58–60,
108, 249n133; as forum for Mexican-
American experience, 143; identification of photographers of, 104,
114, 257n33; lighting of, 100, 101; of
Lincoln, 149–50, 154, 155, 264n54,
265n61, plate 10; as mug shots, 162;
outdoor photography and, 119–20,
122–23, plate 7; in oval vignette, 98,
119; photographic blur in, 98, 256n16;
the real and, 183; realism of, 59–60;
of regional types, 151–52; silhouettes and, 162; studio portraiture
and, 121, 122–24, 259n84, 259n85,
260nn93, 95; subjects outside the
frames of, 139; as a transcription, 161;
as witnesses, 166; wonder gaze and,
182
"Photograph of Lincoln, The" (Los
Angeles Star article): identification of
photograph, 155, 265nn67, 69; poses
in, 155–56, 265n72; symbolic lynching
of Abraham Lincoln and, 149–50,
154, 156, 264n54, 265n61; zoological
analysis in, 149–50, 151, 155–57
Phrenology, 138–39, 157, 202
Physiognomy, physiognomic analysis:
Anglo-Americans and, 203; blushing and, 136–37, 262n10; character
analysis by, 147, 166; criminal type in,
146; Darwin on, 136; facial features
and, 176–77; forehead in, 144, 160,
166, 167; greaser and, 31, 148; impact of, on lynching, 176; of Latinos,
189–90; in literature, 176–77, 181;
of Mexican women, 187; monster
imagery and, 156, 157, 158, 159; moral
character and, 136–37, 147, 158, 166,

262n10; of Murrieta's head, 180–81;
physical appearance and, 160–61, 202;
in portraiture, 161, 176–77, 179–81;
as proof of innocence, 168, 169–70;
racial composition of juries and, 199;
silhouette drawing and, 162, 165; of
Vasquez, 144–45; Walter Benjamin
on, 152, 177, 265n58
Pico, Andrés, General, 77, 191–92, 193
Pierce, C. C., 188, 271n62
Pio Linares band, 194
Pitt, Leonard, 73, 197, 198, 271nn71, 72
Placerville, California (Hangtown),
14–15, 242nn57, 58
Portraiture, 98, 117, 119, 161, 179–81
Positivism, 134, 135, 136, 137, 158, 181,
203
Posses, 4–5, 83–84, 123, 173–75, 177, 183–
85, 190–92, 239n7, 260n92, 271nn72,
73
Postcards, 124; evolution of, 240n16,
257n27; execution of Mexican murderers on, 56, plate 2; frontier justice
images on, 113–14, plate 6; as historical archive, 113–14; lynching
images on, 16, 56, 95, 100, 101, 108,
114–15, 148, 240n16, 257n27, plate 2;
manufacture of, 114, 259n73; physiognomic analysis of, 147; Wild West
images on, 113–14, plate 6
Preston, William, Capt., 43
Prisons: abduction of prisoners from,
12, 50, 52, 86–87, 94, 96, 99, 100,
107–8, 109, 181–82, 196; construction
of, 11, 76; death rows of, 72–73, 75;
executions in, 54; extralegal lynchings inside, 86; lynchings at, 194–95,
273n101; storming of, by mobs, 8,
86, 100, 107–8, 109, 181–82, 194; for
prisoner safety, 11, 66, 70, 84; San
Quentin, 11, 94, 190; state prison of
California, 11, 47–48
Psychic reality, 269n42

Public displays: of bodies, 3, 65, 67, 84, 94, 96, 97, 196, 254n84; of body parts, 174, 177–78, *179*, 196; post-execution vigils and, 71; wonder gaze and, 19, 182–83, 192–93, 201–2

Race, racism: bias and, 4–5, 10, 12–13, 33, 71, 96–97, 101, 134, 169, 197–98, 242n52; bloodlines and, 29, 33, 123, 137, 144, 171; in composition of juries, 199–200; crimes against whites and, 67; death row inmates and, 75; definitions of, 32–33; in determination of guilt, 32; differential treatment and, 7; disappearance (Spencer) and, 29–30; distortions of physiognomic analysis by, 180, plate 11; erasure of identity and, 31, 39–40, 47, 96, 101, 103, 119; ethnicity and, 13–14, 28, 34, 134–35, 146, 242n52; exclusionary acts and, 13; frequency of lynchings and, 9; history of lynching impacted by, 12; identification of, 32–34, 199; Manifest Destiny and, 13, 28, 29, 171, 202; marriage and, 13, 242n54; mutilation of black victims of lynching and, 111; naturalization in United States and, 71; in newspaper accounts, 99–100; physical description of Tiburcio Vasquez and, 144–45; racial mixing, 167–68, 170–71, 176, 180, 198; racial positivism and, 134, 136, 137, 203; social class and, 146, 147. *See also* Greasers; Mexicans; Physiognomy, physiognomic analysis; Spaniards
Ramona (Helen Hunt Jackson), 124, 260nn95, 96
Rancheria tragedy, 36–37
Rangers, 123, 173–75, 177, 184–85, 190–92, 260n92
Rasmussen, Cecilia, 82, 254n84
Ray Golden case, 46, 248n99

Rejali, Darius, 243n1
Rich Bar (mining camp), 8, 9
Ridge, John Rollin (Yellow Bird), 174
Robertson, Joshua (African American), 8–9, 209, plate 1
Robinson, William (alias William B. Heppard), 66
Robles, Nievo, 195, 219
Rodriguez, Richard, 178
Roman Catholicism and death penalty, 64
Romanticization of lynchings, 39, 53, 91
Roosevelt, Franklin D., 44
Roosevelt, Theodore, 246n60
Rousseau, Jean Jacques, 250n4
Rowland, James, 84
Royce, Josiah, 136
Royster, Jacqueline Jones, 42, 111
Rubbish Theory (Thompson), 115–18
Rubottom, Ezekiel, 240n13
Ruggles brothers (John and Charles), hanging of, 49–50, *51*

Sacramento, lynchings in, 66
Samponaro, Frank N., 240n16, 257n27
Sánchez, Tomás, Don, 191
San Francisco: 1851 committee of vigilance in, 41, 66–67, 77; government corruption in, 11; Howard Street Gang in, 103–4; police force in, 76; prison in, 11; Sydney Ducks in, 50; vigilance committee in, 50, 52–53, *52, 53*
San Quentin, 11, 94, 190
Santa Cruz, Arias-Chamales case in, 93–95, 96, 97, 98
Santa Rosa triple lynching, 100–104, 119, 183, 259n70, plate 5
Santos, José, 191, 217, 272n79
Sauripa, Juan (alias of Juan Catabo), 192
Scott, Judge, 193
Scovill flash pistol, 57–58, *58*

Self-alienation, 113, 115, 116, 258n69
Sepulveda, José, 190
Sheldon, John, 37
Shew, William, 267n103
Shipp, Thomas (Marion, Ind.), 105, 257n36
Silhouette drawing, 162, *165*
Silton, Susan, 274n1
Silvas, Juan (alias of Juan Catabo), 192
Silvas, Rodolfo. *See* Silvas trial
Silvas, Ysidro (Pío Linares band), 194–95, 273n101
Silvas trial (Silvas, Rodolfo), 125, 126, 127–30, 143, plate 8
Slavery, 28, 154, 156, 157, 244n27
Smith, Abram (Marion, Ind.), 105, 257n36
Smith, Adam, 250n2
Smith, Shawn Michele, 120
Social class: *cholos* as expression of, 188; community migrations and, 13–14; fantasy heritage of the ranchero and, 122, 123–24, 259n82; housing and, 13–14; injustices of, 143; lynching and, 40–41; mining camp names and, 13; mob participation by, 86, 89, 95, 100–101, 169, 258n55; racial identity and, 146
Social Darwinism, 13, 18, 19, 29, 134, 146
Sonoranians, 41, 67–68, 124, 135, 144, 170, 191, 194, 251n25
Soto, Miguel, 191, 272n80
Southern Commission on the Study of Lynching, 45, *46*
Southern News (pro-Confederate newspaper), 156
Souvenir industry in Europe, 113–14, 258n59, plate 6
Spaniards: greaser and, 30, 137; misidentification of, 34, 72, 94, 190, 270n50; physiognomic analysis and, 144–45; racial categorization of, 24–25, 28; Reginald del Valle, 123

Spectacles: burnings of effigies, 67; cameras as, 97–98; displays of body parts, 3, 174, 177–78, *179*, 196; of executions, 69–70; lynchings as, 35, 96–97, 108; lynchings of women, 185–86; photographs of dead Mexicans and, 97; post-lynching mutilations of black corpses, 111; public hangings, 193; wonder gaze and, 19, 182–83, 192–93, 201–2
Spencer, Herbert, 29–30, 146
Stemler, Garland, 56, 57
Stendhal, Henri Beyle, 176–77
Sterling, Dorothy, 247n95
Stuart, James (Sydney Ducks), 50
Sydney Ducks, 50

Tapia, Luciano (alias Leonardo López), 193
Tar and feathering, 113
Tear gas, 107
Templeton, B. S., lynched by Ku Klux Klan, 111, 221
Texas Rangers, 191, 272n76
Thirty Years of Lynching in the United States, 1889–1918 (White), 45–46, 47
Thompson, John (alias McDermott), 66
Thompson, Michael, 115–18
Thompson, Robert, 81
Three-Fingered Jack, hand of, 174, 177–78, *179*
Thurmond, Thomas H. (Hart kidnapping), 105, 107–8, *109*, 111, 115, 227, 257n39
Tory Conspiracy of 1780, 43
Treaty of Guadalupe Hidalgo, 25, 136
Triple lynchings, 100–104, 119, 183, 259n70, plate 5
Tucker, Hamilton J., 85
Tuskegee Institute, 241n39, 242n51; lynching defined by, 11, 18, 42–43, 111, 182, 246n70; on lynching resulting from rape, 170; lynchings of African

Tuskegee Institute (*continued*)
Americans and, 27; murder trial of Di
Hong and, 267n113; statistical data of,
on lynching, 45–46, 247n95; tradition
of extrajudicial execution and, 65
Twain, Mark, 152, 265n61
Twist, Sheriff, 193
Types: "American," 18, 19, 168; "Anglo-
American," 29; as categorizational
tool, 151; criminal, 146, 147, 264n48;
Mexican, 135; racial mixing of, 176;
regional, 151–52, *153*, 154, 265nn56,
61; Yankee, 167–68

United States Circuit Court for the
District of California, 253n60
United States war with Mexico, 28, 184,
246n60, 272n76

Valento, Charles, 100–104, *106*, plate 5
Valenzuela, Joaquín, 170, 195, 210
Valenzuela, Juan, 191, *192*, 217
Vance, Robert H., 267n103
Vanderwood, Paul J., 240n16, 257n27
Vasquez, Tiburcio (José Jésus López),
141–42, 194; class as racial marker
and, 147; criminality of, 147; physiognomic analysis of, 144–47, plate 9;
spectacle of death of, as forum for
Mexican-American experience,
143; as threat to Anglo-American
supremacy, 171
Vigilance committees: abduction of
suspects by, 67, 170; anti-Latino bias
of, 4–5; cruelty of, 69, 70, 79; discipline of, 89; fining of, 79; general
public and, 66, 94, 183; government
sanctioning of, 18, 108, 109; justification of actions of, 64–66; legal
trials and, 240n14; in Los Angeles,
80, 190, *192*, 193; of miners, 69; response of, to capital offenses, 7; in
Sacramento, 66–67, 70; in San Fran-

cisco, 50, 52–53, *52*, *53*, 65, 66–67, 80,
89; social class of, 40; social contract
and, 69; Sonoranians tried by, 170;
transformation of, 109, 111. *See also*
Law enforcement officers; Lynchings;
Prisons; Vigilance committees in San
Francisco
Vigilance committees in San Francisco:
extrajudicial execution as tradition,
65; extralegal executions in 1851, 66–
67; impact on extralegal executions
in California, 80; notoriety of, 80;
second vigilance committee, *89*
Vigils after executions, 71

Wall, Isaac B., 194
War of reform in Mexico, 190, 271n71
Webb, Clive, 240n20
Welch, Bud, 168, 169–70
Wells, Harry Laurenz, 75
Wells, Samuel R., 160, 167–68
Wells-Barnett, Ida B., 45, 170, 247nn89,
95
Whipping, 112
White, Stephen M., 127
White, Walter, 45–46, 242n51
Whiteness: darkening of, 167–68; iden-
tification of, 199–200; Mexicans and,
72; naturalization in United States
and, 71; racial composition of juries
and, 199–200
White supremacy, 2, 3, 111
Whittaker, Samuel, 50, 209
Williams, Pat Ward, 258n56
Williamson, Thomas, 194
Wilson, James (robbery victim), 66
Wilson, Joseph, 256n14
Winant, Howard, 32–33
Windeler, Adolphus, 8, 241n45
Women: in antilynching movement,
45, 170, 247nn89, 95; blindfolded,
as symbol of justice, 38, 89; execu-
tion of, 75; flogging of, by vigilance

committee, 79; Howard Street Gang assault of, 104; Louise Amelia Knapp Smith Clappe (Dame Shirley), 8, 9, 162, 266n96; lynching of, 19, 185–86; Mexican, 180, 184–85, 187; passivity of, as moral worth, 170; pregnancy and, 186; prostitution and, 186; racial mixing and, 180

Wonder gaze, 19, 182–83, 192–93, 201–2

Work, Monroe N., 44

Wright, Terrence, 256n16

Ygara, José Antonio, 87, 223

Yoakum, Thomas and William, 85–86, 224

Yreka quadruple lynching, 56–57, 249nn128, 129, plate 3

Zangrando, Robert, 170

Zoological methods of physiognomical analysis, 144, 145, 147, 149–50, 156, 159–60, 180, 190

Ken Gonzales-Day is associate professor
of art at Scripps College.

Library of Congress Cataloging-in-Publication Data
Gonzales-Day, Ken.
Lynching in the West, 1850–1935 / Ken Gonzales-Day.
p. cm.
"A John Hope Franklin Center book."
Includes bibliographical references and index.
ISBN-13: 978-0-8223-3781-2 (cloth : alk. paper)
ISBN-10: 0-8223-3781-9 (cloth : alk. paper)
ISBN-13: 978-0-8223-3794-2 (pbk. : alk. paper)
ISBN-10: 0-8223-3794-0 (pbk. : alk. paper)
1. Lynching—California—History. 2. Lynching—California—History—Pictorial
works. 3. Vigilance committees—California—History. 4. Extrajudicial executions—
California—History. I. Title.
HV6468.C2G66 2006
364.1'34—dc22   2006010390